Exercising Discretion

Exercising Discretion
Decision-making in the criminal justice system and beyond

Edited by

Loraine Gelsthorpe
Nicola Padfield

WILLAN
PUBLISHING

Willan Publishing
Culmcott House
Mill Street, Uffculme
Cullompton, Devon
EX15 3AT, UK
Tel: +44(0)1884 840337
Fax: +44(0)1884 840251
e-mail: info@willanpublishing.co.uk
website: www.willanpublishing.co.uk

Published simultaneously in the USA and Canada by

Willan Publishing
c/o ISBS, 5824 N.E. Hassalo St,
Portland, Oregon 97213-3644, USA
Tel: +001(0)503 287 3093
Fax: +001(0)503 280 8832
website: www.isbs.com

First published 2003

ISBN 1-903240-99-9

British Library Cataloguing-in-Publication Data
A catalogue record for this book is available from the British Library

Printed and bound by T.J. International, Padstow, Cornwall
Project management by Deer Park Productions
Typeset by GCS, Leighton Buzzard, Beds.

Contents

Acknowledgements

Thanks are due to the contributors for their patience given this book's long period of gestation (the book has its origins in two day-long highly stimulating and enjoyable seminars devoted to discretion in 2000–2001), and to Keith Hawkins for his serious commitment to the project. We would also like to thank Joanne Garner of the Institute of Criminology for her excellent skills in putting together the final manuscript in preparation for publication. Finally, we would like to thank Brian Willan for his interest and support.

Notes on contributors

Loraine Gelsthorpe is University Senior Lecturer in Criminology and a Fellow of Pembroke College, University of Cambridge. She has carried out a number of research studies since the mid 1980s, including work on police decision-making with regard to juvenile offenders; the operation of multi-agency crime prevention and juvenile panels; the role of the Crown Prosecution Service in juvenile justice, and gender issues in juvenile justice. She has also conducted work on the sentencing of women. Current research interests revolve around links between social and criminal justice (including race and gender issues), community penalties, and youth justice issues. She is currently completing a book on social exclusion, crime and justice. Her publications include *Sexism and the Female Offender* (1989), *Feminist Perspectives in Criminology* (1990 with A. Morris), *Minority Ethnic Groups in the Criminal Justice System* (1993), *Understanding the Sentencing of Women* (1997 with C. Hedderman) and *Community Penalties: Change and Challenges* (2001 with A.E. Bottoms and S. Rex). She chairs the Professional Affairs and Ethics Committee of the British Society of Criminology. She also sits on a number of editorial boards, including the *Howard Journal*, *Women and Criminal Justice*, and *Criminal Justice – The International Journal, of Policy and Practice.*

Adrian Grounds is University Senior Lecturer in forensic psychiatry at the Institute of Criminology, and honorary consultant forensic psychiatrist at Addenbrooke's NHS Trust. His research interests include the needs of mentally disordered prisoners, and secure psychiatric services. He is co-editor of *The Mentally Disordered Offender in an Era of*

Community Care (1993 with William Watson) and *Personality Disorders: Recognition and Clinical Management* (1995 with Jonathon Dowson). Since 1998 he has been one of the Northern Ireland Sentence Review Commissioners.

Keith Hawkins is Reader in Law and Society at Oxford University, and Fellow and Tutor in Law at Oriel College. He took the graduate course in Criminology at the Cambridge Institute of Criminology, followed by a Ph.D. there on decision-making in American parole systems. After a period as Research Fellow of Gonville and Caius College, Cambridge, he moved to Oxford, where he has researched legal decision-making, mostly by focusing on governmental regulation, particularly in environmental pollution and occupational health and safety. He also learned a great deal about practical decision behaviour by serving two terms as a member of the Parole Board for England and Wales. Hawkins is the author of *Environment and Enforcement – Regulation and the social definition of pollution*, and editor of *The Uses of Discretion* (both published by Oxford University Press). *Law as Last Resort: Prosecution decision-making in a regulatory agency,* a study conducted in various inspectorates of the Health and Safety Executive, was published by Oxford University Press in 2002. Hawkins is currently working on a general analysis of legal decision-making with Peter K. Manning.

Katy Holloway completed her Ph.D. in criminology at the University of Cambridge in July 2000. Prior to this she worked as a research assistant for the Metropolitan Police on a project exploring the operational usefulness of offender profiling in serious crime investigations. More recently she has been a Research Associate on the NEW-ADAM project exploring the relationship between drug use and crime. She is currently a Research Fellow at the Centre for Criminology, University of Glamorgan.

Marie Howes is a Social Anthropologist with a background in teaching and probation work. She holds degrees in law and anthropology from Cambridge University. She first worked as a research assistant to Professor David Martin, of the LSE, in Peru. During her anthropological fieldwork with Peruvian immigrants in Chicago she was given research assistant status at the University of Chicago. Most recently she has worked as research assistant on Home Office and Department of Health projects with the Institute of Criminology at Cambridge University and the Institute for the Study of the Legal Profession at Sheffield University.

Vicky Kemp was formerly the criminal policy advisor at the Legal Aid Board responsible for advising the Lord Chancellor's Department on policy development and implementation in respect of criminal legal aid. She represented the Board on the Trial Issues sub-group and was an advisory group member of the JUSTICE Restoring Youth Justice report chaired by Lord Hope of Craighead. Vicky has also worked for the Home Office Safer Cities Unit and then as Northamptonshire County Council's community safety co-ordinator. She is currently completing a Ph.D. on youth justice issues at the Institute of Criminology, University of Cambridge.

Alison Liebling is a University Lecturer in Criminal Justice and Fellow of Trinity Hall. She has carried out several empirical research projects on prison and prison life, including young offender throughcare, suicide and suicide attempts in prison, an evaluation of small units for difficult prisoners, an evaluation of Wolds remand prison, an evaluation of incentives and earned privileges, and staff–prisoner relationships. She is currently working on several projects on prison-related topics: 'Measuring the Quality of Prison Life' and 'Shaping Prison Life'. Her publications include: *Suicides in Prison* (1992), *Deaths in Custody II: Caring for Prisoners at Risk* (ed) (1996), *Privatising Prisons: Rhetoric and Reality* (1997 with A.K. Bottomley), *Security, Justice and Order in Prison* (ed.) (1997), *Deaths Among Offenders: The Hidden Side of Justice* (1998) and *The Prison Officer* (2001 with D. Price). She has published several recent studies in *Punishment and Society, Theoretical Criminology* and *Criminal Justice*.

Nicola Padfield is Lecturer in Criminal Justice, Director of the Applied Criminology and Management (Prison Studies) course at the Institute of Criminology, Cambridge University, and a Fellow of Fitzwilliam College. Nicola Padfield is a criminal barrister by training, whose research interests cover legal topics in a wide range of criminal justice areas. Her books include *The Criminal Justice Process* (1995, 2000), *Sentencing: Theory, Law and Practice* (1996 with Walker), *Criminal Law* (1998, 2002), *A Guide to the Crime and Disorder Act 1998* (1998) and *Beyond the Tariff: Human Rights and the Life Sentence Prisoner* (2002). As well as contributing regularly to various journals, she is editor of the criminal law practitioner's monthly magazine, *Archbold News*.

David Price's Ph.D., completed at the Cambridge Institute of Criminology in January 2001, examined security categorisation within the English prison system. He has also conducted research on staff–prisoner relationships, education in prison and prisoner overcrowding and recently published a book with Alison Liebling entitled *The Prison Officer*. Currently, David Price is working as a computer consultant.

David Thomas QC was, until his recent retirement from Cambridge University, a Reader in Criminal Justice. He remains a Fellow of Trinity Hall and is a practising criminal lawyer whose special research interest is the law of sentencing. His publications include *The Penal Equation* (1978), *Constraints on Judgement* (1979), *Principles of Sentencing* (1979), *Current Sentencing Practice* (continually updated since first publication in 1982) and the *Sentencing Referencer* (updated annually). He is Editor of the *Criminal Appeal Reports (Sentencing)*, Sentencing Editor of *Archbold, Criminal Pleading Evidence and Practice* and Sentencing Case Editor of the *Criminal Law Review*.

Leanne Weber came to England in 1992, having previously worked for some years as a researcher and research manager within the criminal justice system in South Australia. She subsequently completed two post-graduate degrees (in criminology and human rights), worked on research contracts at the Oxford Centre for Criminological Research and Cambridge Institute of Criminology, and acted as an independent research consultant to local government and the independent sector on minority issues. Her most recent empirical work, published in June 2000, was a collaboration with Loraine Gelsthorpe at the Institute of Criminology (*Deciding to Detain: How decisions to detain asylum seekers are made at ports of entry*). She was until recently a Research Associate at the Human Rights Centre, University of Essex, but has now returned to Australia to continue her professional academic career there.

Chapter 1

Introduction

Loraine Gelsthorpe and Nicola Padfield

This book arose out of the realisation that there were a number of people working at the Institute of Criminology in the University of Cambridge who, quite separately, were exploring the concept of discretion. Our different studies, involving discretion and decision-makers in different corners of the criminal justice and penal systems and beyond into the mental health world, and immigration and asylum, have led us to pose some fundamental questions:

How can we define discretion?
How can we evaluate discretion?
How is discretion exercised in different decision-making arenas? And what are the constraints that shape the power to exercise it?
Is the exercise of discretion legitimate?

Discretion is one of the most contentious concepts in criminal justice and related circles because it is so important and yet so difficult to define. Those involved in decision-making processes experience a considerable degree of mandated flexibility in the decisions they can make about individuals, and this immediately draws attention to uncertainties and anxieties about discretion. In many cases, these decisions are life-changing ones, especially when related to processes of gate-keeping – pushing people into or out of criminal justice and other controlling agencies. Indeed, it is the day-to-day discretionary actions of police officers, prosecutors, defence lawyers, judges, psychiatrists, prison, probation and immigration officers, among others, which are the 'stuff of justice' and which make for justice or injustice. Discretion provides all these professionals with the space both to engage in discriminatory activities and to subvert policies that they do not agree with. The concept of discretion is thus critical to the meaning of justice.

In this introductory chapter our aim is to examine some of the meanings and dimensions of the exercise of discretion. Following some preliminary comments about discretion, we do this by distinguishing discretion from its first and second cousins, discrimination and disparity, respectively. Second, we consider how we can evaluate whether discretion is a positive or negative concept. Thirdly, we note the directions taken in explorations of discretion in the socio-legal literature. Within this latter section we outline some general themes, identify some major works and rehearse some questions prompted by legal theorists as to whether the exercise of discretion is legitimate. We conclude this introductory chapter with an outline of what is to follow in the subsequent chapters of the book.

The origins of discretion

In the course of our research into the meaning of discretion, we chanced upon the rather striking claim that discretion in criminal justice was 'discovered' by an American Bar Foundation Survey in 1956 (Walker 1993). Important as the survey may have been, discretion has clearly been around for much longer than this and recognised as such. From Plato onwards, perhaps, discretion has tended to be equated with what remains after one has elucidated what the legislation or law should be. In English legal history, for example, it is clear that there were alternative methods or terms for what we now call discretion: equity, whether administered by the King's courts or by the Chancellor; the Royal pardon; quashing indictments on technicalities of language; and legal fictions such as benefit of clergy or the facility for women to 'plead their bellies' (Oldham 1985, and see Thomas in Chapter 3 of this book). There have been some important historical explorations, not least that by Peter King (2000), who has produced a detailed study of the exercise of discretion between 1740 and 1820.[1] In this major historical study of the exercise of discretion, which draws on primary data concerning property offences from the Essex Record Office, King contrasts the formal criminal law and legal handbook image of justice as rigid and inflexible with the reality on the ground. The administration of justice, in reality, involved several interconnected spheres of contested judicial space, in each of which deeply discretionary choices were made. The key message to emerge from such historical excursions is that however precise the law, theory or policy might be, there is always a certain flexibility, ambiguity or discretion in how it is applied in practice. Put more simply, it relates to differences between what is said to be the case or what might be the case, and what *is* the case; the formal position and the actual practice.

Defining discretion

According to the Oxford English Dictionary, discretion involves a liberty or power of deciding according to one's own judgment or discernment. In the context of our work, the concern is with the way in which individuals and/or groups of officials use their own judgment within a given situation, to take action or not. At its simplest then, discretion refers to the freedom, power, authority, decision or leeway of an official, organisation or individual to decide, discern or determine to make a judgment, choice or decision, about alternative courses of action or inaction. Although each of these terms or phrases convey different shades of meaning, they represent some broad consensus on what is core to the concept of discretion. Judgments or choices are in practice much constrained, not only by formal (and sometimes legal) rules but also by the many social, economic and political constraints that act upon the exercise of choice. In fact, because of these constraints, some might go so far as to suggest that 'discretion' is often a myth (Baumgartner 1992).

One other point that is relevant to make here is that because it extends to all points of decision-making and encompasses procedures and working methods, discretion flows back and forth through all parts of agencies that make up the criminal justice 'system' and related controlling agencies. While 'discretion' is a generic term, it also takes on a different mantle at different points in the system; in the early gate-keeping stages it is sometimes referred to as 'diversion'. But not all diversion is discretionary, some diversion is circumscribed by law (in English law, for example, there has to be acceptance of guilt for there to be diversion from the courts and a caution issued).[2] Diversion commonly channels people out of the criminal justice system, whereas discretion can achieve both 'in and out' actions, though one of the themes in Kemp and Gelsthorpe (Chapter 2 in this volume) is that diversion is very much to be counted within the criminal justice 'system'. Thus some of the terms that are used interchangeably with discretion obfuscate as much as they elucidate. It follows that we wish to make clear the distinction between discretion, discrimination and disparity, for these terms are related, if not also used interchangeably.

Distinguishing discretion from discrimination and disparity

Discrimination is a difficult issue to define and in a neutral sense, to be discriminating can involve the showing of good judgment. There can also be positive (favourable) discrimination. But in the criminal justice context, it is commonly taken to mean unfavourable treatment based on a person's sex, gender, social class, language, 'race', ethnicity, religion, sexual preference, age, disability or any other improper ground. Discrimination is frequently tied to the concept of prejudice; that is, ideas that identify particular groups or individuals as 'inferior' or 'difficult'. Studies of discrimination in the criminal justice system have suggested that it occurs where the law is permissive and individual discretion wide, and that where there are few guidelines as to how a decision should be taken, decision-making is often based on subjective judgments (see Hedderman and Gelsthorpe 1997; Doran and Jackson 2000; Smith 1997; and Bowling and Phillips 2000 for reviews of the evidence).

Disparity is equally difficult to define. In criminal justice circles it is most clearly associated with sentencing and the practice of giving different sentences for similar offences, but it also has wider relevance in terms of offenders and victims being treated differently or unequally throughout the criminal justice system (or a related system) when their circumstances are similar. Discoveries of disparity in the treatment of offenders in the criminal justice system strike at the heart of the ideal that justice is abstract and therefore that all are equal before the law. While disparity is concerned more with differences in outcome than process, it is often used interchangeably with 'discrimination' and most pointedly concerns 'equal treatment'. Indeed, many people appear to believe that fairness necessarily involves treating 'like cases alike'. But equal treatment involves at one extreme the impartial application of existing rules and procedures, regardless of the outcome (procedural justice), and at the other, the idea that any policies or procedures that have the effect of punishing or controlling a higher proportion of one social group than another are unjust, and that law and social policy should be adjusted so as to achieve equal outcomes (substantive justice). Techniques for reducing disparity (discussed by Thomas in Chapter 3 of this volume) include: judicial self-regulation (with courts of appeal, tribunals and the like), statutory sentencing principles (as in penal codes), numerical guideline systems (as in the Minnesota system, with clear classifications of offences and categories of relative gravity, Tonry 1996) and mandatory sentences (prescribed maximum and minimum penalties, Ashworth 1998). Calls to eradicate disparity include calls for equal treatment, but these are not unproblematic. Following critiques of the sentencing of women, for example, both in principle and practice, 'equal' has often come to mean 'like men'. As punishment has become increasingly more severe in England and Wales, the USA and elsewhere, 'equal treatment' with men is far from desirable (let alone 'just', some would say) and so the quest for equal treatment is rightly questioned (Hudson 1998). But since 'disparity' raises questions about difference it also raises questions about the exercise of discretion.

How can we evaluate discretion?

Whereas disparity concerns the consistency with which criteria are applied to cases, and unlawful discrimination commonly refers to the use of illegitimate criteria, both involve the exercise of *discretion*. All this suggests that the exercise of discretion can work in a *negative* way where it leads to unwarranted disparity and discrimination. At the same time, however, it might be suggested that discretion can be linked to justice. Decision-makers may discriminate in a *positive* way too. Thus there is an inherent tension. To be fair, law and policy must be both certain *and* flexible. Critics suggest that negative discrimination occurs where there are unfettered powers of discretion. Immediately, this alerts us to the importance of rules and uniformity of treatment – with the assumption that uniformity of treatment would mean 'better' treatment. Equally, it has to be acknowledged that unfettered powers of discretion can be applied in positive ways too; this perhaps points us in the direction of needing to maintain a balance between uniformity and individualisation of treatment. Having touched on the negative aspects of discretion above, we want to dwell on the positive aspects for a moment by looking at the concept of mercy (that is, compassion or forbearance).

Nigel Walker (1999) in a little known, but important, book of essays, points out that we must recognise mercy as something different from justified mitigation. We have come to expect mitigation in sentencing, for example, in terms of retributive reasoning, which concludes either that the offender's culpability is not as great as the nature of the offence suggests or that, while the offender is fully culpable, there is reason to think that he or she might suffer more than intended. As Walker (1999) outlines, statutory considerations for mitigation include: a plea of guilty and the timeliness of that plea (Powers of the Criminal Courts (Sentencing) Act 2000 (PCC(S)A) s. 152); the totality principle (PCC(S)A 2000 s. 158 (2) b), which serves to ensure that punishments are not excessive; and suspended sentences which can be used in exceptional circumstances for special reasons (the physical or mental state of the offender, for example; see PCC(S)A 2000 s. 118). Non-statutory considerations include motivation, temptation, impulsiveness, entrapment, ignorance, incompetence, necessity and duress, previous good character or meritorious conduct, and remorse.

The boundary between mitigation and mercy is far from clear, but it might be said that the discretion to exercise mercy or 'clemency' takes us beyond these statutory and non-statutory rules, which are tied to logical reasoning about degrees of mitigation, to reflect a degree of compassion. We will all be aware of instances of 'mercy' in this sense – the prison governor who allows a prisoner home leave to attend a funeral, for instance. Walker (1999) also notes that the Crown Prosecution Service may encompass 'mercy' within its decision not to prosecute within the conveniently ambiguous phrase that it is 'not in the public interest' to do so. The chapter by Liebling and Price (Chapter 4 of this volume) in particular, provides further examples of 'mercy'. The general inference here is that decision-makers may resort to what they call 'mercy' when they have vague compassion for the offender, but cannot articulate a precise justification for the decision.

'Discretion' then is a force for ill when it leads to unjustifiable decisions (negative discrimination) and inconsistency (disparity), but it can be a good thing in that it provides a mechanism to show mercy which, even if defying precise definition, many would recognise as being necessary to the conception and delivery of justice. It allows for justice to become 'humane'. Evaluations of discretion thus involve a careful assessment of the balance achieved between these things, for one person's mercy may be another's negative discrimination.

Socio-legal research on discretion[3]

It is within the socio-legal realm that our knowledge of both the meaning of discretion and our knowledge of the manner in which it is exercised best come to the fore. The considerable literature questions the authority to make choices or judgments about different courses of action, the factors (criteria or standards) which do or should determine the choice, and what processes underpin the reasoning behind the actual decisions that are made.

Socio-legal explorations have identified a number of variables that may influence the exercise of discretion in criminal justice and related systems. These include: i) process, ii) environment, iii) context, and iv) illicit considerations (for example, the social class, ethnicity or sex of the accused). Focusing on 'process' for a moment, we can see that there are numerous opportunities to 'screen out' or 'divert' cases based on legal or practical criteria. We can also see that there might be informal modes of disposition alongside the formal ones (the police decision to take 'no further action' springs to mind; this non-disposition sits alongside charging, summonsing, cautioning, reprimand or warning possibilities; see Banton 1964; Bittner 1964; Steer 1970; Cain 1973; McConville, Sanders and Long 1991; Sanders and Young 2002). Alongside these informal mechanisms there are inducements to choose certain alternatives (negotiated pleas, for example; see Baldwin and McConville 1977; Sanders and Young 2002).

The exercise of discretion by officials clearly takes place within a particular environment or cultural context, both in terms of the large social and political system and in terms of local factors. These environmental factors are described most frequently as the 'local community'. For example, Bottomley argues:

> From the start, therefore, different members of society are shown to have conflicting views about the nature of 'crime' and the appropriate measures to be taken against suspected 'criminals'. Throughout the subsequent stages of the process, decision makers are directly and indirectly influenced by a variety of 'community' factors, in which the interests and pressures of a local community can be seen as a microcosm of the forces at work in society at large: the exercise of police discretion may differ according to the social characteristics of the communities in which it operates, as may the sentencing practices of magistrates' courts; decisions about the location of prisons and the allocation of prisoners to them often takes into account the views of the local community, as do many parole board decisions about the release of a prisoner to a particular locality.
>
> (Bottomley 1973: 225–6)

These communal or environmental influences require greater attention than we give them here, because they are not normally recognised in the legal literature and because there is no consensus on the legitimacy or otherwise of their role. But certainly, the environment or community serves to constrain the exercise of police and criminal justice agency discretion by reporting or not reporting crimes, by participating in the criminal justice process as complainants or jurors (or, under the 1999 Youth Justice and Criminal Evidence Act's Referral Orders, as youth panel members), by expressing views through specific interest groups (for example, neighbourhood watch schemes, police liaison committees), and by expressing views through the media. More than this, it might be argued that the local political culture will determine 'police styles'. In an early review of policing, for example, Sherman concluded:

> Theoretically, the community level of explanation should receive the most attention, since it ought to be the most powerful level, if only indirectly. It is assumed to shape the causal factors at all the other levels ... Even if it does not shape them, it may still over-ride other levels of influence. Rossi and his colleagues found, for example, that in comparing city of employment and officers' personal characteristics as explanations of the use of aggressive detection tactics, 67% of the explained variance was uniquely attributable to the city.
>
> (Sherman 1980: 94)

Similar points about local community and 'background expectancies' (Cicourel 1976) have been made with regard to sentencing (Hood 1962; Levin 1977; Parker et al. 1989). National and local 'political' pressures on the Parole Board are made evident in Padfield and Liebling's discussion (Chapter 5 of this volume), while broader environmental or cultural factors and sentencing are addressed by Downes (1988) and Garland (2001).

Contextual variables such as organisational, occupational and situational factors are also relevant here. The key issue is the degree to which an organisation can control the behaviour of its members (by specifying rules or policies, by offering incentives or punishments so as to ensure conformity, by monitoring and supervising behaviour, or by allocating priorities or establishing performance standards, for example). Studies on occupational roles, too, elucidate the working philosophies of different professional groups within the criminal justice system (see, for instance, Skolnick 1966; Pepinsky 1976; Holdaway 1979, 1983; Manning 1978; McCabe and Sutcliffe 1978; Grimshaw and Jefferson 1987; Gelsthorpe and Giller 1990; Young 1991; Fielding 1994).[4] With regard to the police, for example, dominant themes that emerge include: the need to remain in control in encounters with the public, the search for excitement in an otherwise routine existence, and administrative biases (that is, the need to achieve certain performance indicators – whether this is to 'feel a certain number of collars' on any one day or to show success in dealing with a particular kind of crime (for example, burglary) to the neglect of other pressing crimes and nuisance behaviours). Thus these 'internal' organisational and occupational factors may be as important as the legal rules which guide action. Skolnick's (1966) conception of the police officer as a 'craftsman' (sic), rather than as a 'legal actor', for example, captures this well.

Officials working within the criminal justice system are prohibited from basing their decisions upon arbitrary or irrelevant standards, and they are required to apply rules impartially. These injunctions are normally interpreted in the socio-legal literature as precluding decisions based on distinctive characteristics of individuals: race, ethnicity, social class, socio-economic status, sex or sexual orientation, for example. But illicit considerations in the exercise of discretion are far from rare. With regard to police decision-making, for example, we learn from research studies (not incontrovertibly, it should be acknowledged) that ethnicity can be an influence on decisions to stop and search people on the street (Willis 1983; Jones, MacLean and Young 1986; Home Office 2000). And even clothing (base ball caps and hooded jackets, for instance) and the type and cost of cars can influence decisions in this regard (Quinton, Bland and Miller 2000).[5] In the courtroom, we learn that the appearance of gender-appropriate or inappropriate behaviour can influence decisions (Edwards 1984; Eaton 1986; Worrall 1990; Gelsthorpe and Loucks 1997).[6]

There is one other related point that we want to make here. It concerns power. As previously indicated, the exercise of discretion necessarily involves a power to decide, to choose, to discern or to determine. This leads not only to considerations of the misuse of power (biased decision-making where illicit factors are given weight in the decision-making process), but also to considerations of controls (internal or external) and accountability (Davis 1969; Reiss 1974).[7] Since this theme concerns the legitimacy of the exercise of discretion, one of the fundamental questions that emerged from the seminar discussions which led to this book, we do not address it here, but it is a persistent theme throughout the chapters.

This dip into the socio-legal literature in the area of criminal justice demonstrates the importance of considering factors such as process, environment or culture, organisational culture and occupational culture, as well as illicit variables, all of which go well beyond the law, when trying to understand the exercise of discretion. Moreover, considerations of the exercise of discretion involve reflections on power: who has the authority to decide, to choose, to judge. Many of these themes emerge not only in significant contributions to the socio-legal field (some of which we note below), but also in the pages of this book.

Notwithstanding the general commentary on the dimensions of discretion above, this introduction would be incomplete without acknowledgement of some of the major socio-legal and criminological works that have explored the concept of discretion. With different degrees of emphasis, key authors such as Davis (1969, 1976), Bottomley (1973), Galligan (1986) and Hawkins (1992) explore the four fundamental questions that we set out at the beginning of this chapter. Again, we are necessarily selective here, but few would dispute that one of the first serious attempts to analyse discretion emerged in 1969 with the publication of Kenneth Culp Davis' *Discretionary Justice*. In a critical exposition of the concept of discretion in the application of criminal justice, Davis explores what can be done to ensure that 'where law ends tyranny will not begin' (1969: 3). His particular concerns were that US administrative systems at that time had created excessive discretionary power. His treatise on discretion thus serves as a corrective as he sets out the case for a more balanced approach. His claim is that while discretionary power is necessary, the 'huge quantities of unnecessary discretionary power' should be cut back (1969: 217) in order to ensure justice for individuals. While not being an advocate of improved statutory standards on their own, as an alternative to discretion, he argues that more elaborate administrative rule-making may be a key to justice, if accompanied by better structuring and checking of discretionary power.

Davis also highlights 'openness' as being a key to the fair exercise of discretion: openness in plans, openness in policy statements, and open findings and reasons. As he puts it, 'openness is a natural enemy of arbitrariness, a natural ally in the fight against injustice' (1969: 226). With this in mind, among other things, Davis also proposed eliminating barriers to judicial review and the setting up of a Federal Appeals Tribunal so as to ensure access for those who felt that the exercise of discretionary power had been unjust. In an interesting response to Davis' rather negative view of discretion, Baldwin and Hawkins (1984) point to the need to look at the operational strengths and weaknesses of various control devices, rather than assuming that powers of regulation should be extended. In other words, more control does not necessarily mean better control. This is a useful point to bear in mind when considering the new research findings that are described in this book.

In a subsequent exploration of discretion, Davis explores discretionary justice in Europe and America (1976). Having claimed that Americans had failed to solve many problems in the exercising of discretion, the aim here was to compare different perspectives. Various contributors to the book thus explore the situation in Germany, the Netherlands, Denmark, Italy and France, as well as more generally within the Europe. What is particularly telling in this collection of essays is the way in which Davis exhorted his European colleagues to carry out interviews with administrators to find out how decisions were made and discretion exercised in practice. Thus the essays focus on discretionary power behind the scenes, so to speak.

Keith Bottomley similarly explores the meaning and exercise of discretion in *Decisions in the Penal Process* (1973). The book asks questions regarding the stages in the process of dealing with offenders in which decisions are made, and asks about the nature of those decisions. Bottomley pursues an analysis that takes us to the heart of matters by focusing on *'what is'* – on the actual operation of things, rather than simply what the law or rules say. The book starts with some discussion about social attitudes towards crime, and patterns of reporting and recording crimes. The power to exercise discretion is also explored in his analysis of police law enforcement, pre-trial decision-making, sentencing, prison classification and parole. In an insightful conclusion to the book, Bottomley identifies tensions between the notion of structural unity and common purpose in the processing of offenders, and the reality of the system that revolves around a multiplicity of conflicting values and aims. Thus there is no authoritative resolution of the principle objectives and this inevitably influences the exercise of discretion; there are both ideological differences and operational differences in each part of the process. Of course, there have been many attempts to create more of a coherent system since Bottomley (1973) first drew attention to these issues, not least the government's attempt to promote 'joined up thinking' (Cavadino and Dignan 2001; Faulkner 2001). But in anticipating moves towards integration and greater control through open procedures and decision-making, as advocated by Davis (1969) and fellow American, Walker (1993), Bottomley is arguably right to think that some of the prescriptions for integrating the operation of the criminal justice system might be unrealistic. As he states:

> It is important to recognize the existence of interaction between the different parts of the system, that the 'output' of one stage provides the 'input' for another, and that for the system to be 'rational' there would need to be an overall goal towards which each and every part was directed, but in fact the complex socio-political nature of crime and society's response to criminal behaviour seems to rule out the possibility of any real integration or 'rationality' throughout the penal process.
>
> (Bottomley 1973: 225)

Thus, in this important analysis of the reality of decision-making, Bottomley is acknowledging the fact that conflicts and ambiguities are inherent in the system. At the same time, he is suggesting not only that discretion is indispensable for justice, but that it is right for us to question the various official claims about the principles which are intended to inform the process of decision-making. While short on practical suggestions as to how this can be done, Bottomley favours society as a whole being the arbiter, the judge of what principles *ought* to underlie the penal process.

Denis Galligan's (1986) contribution is a legal one. The main focus of his book *Discretionary Powers* is to explore some of the issues that emerge with respect to discretionary powers in the hands of administrative officials. He grapples with the different legal perspectives on discretion; on the one hand there is acceptance of its inevitable existence, and a feeling that the proper legal strategy is to keep it to a minimum so as to limit damage. It is believed that this can be done by regulating its exercise through fixed and certain rules. On the other hand, jurisprudential debate about judicial reasoning is centrally about discretion. Galligan's exploration prompts us to emphasise the significance of the legal theory perspectives on discretion.

Legal philosophers have long sought to explain justice, law and rights, and these central issues in jurisprudence underlie our work (see Simmonds 1986, which remains the leading introduction to these issues). Each empirical study in this book questions whether or not the decision-making processes under the microscope are 'fair'. One thing is clear: the English courts seem to have become more interested in 'procedural justice' than 'substantive justice'. It is a common theme in our work that decision-makers seem preoccupied with fair procedures. Whether outcomes are fair is a more difficult issue. John Rawls' *Theory of Justice* (1972) has influenced current thinking on this subject perhaps more than any other. We assume that our courts give fair *and* just punishment, but Rawls argues that the concepts of justice and fairness are essentially the same. Many readers will be familiar with his story about a group of men and women who do not belong to any particular society, and have come together in a kind of constitutional convention to choose fundamental rules for a new society. There is nothing particularly distinctive about these people; they have specific identities, weaknesses, strengths and interests. They suffer from amnesia, however, and they have no idea who they are, whether they are young or old, black or white, talented or stupid. In particular (and crucial to Rawls' argument), they do not know what their beliefs are regarding what is valuable in life. Each person has some sort of rational plan of life, but they do not know the details of this plan. Indeed, they are separated from their own personalities by what Rawls calls a 'veil of ignorance'. Rawls contends that the construction of rules will reflect what people believe is best for them – as individuals. Each person would be interested in establishing the fairest rules because they would not be protected by social or any other advantages. Thus, Rawls considers that the basic institutions of a society would be chosen by rational people under conditions that ensure impartiality. From this original position, just two principles of justice would emerge: first, everyone would have basic liberties, such as equal liberty to speak, freedom of conscience, freedom to hold personal property, to be protected in their person, not to be arrested suddenly and without cause, and so on. Indeed, these are what we might call conventional liberties. Rawls' second principle relates to social and economic equality. He argues that no difference in wealth should be tolerated unless that difference works for the benefit of the worst-off group in society. The first principle takes priority over the second in that it is only when the first principle is completely satisfied that we can apply the second principle at all. Rawls' thinking has come under attack, not least from those who believe that the idea of a rational agent (person) situated behind a 'veil of ignorance' is faulty (see Gelsthorpe 2001). This said, the first principle makes clear that there are some basic liberties. The list is not self-evident, however. The second criticism here is that these so-called rational people may not appreciate alternative standpoints. Impartiality and objectivity are vital to the theory, but the danger is that what Rawls may presume to be universal is in fact partial (Young 1990; Hudson 2001). Hudson (1998), in particular, has sought to reconstruct theories of justice based on difference.

Dworkin (1977) builds on Rawls to argue that one right is fundamental: the right to equality, what he calls the right to equal concern and respect. He explores the nature of legal decision-making, concentrating on the role of judges and legislators. Law can be seen as a system of rules, but the jurisprudential problems arise when considering judicial discretion. What is it that a judge is doing in 'hard cases', when the existing rules of law do not give an easy answer? Sometimes the judges must 'discover' the law in order to reach the 'right' answer. Only David Thomas looks at judicial discretion in this book (see Chapter 3), and only in the context of sentencing where all cases may be seen as 'hard cases'. Legal theorists have struggled to explain 'hard cases' – for example, Hart (1961), whose *Concept of Law* is a classic 'positivist' explanation, concludes that, where rules conflict or where there are irreconcileable rules, a judge must use his or her discretion, his or her own conception of what is 'just' to 'invent' the law. Dworkin does not accept that law is simply made up of rules.

Dworkin (1977) challenges Hart and other legal positivists in *Taking Rights Seriously*. As the title of his book suggests, Dworkin defends the case for individual rights. In his analysis, Dworkin holds that courts should decide hard cases on grounds of principles, not policy: principles define rights, and individual rights operate as 'political trumps held by individuals' (1977: xi). Policies merely define collective goals. Dworkin is keen to marginalise the role of discretion in defending his theory of law and does this by arguing that judicial decisions are based on arguments of principle. For Dworkin, the word 'discretion' can be used in various ways. He identifies two 'weak senses'. The first weak sense suggests simply that an official must use judgment in applying the standards set by authority. The second weak sense is where an official is a final arbiter because no-one will review his or her exercise of judgment. Alternatively, discretion in a 'strong sense' is used to show that on some issues an official is simply not bound by standards set by the authority in question. It is this 'strong' sense of discretion which really interests Dworkin, for it is here that a sentencing judge may have discretion. He points out that 'discretion, like the hole in a doughnut, does not exist except as an area left open by a surrounding belt of restriction. It is therefore a relative concept' (1977: 39).

As previously indicated, underlying any discussion of discretion lies an argument about justice-as-fairness. To be fair, the law must be applied consistently. Is flexible decision-making unpredictable decision-making? Thereby hangs one of the central dilemmas of discretionary decision-making: finding the balance between certainty and flexibility. It is no accident that all those whose decisions are examined in this book have been given authority, either directly or indirectly as part of their jobs, to exercise discretion. The police, the Parole Board, the Mental Health Review Tribunal and the Immigration Service Adjudicator (to name but four of those whose decisions we scrutinise) operate in a world where the formal legal constraints on their powers are limited. The 'frames of reference' within which they operate have not been tightly constrained by the law.

The emphasis on formal justice means that the decision-maker is often *process orientated*; much time is spent considering whether the right procedures have been followed rather than whether the right conclusion has been reached. Few would doubt the importance of fair procedures. Not only are they instrumental on outcomes, but they serve other important (political) values such as representation and participation too. They may also encourage the treatment of the subject of the decision as a responsible agent. However, there is also a growing awareness that an over-concentration on fair procedures can lead to myopia. As Lacey suggests:

> The contribution made by procedural reforms on criminal justice to the wider goal of fairness of outcome is seriously limited by the fact that one of the major problems ... is that the legal and indeed political systems generate no relatively determinate criteria as to what counts as a fair or correct outcome.
>
> (Lacey 1987: 226)

One might go further to suggest that a concentration on procedural fairness may allow the decision-maker to fail to recognise the essential 'blur' at the centre of their enterprise. One of the ambitions of this collection of essays is to tease out some of these uncertainties with which decision-makers operate.

Another major concern of legal theorists has been the need for accountability and control (Birkenshaw 1985; Harlow and Rawlings 1997). Limiting discretion is not necessarily a good in itself (see Baldwin and Hawkins 1984), but a system of adequate control devices is essential. Hence lawyers' preoccupation with judicial review, Ombudsmen and other complaints mechanisms. However, the main thrust of the work within this book follows in the socio-legal tradition of Keith Hawkins: that is, on the decision-making process itself. This is not to say that the work of legal theorists is ignored. Lacey highlights something of the interdependence of jurisprudential and social science approaches, concluding that, 'we need to integrate empirical, interpretive, and normative questions in an attempt both to understand discretion and, ultimately, to ensure the legitimacy and effectiveness of the exercise of social power in particular contexts' (1992: 388).

Keith Hawkins' work on discretion has been hugely important in socio-legal circles. In earlier consideration of issues Hawkins points out the need to think about a number of key areas: the decision-making process as a highly subtle, shifting, dynamic matter; the problematic nature of the material for decision; broader ideological, symbolic, socio-political, economic, organisational and interactional constraints on decision-makers; and the multifarious meanings and interpretations that are given to discretion (1983a, 1983b, 1984). As the chapters that follow reveal, it is this work and the later book on *The Uses of Discretion* (Hawkins (ed.) 1992) that has inspired much of our collective thinking about discretion. Contributors to *The Uses of Discretion* question the part that legal rules play in action by legal officials alongside a range of other social, political, economic, and organisational constraints which shape the way in which discretion is exercised. Contributors also compare the advantages and disadvantages of rules and discretion, and debate what would be an appropriate mix. As a contributor, Schneider (1992), for example, identifies four types of discretion: i) 'khadi discretion', which revolves around an individual making decisions about individuals on the basis of a range of factors reflecting legal, ethical, emotional and political interests; ii) 'rule-failure discretion', which is where discretionary authority is established in anticipation of complex cases that will defy any rules; iii) 'rule-building discretion', which is where decision-makers are granted discretionary authority in the belief that better rules will emerge from this experience; and iv) 'rule-compromise discretion' which, as the name suggests, involves compromise where there is an absence of agreement over appropriate rules. Identification of different types of discretion leads to consideration of constraints on decision-making and to mechanisms of accountability. Contributors to *The Uses of Discretion* also look at the way in which both formal rules and procedures and the exigencies of every day practice limit and shape decision-making on the ground. Such constraints range from regulatory inspection to decision-makers' socialisation and training. And they look not only at the relationship between law and other forms of constraint on the exercise of discretion, but at the implications of discretion for theories of law.

The aim of this book

This book makes no attempt to address all the questions and issues raised by previous authors; its modest aim is to add to a descriptive understanding of the uses of discretion in contemporary criminal justice and related circles. In this way we believe that it will help keep debates about the meaning and uses of discretion alive. We think our revisiting of discretion timely in a context of increasing attempts to control judicial discretion through statutory means – criteria for custody (Ashworth 2002), jury trials (Jackson 2002; Doran 2002) and through the Home Secretary's interventions (regarding lifers, for example, when mandatory life sentences were introduced for a second serious offence; see Ashworth, 2002 and Henham, 1998). A further example of attempts to limit discretion emerges through the newly established youth justice system, with its structured approach to pre-court decision-making through clear rules which set out the criteria for the issuing of reprimands and warnings. This system was arguably set up partly in response to criticisms that too many young offenders were being diverted away from formal criminal justice procedures, or were being cautioned too often (Muncie 1999; Gelsthorpe 2002). Decisions about the detention and removal of selected asylum seekers emphasise that decision-making is made in a political context (Weber and Gelsthorpe 2000; Weber and Landman 2002). In the mental health field, official enquiry after enquiry has questioned decisions to release offenders into the community, yet it is clear that decisions are influenced not only by medical risk assessments, but by practical considerations such as bed space and costs (Melzer et al. 2000; House of Commons 2000).

About this book

The order of the chapters which follows is simple: we start with the more obviously 'core' criminal justice concerns and move steadily outwards. A feature of many of the decisions which we explore is their difficult nature: there is little that is 'routine' in deciding who should get one of the limited numbers of secure hospital beds, or whether to take the 'risk' of releasing a mentally ill patient or a life sentence prisoner.

Key questions recur: the role of intuition, or the nature of an independent decision, for example. A common feature, too, perhaps is as Hawkins (1992) suggests, that the ostensible criteria (often legal) turn out on close inspection to be less important than other criteria. There are notable differences between theory, policy and practice.

In the first substantive chapter, Vicky Kemp and Loraine Gelsthorpe explore discretion in pre-court decision-making. The discretion not to prosecute young offenders has been a feature of police decision-making since its inception. Kemp and Gelsthorpe review developments in police discretion with regard to young offenders and then focus on one particular local authority area, well known for its propensity to divert young offenders from prosecution. They consider some contemporary issues concerning police discretion: the impact of the Crime and Disorder Act 1998, issues which revolve around netwidening, and the application of legal criteria in the decision-making process, for example. Who makes decisions, the limits of internal review, and negative un-intended consequences of policies all come to the fore and point to the need for checks and balances in the regulation of discretion on the ground.

A chapter on discretion in sentencing by David Thomas follows. Contrary to the image often presented by the media, a sentencing judge does not have untrammelled discretion when deciding what sentence should be imposed on an offender in an individual case. Thomas' historical account makes clear that judicial discretion in sentencing is of relatively recent origin. As the discretion grew, so did the need to control it, hence the birth of the Court of Criminal Appeal in 1907. Thomas makes the important point that until the 20th century, sentencing was merely a matter of quantifying punishment; the choice between competing penal objectives has arisen with the developments of alternatives to custodial sentences. Thomas also traces the changes in parole and early release rules in the 20th century, commenting that the effective authority of the judiciary, and therefore of the importance of the decisions which they made, has been reduced by these changes. Particularly pertinent for the study of discretion is Thomas' analysis of 'judicial self-regulation', which, he concludes, has reached 'a reasonably high level of sophistication'.

Thus there is considerable value in taking an historical approach in order to understand the changing role of discretion in sentencing and in order to understand both internal and external pressures on judicial decision-making. We also see revealed a particular tension between Parliamentary regulation and judicial regulation.

Many studies of the criminal justice system end with the imposition of the sentence. But for the offender committed to prison this is just the beginning. The next two chapters explore two areas where the prisoner is especially liable to the vagaries of discretionary powers. First Alison Liebling and David Price consider the exercise of discretion in the work of prison officers, drawing on their own recent research carried out in a single maximum security prison in England (Liebling and Price 1999). Rules may be the anchor in a world of uncertainty, but their flexible interpretation and application is a key feature of effective prison work, as well as a key feature in its corruption. As they argue, norms of reciprocity exist between the enforcer and the enforced, which result in rules being suspended in the interests of long-term interests. Liebling and Price explore similarities between the work of prison officers and the work of regulation inspectors, and between prison officers and police officers. In many ways, the work of a prison officer can be regarded as 'policing the community', where the enforcement of the 'law' is sometimes suspended in the interests of order. They point out that prison officers cannot enforce all the rules if they want to get to the 'end of the day', without difficulty: what they term the 'unexercise of power' in prison is significant. Officers need to secure co-operation from prisoners, but in ways that retain and enhance legitimacy: rules are resources to be drawn upon. Liebling and Price explore links between the use of formal and informal power, and the nature of relationships between staff and prisoners. They suggest that the closer the relationships, the higher the ratio of informal to formal power used.

Whilst many studies focus on the abuse of power, Liebling and Price focus also on the under-use of power. They argue that more attention should be paid by those interested in the use of discretion to the use of discretion in prison life, and to the principles and beliefs underlying its use. Interestingly, in their description of the negotiated controlling relationships between prison officers and prisoners, the authors also exemplify 'discretion' as mercy in its most positive, compassionate sense (see earlier comments on mercy on pages 5–6).

The second prison-based chapter is by Nicola Padfield and Alison Liebling, with Helen Arnold, and concerns discretion and the release of life sentence prisoners. This chapter arises from research into the release of life sentence prisoners carried out in 1999, which involved an observational study of the nature and quality decision-making at Discretionary Lifer Panels of the Parole Board (Padfield and Liebling 2000). These panels have been given the responsibility by Parliament to direct the Home Secretary to release a life sentence prisoner only if they are satisfied that it is no longer necessary for the protection of the public that the prisoner should be confined (section 28(6) of the Crime (Sentences) Act 1997). The decision-making process is thus primarily about risk and its assessment, with an extremely difficult (and arguably high-risk) population. About 300 cases are considered each year. Only about 10 per cent of cases are directed for release and perhaps a further 20 per cent of cases are recommended for transfer to open prison conditions. Padfield and Liebling argue that discretion, whilst ostensibly in the hands of the Parole Board, actually lies elsewhere. They explore the many decisions (those of the sentencing judge, the Prison Service, probation officers, and not least the prisoner himself and his legal representatives) that have to be taken before a discretionary life sentence prisoner is released from, or recalled into, prison. They question the relationship between the decisions taken by the key 'players' within the system and the culture of caution in which all players operate.

The emphasis is thus on the broader constraints within which the Parole Board operates. The difficulty of the task which lies before them in terms of predicting risk of reoffending perhaps helps explain the willingness of the Parole Board to accept these constraints. Nevertheless, the research findings point to the need for greater openness and accountability in the process – especially since decisions are being made in a 'blame' and risk-averse culture.

The next three chapters move further afield to mental health and asylum seekers, but again the same themes recur. First, Adrian Grounds,

Marie Howes and Loraine Gelsthorpe look at discretion with regard to offenders' routes into forensic psychiatric units. They discuss psychiatrists' views of their decision-making processes when admitting offenders into medium secure care. The chapter is based on research which was part of a wider project, commissioned by the Department of Health, to examine current resources and practices with a view to assisting future planning and provision (Melzer et al. 2000). 'Medium secure care' is a nebulous region located somewhere between maximum security and the local locked wards' security – decisions on detention are perceived to be clinically-based, with the consultant's word the final arbiter, though with a degree of consensual exchange in the process. The authors' discussion touches on ways in which the training, belief systems and values of the consultants have had to be accommodated within increasingly political and economic agendas. Here, too, a hierarchy of managerial and other non-clinical constraints have an impact on their decision-making role. In particular, two linked aspects come to the fore. One is the difficulty of achieving and maintaining the balance between the individual patient's rights and needs and the proper concern for public safety. The other is a focus on risk. In one sense, medium secure care always involves a degree of created risk as it prepares patients for moving on and out of that level of security. As with the discussion of limitations on parole board discretion, the increasing importance given to the prediction and calculation of risk underlies this chapter. But there are some interesting differences between this and the criminal justice world too. Whereas a limit on the number of prison places would be politically unpalatable, it is clear that those working in the mental health field operate under practical constraints which revolve around limited capacity (bed space). Thus there is a concomitant need to prioritise cases. The evidence outlined here also points to an interdependence between agencies. An agency ostensibly outside the criminal justice system is actually dependent on it, as blocks and delays between prisons and medium secure units (MSUs) lead to problems of depriving patients of treatment. There are problems between mental health agencies, too, where different levels of security operate, meaning that patients cannot be transferred to an appropriate MSU for treatment. All these constraints perhaps lead psychiatrists to doubt their decisions and to wish that they had made different decisions, a point which is particularly significant in a context which values psychiatrists' scientific assessment of risk *and* their intuition. With the borders between private and public health care becoming increasingly blurred, there are also some questions here as to whether decision-making might be different in the independent sector.

Next, Katy Holloway and Adrian Grounds explore discretion in the decisions to release mentally disordered offenders. This chapter is concerned with the operation of the Mental Health Review Tribunal system and presents an empirical investigation of tribunal decision-making in restricted cases. Given that the first priority of a tribunal is to safeguard patients, the authors consider how effectively tribunals are fulfilling their fundamental role in the current climate of heightened concern for public safety. They describe a retrospective file study of hearings which was conducted to explore the factors predictive of tribunal outcome. Perhaps unsurprisingly, the factor of greatest influence was the written opinion of the responsible medical officer. Second, a questionnaire survey of tribunal members was designed to explore how members used the evidence and applied the discharge criteria when making their decision. The medical evidence, particularly that of the medical member, was reportedly of most assistance to the members. The evidence of the Home Secretary and the social worker were rarely of assistance. Perhaps most troubling is their finding that questionnaire responses also indicated that a number of patients had not been discharged in spite of majority (or unanimous) agreement that they had satisfied the discharge criteria. Holloway and Grounds' third study, observational in nature, reveals the negative effect of a heavy caseload on the quality of tribunal decision-making. They conclude that tribunals are failing in their duty to protect some patients from unjustified detention. This failure, however, is not solely a result of preoccupation with issues of public safety: they identify problems with the process of decision-making itself, in the rules governing the tribunal process, in the tribunals' powers (or lack thereof) and in the evidence upon which their decisions must be based.

There is a startling conclusion here (page 150) that some patients are not discharged despite agreement that the discharge criteria have been satisfied, a point which strikes at the heart of principles of fairness. Two other points seem particularly noteworthy in this account of decision-making: the importance of the concept of 'independence' to the Mental Health Review Tribunal and the dominance of the medical officer's written evidence. These points clearly create a tension.

The penultimate chapter is devoted to discretion and the detention of asylum seekers, a topic which is politically charged and widely neglected by academics. It draws on interviews conducted with immigration officers (see Weber and Gelsthorpe 2000). Weber examines the individual differences in decision-making styles which were identified in that research, and considers whether the concept of individuals as role-, rule- or value-orientated might help to explain the differences observed in the way immigration officers exercise their discretion. She draws on a typology formulated by social psychologists Kelman and Hamilton (1989) to explain the propensity of organisational actors to actively participate in, or tacitly consent to, large-scale harmful acts ranging from bureaucratic bungles (such as the 1986 Space Shuttle disaster) to military massacres (such as the My Lai killings). Although not immediately identifiable with these high-profile 'crimes of obedience', Weber considers that the detention of asylum seekers is an example of the routine production of harm, since the administrative decisions made by junior officials on a day-to-day basis can lead to long periods of detention for people not accused of any crime, many of whom will later prove to be 'genuine refugees' or to be particularly vulnerable to the effects of incarceration. After considering the evidence obtained from the interviews, Weber concludes (albeit tentatively) that officers who identify closely with their role (dubbed 'entry controllers') are the most likely to actively seek to detain asylum seekers, while those who have a clear set of personal values which are at odds with the use of detention (dubbed 'critical thinkers') are most likely to resist its use. Both these groups, she argues, seek to exercise their personal discretion more actively than their colleagues, identified as 'bureaucrats' or 'humanitarians', who may go along with prevailing practices, although for different reasons.

What is particularly interesting here is the distinction drawn between roles, rules and values among immigration officers and how these roles can shape decisions. The account of immigration officers' decision-making also highlights the importance of the individual, both in relation to why certain asylum applicants are singled out, and in relation to immigration officers as individuals and not simply functionaries.

Finally in what serves as an epilogue, Keith Hawkins comments on both common and distinctive themes in the other chapters in the book. He reflects on criminal justice decision-making under the title 'Order, rationality and silence'. He returns to the issue of 'framing', which, as he puts it, involves making sense of signals from the surround and the field. Thinking about framing processes has helped many of the contributors to this book interpret the decision-making processes they analysed. The chapters, combined, focus on instrumental and expressive conceptions of decision-making and highlight the importance of understanding precisely what is going on in the process of making decisions. The fact that the chapters are all rooted in empirical evidence adds much to our knowledge here, and it is arguable that it is only by immersing ourselves in the day-to-day decision-making of different agencies and systems that we can evaluate both the role and regulation of discretion. But the chapters also highlight difficulties – particularly with regard to serial decision-making and the way in which different frames of reference and organisational contexts shape the results. To judge from these chapters, the role of status, expertise, and charisma all emerge as ways of resolving differences between decision-makers, but there are questions as to whether these are the appropriate resolutions.

Hawkins notes, in his concluding chapter, three sorts of silence in much existing research: lack of attention to the wider forces at play, to other important interested individuals or groups, and to parallel decision-making. There is, of course, a danger that where research is focused on the decision-makers, it may exclude the subjects of the decision, and Hawkins makes a plea that researchers ought not to forget the subjects of criminal justice decisions, nor the audience for such decisions. We can only plead that a better understanding of the frameworks within which the decisions we review are made is in the interests of both subject and audience.

Notes

1 See also the work of Hay (1975); Linebaugh (1992); Morgan and Rushton (1998).
2 For an outline of pre-court processing options for both adults and juveniles, see Sanders and Young (2002). It should be noted that juveniles are no longer cautioned; a system of reprimands and warnings is in place instead.
3 We are necessarily selective in referring to the literature here; our purpose is merely to provide some examples of research studies where the exercise of discretion has been the focus of attention. But looking more broadly at the literature, Richardson's (1982) investigation of the regulation and control of pollution, Hawkins's (1984) analysis of the regulation of the environment and Baldwin's (1985) account of the uses of discretion in the regulation of the airline industry are considered very important.
4 See Bowling and Foster (2002), for an overview of research on policing.
5 For an overview of the evidence see Smith (1997) and Bowling and Phillips (2002).
6 See Gelsthorpe (2001) for an overview of the research evidence in this area.
7 Salem (1983) also explores this in her theoretical analysis of the concept of discretion.

References

Ashworth, A. (1998) 'Four techniques for reducing disparity', in von Hirsch, A. and Ashworth, A. (eds.) *Principled Sentencing: Readings on Theory and Policy*.

Oxford: Hart Publishing.

Ashworth, A. (2002) 'Sentencing' in Maguire, M., Morgan, R. and Reiner, R. (eds.) *The Oxford Handbook of Criminology*, 3rd edn. Oxford: Clarendon Press.

Baldwin, J. and Hawkins, K. (1984) 'Discretionary Justice: Davis Reconsidered'. *Public Law*, 570–99.

Baldwin, J. and McConville, M. (1977) *Negotiated Justice: Pressures to Plead Guilty*. London: Martinson.

Baldwin, R. (1985) *Regulating the Airlines: Administrative Justice and Agency Discretion*. Oxford: Clarendon Press.

Banton, M. (1964) *The Policeman in the Community*. London: Tavistock.

Baumgartner, M. (1992) 'The Myth of Discretion' in Hawkins, K. (ed.), *The Uses of Discretion*. Oxford: Clarendon Press.

Beck, K. (1992) *Risk Society: Towards a New Modernity*. London: Sage Publications.

Birkenshaw, P. (1985) *Grievances, Remedies and the State*. London: Sweet and Maxwell.

Bittner, E. (1964) 'The Police on Skid-Row: A Study of Peace Keeping'. *American Sociological Review*, 32, 699–715.

Bottomley, K. (1973) *Decisions in the Penal Process*. London: Martin Robertson.

Bowling, B. and Foster, J. (2002) 'Policing and the Police', in Maguire, M., Morgan, R. and Reiner, R. (eds.) *The Oxford Handbook of Criminology*, 3rd edn. Oxford: Oxford University Press.

Bowling, B. and Phillips, C. (2002) *Racism, Crime and Justice*. London: Longman.

Cain, M. (1973) *Society and the Policeman's Role*. London: Routledge and Kegan Paul.

Cavadino, M. and Dignan, J. (2001) *The Penal System: An Introduction*. London: Sage.

Cicourel, A. (1976) *The Social Organisation of Juvenile Justice*. London: Heinemann. (revised edition; first published in 1968)

Davis, K. (1969) *Discretionary Justice: A Preliminary Inquiry*. Baton Rouge, Louisiana: Louisiana State University.

Davis, K. (1976) (ed.) *Discretionary Justice in Europe and America*. Urbana, USA: University of Illinois Press.

Doran, S. (2002) 'Trial by Jury' in McConville, M. and Wilson, G. (eds.) *The Handbook of the Criminal Justice Process*. Oxford: Oxford University Press.

Doran, S. and Jackson, J. (2000) (eds.) *The judicial role in criminal proceedings*. Portland, Oregan: Hart Publishing.

Downes, D. (1988) *Contrasts in Tolerance*. Oxford: Oxford University Press.

Dworkin, R. (1977) *Taking Rights Seriously*. London: Duckworth.

Eaton, M. (1985) *Justice for Women?* Buckingham: Open University Press.

Edwards, S. (1984) *Women on Trial*. Manchester: Manchester University Press.

Faulkner, D. (2001) *Crime, State and Citizen*. Winchester: Waterside Press.

Fielding, N. (1994) 'The organisational and occupational troubles of community police'. *Policing and Society*, 4(3), 305–22.

Galligan, D. (1986) *Discretionary Powers: Legal Study of Official Discretion.* Oxford: Clarendon Press.

Galligan, D. (1996) *Due Process and Fair Procedures.* Oxford: Clarendon Press.

Garland, D. (2001) *The Culture of Control: Crime and Social Order in Contemporary Society.* Oxford: Oxford University Press.

Gelsthorpe, L. (2001) 'Critical decisions and processes in the criminal courts' in McLaughlin, E. and Muncie, J. (eds.) *Controlling Crime.* London: Sage (in association with The Open University).

Gelsthorpe, L. (2002) 'Recent Changes in Youth Justice Policy in England and Wales' in Weijers, I. and Duff, A. (eds.) *Punishing Juveniles: principle and critique.* Oxford: Hart.

Gelsthorpe, L. and Giller, H. (1990) 'More justice for juveniles: does more mean better?', *Criminal Law Review,* 153–64.

Gelsthorpe, L. and Loucks, N. (1997) 'Magistrates' explanations of sentencing decisions' in Hedderman C. and Gelsthorpe, L. (eds.) *Understanding the Sentencing of Women,* Home Office Research Study 170. London: Home Office Research, Development and Statistics Directorate.

Grimshaw, R. and Jefferson, R. (1987) *Interpreting Policework.* London: Allen and Unwin.

Harlow, C. and Rawlings, R. (1997) *Law and Administration,* 2nd edn. London: Butterworths.

Hart, H. (1961) *The Concept of Law.* Oxford: Clarendon.

Hawkins, K. (1983a) 'Thinking about legal decision-making' in Shapland, J. (ed.) *Decision-making in the Legal System: Issues in Criminological and Legal Psychology,* 5. British Psychological Society.

Hawkins, K. (1983b) 'Assessing Evil: Decision Behaviour and Parole Board Justice'. *British Journal of Criminology,* 23, 101–27.

Hawkins, K. (1984) *Environment and Enforcement: Regulations and the Social Definition of Pollution.* Oxford: Oxford University Press.

Hawkins, K. (1992) 'Using Legal Discretion' in Hawkins, K. (ed.) *The Uses of Discretion.* Oxford: Clarendon Press.

Hay, D. (1975) 'Property, Authority and the Criminal Law' in Hay, D. et al. (eds.) *Albion's Fatal Tree: Crime and Society in Eighteenth Century England.* London: Allen Lane.

Hedderman, C. and Gelsthorpe, L. (1997) (eds.) *Understanding the Sentencing of Women.* Home Office Research Study 170. London: Home Office Research, Development and Statistics Directorate.

Henham, R. (1998) 'Making Sense of the Crime (Sentences) Act 1997', *Modern Law Review,* 61, 223.

Holdaway, S. (1979) (ed.) *The British Police.* London: Edward Arnold.

Holdaway, S. (1983) *Inside the British Police.* Oxford: Blackwell.

Home Office (2000) *Statistics on Race and the Criminal Justice System 2000: A Section 95 Report.* London: Home Office.

Hood, R. (1962) *Sentencing in Magistrates' Courts.* London: Stevens.

House of Commons (2000) *Health Committee Fourth Report – Provision of NHS*

Health Services. HC 373-1. London: Stationery Office.

Hudson, B. (1996) *Understanding Justice*. Buckingham: Open University Press.

Hudson, B. (1998) 'Doing Justice to Difference' in Ashworth, A. and Wasik, M. (eds.) *Fundamentals of Sentencing Theory*. Oxford: Clarendon Press.

Hudson, B. (2001) 'Punishment, rights and difference: defending justice in the risk society' in Stenson, K. and Sullivan, R. (eds.) *Crime, Risk and Justice*. Cullompton, Devon: Willan Publishing.

Jackson, J. (2002) 'The adversary trial and trial by judge alone' in McConville, M. and Wilson, G. (eds.) *The Handbook of the Criminal Justice Process*. Oxford: Oxford University Press.

Jones, J., MacLean, B. and Young, J. (1986) *The Islington Crime Survey: Crime Victimisation and Policing in Inner City London*. Aldershot: Gower.

Kelman, H. and Hamilton, V. (1989) *Crimes of Obedience: Toward a Social Psychology of Authority and Obedience*. London: Yale University Press.

King, P. (2000) *Crime, Justice and Discretion in England 1740–1820*. Oxford: Oxford University Press.

Lacey, N. (1987) 'Discretion and Due Process at the Post-Conviction Stage' in Dennis, I. (ed.) *Criminal Law and Justice*. London: Sweet and Maxwell.

Lacey, N. (1992) 'The Jurisprudence of Discretion: Escaping the Legal Paradigm' in Hawkins, K. (ed.) *The Uses of Discretion*. Oxford: Clarendon Press.

Levin, M. (1977) *Urban Politics and the Criminal Courts*. Chicago: University of Chicago Press.

Liebling, A. and Price, D. (1999) *An Exploration of Staff–Prisoner Relationships at HMP Whitemoor*. Prison Service Research Report No. 6.

Linebaugh, P. (1992) *The London Hanged: Crime and Civil Society in the Eighteenth Century*. Cambridge: Cambridge University Press.

McCabe, S. and Sutcliffe, F. (1978) *Defining Crime: A Study of Police Decisions*. Oxford: Basil Blackwell.

McConville, M., Sanders, A. and Long, R. (1991) *The Case for the Prosecution: Police Suspects and the Construction of Criminology*. London: Routledge.

Manning, P. (1978) 'Organisation and environment: influences on police work' in Clarke, R. and Hough, J. (eds.) *The Effectiveness of Policing*. Farnborough: Gower.

Melzer, D., Tom, B., The Mental Health Policy Research Group (2000) *Pathways into medium secure psychiatric provision in England and Wales*. Report to the Department of Health. Cambridge, The Epidemiology Policy Group, Department of Public Health and Primary Care, University of Cambridge.

Morgan, G. and Rushton, P. (1998) *Rogues, Thieves and the Rule of Law: The Problem of Law Enforcement in North-East England 1718-1800*. London: University of Central London Press.

Muncie, J. (1999) *Youth and Crime. A Critical Introduction*. London: Sage.

Oldham, J. (1985) 'On Pleading the Belly: A History of the Jury of Matrons'. *Criminal Justice History*, 6, 1–64.

Padfield, N. and Liebling, A. with Arnold, H. (2000) *An Exploration of decision-making at Discretionary Lifer Panels*. Home Office Research Study No. 213. London: Home Office.

Parker, H., Sumner, M. and Jarvis, G. (1989) *Unmasking the Magistrates: The 'custody or not' decisive in sentencing*. Milton Keynes: Open University Press.

Pepinsky, H. (1976) 'Discretion and crime legislation' in Evans, M. (ed.) *Discretion and Control*. Beverly Hills, CA: Sage.

Quinton, P., Bland, N. and Millar, J. (2000) *Police Stops, Decision-making and Practice*. Police Research Series Paper 130. London: Home Office.

Rawls, J. (1972) *A Theory of Justice*. Oxford: Oxford University Press.

Reiss, A. (1974) 'Discretionary Justice' in Glaser, D. (ed.) *Handbook of Criminology*. Chicago: Rand McNally.

Richardson, G. (assisted by Ogus, A. and Burrows, P.) (1982) *Policing Pollution: A Study of Regulation and Enforcement*. Oxford: Oxford University Press.

Salem, S. (1983) *Discretion in Criminal Justice: a theoretical analysis of the concept and a proposed framework for examining its exercise in the criminal justice process*. Ph.D. thesis, University of Cambridge (unpublished).

Sanders, A. and Young, R. (2002) 'From Suspect to Trial', in Maguire, M., Morgan, R. and Reiner, R. (eds.) *The Oxford Handbook of Criminology*, 3rd edn. Oxford: Oxford University Press.

Schneider, C. (1992) 'Discretion and Rules: A Lawyer's View' in Hawkins, K. (ed.) *The Uses of Discretion*. Oxford: Clarendon Press.

Sherman, L. (1980) 'Causes of police behaviour: the current state of quantitative research', *Journal of Research in Crime and Delinquency* 17, 69–100.

Simmonds, N. (1986) *Central Issues in Jurisprudence: Justice, Law and Rights*. London: Sweet and Maxwell.

Skolnick, J. (1966) *Justice without Trial: Law Enforcement in Democratic Society*. New York: John Wiley.

Smith, D. (1997) 'Ethnic Origins, Crime and Criminal Justice' in Maguire, M., Morgan, R. and Reiner, R. (eds.) *The Oxford Handbook of Criminology*, 2nd edn. Oxford: Oxford University Press.

Steer, D. (1970) *Police Cautions: A Study in the Exercise of Police Discretion*. Oxford: Basil Blackwell.

Tonry, M. (1996) *Sentencing Matters*. New York: Oxford University Press.

Walker, N. (1999) *Aggravation, Mitigation and Mercy in English Criminal Justice*. London: Blackstone Press Ltd.

Walker, S. (1993) *Taming the System: The Control of Discretion in Criminal Justice 1950–1990*. New York: Oxford University Press.

Weber, L. and Gelsthorpe, L. (2000) *Deciding to Detain: How Decisions to Detain Asylum Seekers are Made at Ports of Entry*. Cambridge: Institute of Criminology.

Weber, L. and Landman, T. (2002) *Deciding to Detain: the organisational context for decisions to detain asylum seekers at UK ports*. Colchester: Human Rights Centre, University of Essex.

Willis, C. (1983) *The Use, Effectiveness and Impact of Police Stop and Search Powers.* Home Office Research and Planning Unit Paper 15. London: Home Office.

Worrall, A. (1990) *Offending Women: Female Lawbreakers and the Criminal Justice System.* London: Routledge.

Young, I. (1990) *Justice and the Politics of Difference.* Princeton, USA: Princeton University Press.

Young, M. (1991) *An Inside Job: Policing and Police Culture in Britain.* Oxford: Clarendon.

Chapter 2

Youth justice: discretion in pre-court decision-making

Vicky Kemp and Loraine Gelsthorpe

Introduction

In this chapter we consider the nature of police discretion in the context of a study of Northamptonshire's pre-court decision-making process, carried out between January 1999 and April 2000. We begin, however, with a brief historical overview of police cautioning practice. The overview raises a number of issues that are then addressed in the context of our analysis of the way police decision-making may have changed. Northamptonshire is an area well known for its policy not to prosecute young offenders,[1] but the youth justice reforms of the Crime and Disorder Act 1998 (a new system of reprimands and warnings as well as provisions to reduce delays) have inevitably affected the way decisions whether or not to prosecute young people are taken. These decisions are increasingly important now that pre-court decisions are seen increasingly not as alternatives to court, but as a first step towards it.

A brief history of cautioning practices

The police have long enjoyed a wide discretion, including informal measures such as a 'clip around the ear', the 'flick of a policeman's rolled cape' or the confiscation of 'toys, marbles or hoops' (Emsley 1983; Pearson 1983). The first record of a police warning was in 1833 (Steer 1970), four years after the creation of the Metropolitan Police, but it was not until 1853 that official police policy was changed to encourage informal warnings for minor offences (Steer 1970: 54–55).

The setting up of separate courts for juveniles under the Children Act of 1908 was intended to lead the police to bring more children before the court, since magistrates would have a dual role in court, providing both *welfare* and *justice*. Indeed, a Departmental Committee on the Treatment of Young Offenders (the Molony Committee), undertaking the first review of the juvenile courts in 1927 (Home Office 1927), actively encouraged the prosecution of young offenders. The Committee hoped that once it was recognised that 'the courts are specially equipped to help rather than punish the young offender' the reluctance to prosecute would disappear (Home Office 1927: 23). Not surprisingly, the Molony Committee found the use of informal warnings to be objectionable '... usurping the functions of a tribunal' and 'outside the proper duties of the police' (Home Office 1927: 22). Committee members accepted, however, that the police could 'turn a blind eye' to first-time offenders, but only when dealing with 'minor offences' and 'if applied with judgment and good sense' (Home Office 1927: 22). The juvenile courts thus came to have an early 'net-widening' effect, by drawing into the criminal justice system both the deprived and depraved the child.

A further review of the juvenile justice system in the 1960s led to the Children and Young Persons Act 1969, which adopted a predominantly welfare approach, promoting the provision of welfare in court, but also encouraging diversion from court (see Gelsthorpe and Morris 1994). A Home Office guide to the 1969 Act encouraged the police to extend the use of cautions and the involvement of other agencies (Home Office, 1970). By the late 1960s a number of areas had also established 'juvenile liaison bureaux' or 'juvenile liaison schemes' to deal with referrals from the police, all of which facilitated an increase in cautioning.

During the 1980s, diversion from court was repeatedly advocated in government documents, and social workers sought to influence other agencies to keep juveniles out of court and custody. Home Office circulars in 1985 and 1990 encouraged greater use of cautioning (Home Office 1985; 1990). By the early 1990s, the effectiveness of this 'new orthodoxy' (Jones 1984) was evident as the number of young offenders both at court and in custody had reduced dramatically. Largely as a result of Evans and Wilkinson's (1990) research into the 1985 Circular, H.O. Circular 59/90 was issued, giving clearer guidance to police forces, and urging more consistent use of diversionary courses of action (see also Wilkinson and Evans 1990). The 1990 Circular also introduced National Standards.

Some of the professional and academic concern throughout this period revolved around the issue of 'net-widening' (Ditchfield 1976). Were cautions being used as an alternative to prosecution or were young people being cautioned where previously no action would have been taken? Theorists were concerned at the widening of the 'net of social control', the increased power of the state (Austin and Krisberg 1981; Cohen 1985, Garland 1996). Yet by 1994, drawing on research findings, Gelsthorpe and Morris concluded that 'net-widening is not now occurring' (1994: 978).

Theoretical concerns were fuelled by empirical research which raised serious questions about gender and racial discrimination in police decision-making. Early evidence in America suggested that extra-legal factors such as demeanour, attitude and appearance, as well as perceived levels of parental control, could influence decisions in favour of or against diversion (see Piliavin and Briar 1964, for example). In England and Wales analysis of police decision-making revealed that factors such as age, class, ethnicity and parental control could shape police decisions (see, for example, Bennett 1979; Fisher and Mawby 1982; Landau and Nathan 1983; Smith and Gray 1983). Gelsthorpe's (1989) study of the treatment of girls in the criminal justice system included the observation that there was a higher use of police cautioning for girls than boys for the same type of offences. But the real cause of change in cautioning policy in the 1990s was the change in political mood. Bottoms coined the phrase 'popular punitiveness' to reflect the political mood and to convey the notion of politicians 'tapping into, and using for their own purposes, what they believe to be the public's generally punitive stance' (1995: 40).

Thus it was no surprise that Home Office Circular No. 18/1994 sought to limit the use of cautions (Home Office 1994). The Code for Crown Prosecutors was also revised at this time to bring it into line with the seemingly more restrictive approach. The original message that Crown Prosecutors should 'divert juveniles from court whenever possible' was replaced by the statement that 'Crown Prosecutors should not avoid prosecuting simply because of the defendant's age' (Crown Prosecution Service 1986; 1994). Figure 1 below shows graphically that the changes were successful in reducing the proportion of cautions for young offenders who have been found guilty or cautioned.

It was not only the Conservative government that sought to adopt more popular and punitive responses to young offenders. A priority for the newly elected Labour government in May 1997 was reform of the youth justice system. Influenced by the Audit Commission report *Misspent Youth* (1996) and a report for the Home Office on reducing delays at court (Home Office 1997a), the intention of the Labour government was to be 'tough on crime' and this was reflected in the White Paper *No More Excuses* (Home Office 1997b), which set out the

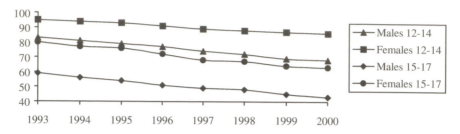

Source: Home Office Criminal Statistics(2001).

Figure 1 *Young offenders cautioned as a percentage of those found guilty or cautioned from 1993–2000*

reforms of the system.

The Crime and Disorder Act 1998 introduced three key changes which had implications for pre-court decision-making. First, each local authority was to form a multi-agency Youth Offending Team (YOT) in order to co-ordinate the provision of youth justice services (Section 39). Secondly, the Act set limits to reduce delays in proceedings (Sections 46 and 50), and thirdly, the cautioning scheme for young offenders was replaced with a new system of reprimands and warnings (also referred to as the Final Warning Scheme) (Sections 65 and 66). All children warned were to be referred to the YOT. The new scheme was designed to limit police discretion with regard to young offenders. Placing the final warning scheme on a statutory basis, the government intended to 'ensure that more consistent action is taken, before a young offender ever appears in court' (Home Office 1997b: 17). Guidance to the police states that only one reprimand may be given. Where an offender has already received a reprimand, the minimum response will be a final warning. Only one warning may normally be given, but a second warning is available where the previous offence was committed more than two years ago, and the offence is minor. Where an offender has already been warned, a further offence should normally result in a charge (Home Office 1999a: Annex C: 9). A conviction at any stage means that a young offender cannot receive a reprimand or warning and must instead be charged.

One other major change brought about by the Crime and Disorder Act 1998 concerns the setting up of the national Youth Justice Board. The introduction of the Board was to give strategic direction, to set standards for, and measure the performance of the youth justice system as a whole. There is thus suggestion of a regulatory role here.

Northamptonshire pre-court diversion: a history of change

We now turn our attention to police practice in Northamptonshire to examine the impact of the changes in practice. The county agencies in Northamptonshire have long supported a multi-agency approach to pre-court diversion. The first two experimental Juvenile Liaison Bureaux (JLB) were set up in 1981. Seconded to each was a police officer, a social worker, a probation officer, a teacher and a youth worker (Blagg et al. 1986). In 1984 another JLB was established (Davis et al. 1989), and in 1986 two experimental Adult Reparation Bureaux were introduced to provide pre-court diversion for adults (Dignan 1990). By 1985 the Northamptonshire police force had achieved the highest cautioning rate in England and Wales at 84 per cent of males aged 10 to 17 for indictable offences (Home Office 1986). Following the 14/1985 Circular, the low rate of prosecution in Northamptonshire continued.

In 1992, influenced perhaps by public fears over the police failure to respond to repeat offenders (Littlechild 1997), a review of pre-court diversion in the county led to the police 'taking back' responsibility for the decision-making process (Northamptonshire County Council 1992). Previously young offenders had been automatically referred to the Juvenile Liaison Bureaux (JLB), and the vast majority of disposal recommendations made by the JLB had been accepted by the police (Blagg et al. 1986; Davis et al. 1989). The juvenile and adult schemes were brought together in 1993 to form the County Diversion Unit (Hughes et al. 1998). Now it was the police alone who were to decide on disposal decisions. Referrals to the Diversion Unit were pre-selected by the police. The consequence of this change was that 'the previous social work-derived "systems" based approach appears to have taken a back seat to a police-driven agenda' (Hughes et al. 1998: 22).[2]

Although they took back responsibility for decision-making, the police did not seek to limit the number of cautions as required by the Home Office Circular of 1994. Rather than give in to central pressure to limit the number of cautions (see Her Majesty's Inspectorate of Constabulary 1994, for example), it was agreed locally that the police would allow young offenders to be diverted four or five times (depending on the seriousness of the offence) prior to prosecution (Northamptonshire Police 1994). While the Northamptonshire police force operated against national guidelines, however, its approach was endorsed by the Audit Commission in 1996, who particularly recommended the practice of combining a caution with an intervention (often referred to as a 'caution plus') as a model of good practice (Audit Commission 1996). Northamptonshire's 'caution plus' scheme was also later commended by the Home Office and cited in the White Paper as a successful programme on which final warning interventions could be built (1997b: 17).

Northamptonshire's approach to pre-court decision-making

Further change took place in 1998 when the Diversion Unit was merged with the Youth Justice Team to form the Northamptonshire YOT, following the enactment of the Crime and Disorder Act 1998. (Figure 2 below shows the key transitions between the different pre-court decision-making systems in existence in Northamptonshire; the change mentioned above relates to stages 2 and 3.)

This chapter is in part based on empirical research carried out over a 16-month period from January 1999 to April 2000.[3] What we focus on here are certain issues relating to the uses of discretion within the pre-court decision-making processes, as the county incorporated the national framework for decision-making following the 1998 Crime and Disorder Act. It should be made evident, of course, that with some modifications concerning the number of chances any one offender might have before prosecution, the architects of the national framework itself drew heavily on the much vaunted Northamptonshire pre-court system.

The study included observation of the YOT pre-court process, and semi-structured interviews with police and YOT representatives. Three samples of cases were analysed. The first comprised 910 decisions made by the police from January to March 1999, extracted from the YOT database. The second sample comprised 124 police report forms, submitted by the police to the local Police National Computer Bureau during September 1999. In addition to the name, sex, ethnic background, type of offence and disposal decision, the forms also included a brief description of the offence and previous disposal decisions.[4] The third sample comprised 20 cases of juveniles which were examined in some depth through observation of pre-court YOT meetings and visits by YOT workers to victims and offenders, and by examination of case files and interviewing caseworkers.

Whose decision?

At the time of the research, there were two key groups of decision-makers in Northamptonshire Police: custody officers who made the first disposal decisions, and process-markers who received cases referred by custody officers for review. The process-markers were based in administrative support units situated within each of the four police

¹An informal warning.
²In some cases 'offence analysis work' or reparation might be undertaken as part of the caution. This came to be known as a 'caution plus'.

Diversion Unit: a 'justice approach' 1993–2000¹

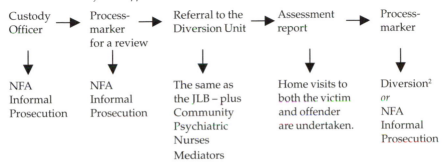

¹It was this model of pre-court decision-making that was in operation at the time of this case study.
²Young offenders diverted for an intervention have either a caution or an informal warning recorded.

Youth Offending Team: a new approach? 2000-onwards

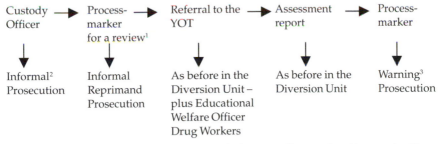

¹There is now a centralised Criminal Justice Unit which reviews all cases referred by custody officers. The Unit includes process-markers and Crown Prosecutors. The process-markers review all cases recommending a pre-court disposal.
²Informal warnings continue to be used for first-time minor offenders.
³The vast majority of warnings include an intervention.

Figure 2 *Juvenile Liaison Bureaux: a 'welfare' approach to pre-court decision-making 1981–1993*

divisions. They were responsible for reviewing cases 'reported for summons' by custody officers, who recommended either prosecution or diversion (which entails an intervention and the subsequent recording of a caution[5] or informal warning). It was also within these units that police files were prepared for court.

It has long been recognised that in the police context organisational rules and occupational pressures operate 'sometimes fuelled by the unrealistic expectations of the public and others' (Hawkins 1992: 22). Research into the police organisation has identified a 'cop culture' such that decisions are made within the context of policing norms (Reiner 2000). This 'cop culture' encourages officers both to support colleagues' decisions, and to believe that rules are there to be used and bent (Sanders 1988; McConville et al. 1991; Ashworth 1998). With a policy commitment to support pre-court diversion in Northamptonshire, custody officers would refer the majority of cases for a diversionary review; indeed, the culture of diversion led to the process-markers being dominant. Curiously, despite the on-going changes brought into relief by the 1998 Crime and Disorder Act and its youth justice reforms, which set store by limiting discretion to divert and promoted early intervention, high-ranking police officers at management level still assumed that it was process-markers' decisions that were dominant as they provide a review function. They seemed not to be aware of the police 'claw-back' on the ground in terms of decision-making power. This became manifest in the changing relationship between the custody officers and the process-markers with custody officers assuming their naturally 'senior' positions in the police hierarchy. Custody officers are required by law to be serving police officers holding the rank of sergeant, while the process-markers are civilians. Interestingly, three of the five process-markers had previously been in the police force, two as inspectors and one as a sergeant, which seemed to earn them respect from their police colleagues. Two process-markers had no operational experience of the police force.

The process-markers were reliant on custody officers referring on for review all appropriate cases (bearing in mind that in some cases no further action would be deemed appropriate, in some cases there would be an informal warning, and in some cases direct charges would be brought). An important influence on the diversionary process, therefore, was the extent to which there were good working relations between the decision-makers operating in the same police division. In interview, the former police process-markers and one of the two civilian process-markers reported having good working relationships with the custody officers. It may be significant that the other process-marker was the only woman amongst the decision-makers. She was concerned that because of the personal tensions she experienced, custody officers would be more likely to charge in borderline cases rather than referring them to her for internal review. Certainly, research studies have identified a 'machismo' element within the culture of the police, in which female police officers are considered to be inferior to their male colleagues and in which male officers adopt a tough stance (Reiner 2000). Thus the pattern of decision-making may reflect the gendered dynamics of the office culture to a degree. But, equally, it seemed that the female process-marker stuck more rigidly to national guidelines,[6] while her closest male civilian colleague, who tended to seek the advice of custody officers when making decisions, was more influenced by the local culture.

The process-markers who had direct experience of working within the organisation of the police also seemed to enjoy the flexibility of the decision-making process, whereby the legal rules provided little or no barrier to simple endorsement of the recommendations of custody officers, even if this resulted in decisions outside Northamptonshire's matrix guidelines. Again, the interpersonal office dynamics appear to come to the fore in the decision-making process.

The three-month sample of cases analysed showed that the custody officers' decisions were dominant.[7] Overall, custody officers made 701 of the 910 decisions. It was also custody officers who made the majority of prosecution decisions.[8] The majority of custody officers' recommendations to process-markers were also accepted, thus suggesting that either the custody officers were very persuasive in their recommendations or that the process-markers' review was neither independent nor rigorous.[9] A breakdown of the decisions made by custody officers and process-markers is shown in Figure 3 below.

'Speeding up' the decision-making process

The political pressure to reduce delays at court arguably consolidated the position of custody officers as the dominant decision-makers. From October 1998 Northamptonshire was included in a Home Office pilot project to 'speed up' decision-making following provisions contained in the 1998 Crime and Disorder Act to do this. As a consequence of involvement in the pilot project, custody officers were under pressure to make decisions more quickly. In practice, decisions to prosecute could be made more quickly than those requiring internal review by the process-markers.

There is evidence from a Home Office study of police decision-making that the Northamptonshire Police maintained a commitment to

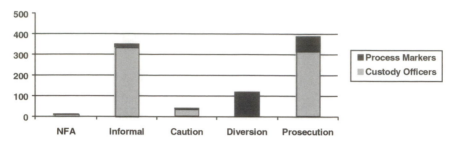

The 910 decisions included: 11 NFAs, 350 informal warnings, 41 cautions, 119 diverted for an intervention, and 389 prosecutions.

Source: Police decisions extracted from the YOT database.

Figure 3 *Pre-court disposal decisions for young offenders in Northamptonshire from January to March 1999*

pre-court diversion at least until early in 1996 (Bucke and Brown 1997). In 1999, however, process-markers complained that the emphasis on speed was undermining a policy of diversion. An increase in the number of young offenders prosecuted is reflected in the official statistics. Such change, however, was happening well before the provisions to reduce delays were implemented. Changes in the number of young offenders prosecuted from 1993 to 2000 are reflected in Figure 4 below.

The official statistics show a sharp rise in the number of young offenders prosecuted from 1996 to the end of 1999. One assumption that could be made is that the policy of diversion in Northamptonshire was becoming less influential by 1996. The increase in the number of prosecutions of young offenders does not seem to reflect a growth in youth crime, as the police arrest figures of young offenders in Northamptonshire had reduced by 17 per cent from 1996 to 2000.[10] One reason could have been custody officers coming under increased pressure to speed up the decision-making. Certainly, in interview, process-markers and YOT managers perceived that the provisions to reduce delays had led to a dramatic increase in the number of young offenders prosecuted. Thus, while the official figures reveal that such increases were taking place before October 1998, the pilot project helped to raise awareness locally that there was a significant increase in the number of young offenders prosecuted. The apparent decline in prosecutions in 2000 perhaps reflects a police response to concerns about the increase.

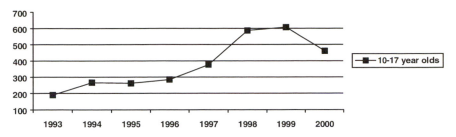

Source: Home Office Criminal Statistics (1994 to 2001 annually).

Figure 4   *Young offenders found guilty of indictable offences at Northamptonshire magistrates' courts from 1993–2000*

Applying the rules

The 'rules' that decision-makers were required to apply when making disposal decisions included the Charging Standards, which set out national guidance, and a locally-devised decision-making matrix which required decision-makers to undertake a 'gravity assessment exercise'. These were brought together into a single document known locally as *Charging Rules and the Decision-Making Matrix* (Northamptonshire Police 1994). This was to operate alongside Home Office Circular 18/1994, which sets out the cautioning criteria for police to ensure that there is: i) evidence of the offender's guilt sufficient to give a realistic prospect of conviction, ii) an admission, and iii) that it is in the public interest to prosecute (Home Office 1994: 5).

As the matrix encourages the police to concentrate on the seriousness of the offence when making a decision, the offence type recorded is clearly vital. In applying the gravity scores in Northamptonshire, custody officers and process-markers were required to record a seriousness score for the offence of between 10 and 40 (in multiples of 10). This approach meant that a different score could be recorded for the same offence type. Thus for an offence of robbery, for example, a seriousness score of 40 could be recorded in more serious cases, but in more minor offences (school bullying, for instance), a score of 10 could be recorded. This flexibility was important as it enabled decision-makers to consider the seriousness of the offence within the same offence types. Such flexibility can also lead to inconsistencies and a lack of fairness within the process, however. In two separate cases, for example, two female offenders (both aged 12 and with one previous informal warning each) were dealt with for a similar type of offence. Both girls had entered a dwelling-house as trespassers, neither had any intention to steal but they caused damage by painting on a wall. In one girl's case, an offence of dwelling-house burglary was recorded, with a score of 40. In the other girl's case an offence of 'criminal damage' was recorded, with a score of 10. Similarly, in two further cases, this time for the offence of 'taking a car without the owner's consent', one offence was given a score of 40 and the other 10. Moreover, despite the matrix seriousness score going up to 40, a score of 60 was recorded against one young offender for an offence of dwelling-house burglary. Thus we learn of inconsistencies in the application of the rules. The effect of recording a more serious offence type was not necessarily intended to encourage a prosecution decision, however. This was evident in a case where an offence of rape was recorded. Rape is an offence that the police are mandatorily required to charge, but the police decision was to recommend that the young offender be diverted to the YOT for a 'caution plus', while leaving the offence type recorded as 'rape'. From the offence description, however, it was evident that rape had not occurred, as it was explicitly stated by the victim that 'sexual intercourse did not take place'. Instead the incident involved 'fondling' between the young offender and his step-sister. With some prompting from the YOT manager who chanced upon the paper-work, the process-marker changed the offence type to 'indecent assault' and referred the case to the YOT.

The gravity assessment exercise under the national final warning scheme operates on a different basis to the matrix operating in Northamptonshire, although there are similarities. The Association of Chief Police Officers has set out a list of 'gravity factors' that are incorporated into Home Office (1999a) guidance to the police. These guidelines are intended to guide police decisions and encourage greater consistency in decision-making both within and between police force areas (Home Office 1999a). Assessment is based on the seriousness of the offence, with the custody officer normally calculating the score when deciding whether to record a reprimand, warning or prosecution decision. In the final warning scheme it is the seriousness of the offence and the number and type of previous disposals that determine the police decision.

The Home Office guidance (1999a) has categorised different offence types into four different seriousness scores. A score of 1 is used for very minor offences such as being 'drunk and disorderly', having an air weapon in a public place, obstructing the police and all non-recordable offences. Despite the trivial nature of these offences, there is no flexibility in the rules to allow the police not to prosecute such offences if the offender has previously received a warning (Home Office 1999a: Annex C: 7). Similarly, a score of 2 is used for offences such as common assault, possession of a class 'B' or 'C' drug, and forgery offences. The majority of offences are categorised with a score of 3 or 4 depending on the seriousness. Burglary of a non-dwelling, for example, has a score of 3, while burglary of a dwelling has a score of 4. Assault occasioning actual and grievous bodily harm scores 3, and wounding with intent scores 4. Having decided the appropriate offence category, the gravity score 'can be up-graded or down-graded by one point irrespective of the number of factors present' (Home Office 1999a: Annex C: 5). With a score of 2, for a first offence, the recommendation is to reprimand, but with a score of 3 the young offender would normally be warned. A score of 4 normally leads to a charge.

In theory, the structured national gravity scores used under the final warning scheme would seem to address the problems identified in Northamptonshire, where different seriousness scores were recorded for very similar offences. But different problems emerge in their application. In particular, with the stipulation that formal action be taken in respect of all offences (and with a strict limitation on the number of pre-court disposals allowed), application of the national gravity factors is likely to increase dramatically the number of young offenders prosecuted. In particular, it has been found in national research findings that *many* young offenders receive a warning for the first offence rather than a reprimand (Holdaway et al. 2001). For a second offence in such cases, the rules stipulate prosecution, irrespective of the possible minor nature of the offence. The final warning scheme seeks to strictly limit the police use of informal warnings and the recording of 'no further action' is discouraged. Circular 9/1999 states that 'no action' decisions are not a method of disposal, but an acknowledgement that no action is appropriate in a particular case (Home Office 1999a). The guidance indicates that, 'no substantive offence can be mitigated down to warrant no further action, using the gravity factor decision process alone' (Home Office 1999a: Annex C: 8).

Research findings relating to inconsistencies in decision-making in Northamptonshire[11] have been mirrored at a national level. From analysis of 1,700 final warning decisions in four areas, for example, we learn that one per cent of young offenders received *two* reprimands, and two per cent received a second warning within two years of the previous warning (Holdaway et al. 2001: 72), contrary to the statutory rules. Further, in Liverpool, of 900 reprimand and warning decisions, 6.5 per cent of young offenders were found to receive a reprimand *after* a previous warning (Evans and Puech 2001: 803).

Inconsistencies have also been found in the use of the national gravity assessment exercise. In four police areas, the final gravity score was not recorded in 38 per cent of cases (Holdaway et al. 2001). When the police were asked about the assessment exercise 'many mentioned erroneous criteria used to make a decision about whether or not a young person should be finally warned' (Holdaway et al. 2001: 74). Other factors influenced them too in Northamptonshire and at a national level: the perceived personality of the offender, the likelihood of the young person to co-operate with the YOT, police officers' views about 'fairness', their perceptions of offenders' remorse, and the 'supposed views of a victim' all featured (Holdaway et al. 2001: 74; Kemp 2003).

In Liverpool, some police officers were found to rely on their previous experience of cautioning when deciding on the appropriate disposal, and the gravity scores would be applied retrospectively to justify a particular decision (Evans and Puech 2001: 798). In a third of their sample of 90 cases, Evans and Puech found inconsistencies in police decision-making (2001: 799). From all of this we surmise that application of the national gravity assessment exercise is seemingly, and as yet, ineffective in ensuring fairness, consistency and accountability within the pre-court system.

Towards a conclusion

The national youth justice reforms encourage a policy of positive 'early intervention' (Home Office 1997b; 1999a) but it is clear that these may lead to 'net-widening' in the pre-court process. In practice, by requiring the police to focus on the offence seriousness, it was found that many young offenders were not reprimanded for a first offence, but warned (Holdaway et al. 2001: 61). The final warning scheme was also intended to 'ensure that more consistent action is taken, before a young offender ever appears in court' (Home Office 1997b: 17), which would also mean that many would then be prosecuted for a second offence.

The final warning scheme encourages the police to respond formally when dealing with young offenders, even for minor offences. In the circumstances, informal warnings are strictly limited normally to 'non-recordable offences' or in cases of 'anti-social behaviour which falls short of inherently criminal activity' (Home Office 1999a: 3). The emphasis on responding formally is likely to encourage the police to record reprimands and warnings in cases which would previously have been dealt with informally or discontinued. In their study of developments in Liverpool, Evans and Puech found that a 'significant minority of offences are very minor', and YOT workers commented on how the police were processing offences that previously would have been dealt with informally (2001: 796).

Research findings since the implementation of the reforms also suggest that some referrals to the YOTs were because of concerns over welfare issues, rather than on the basis of an offence having been committed. Indeed, critics of the reforms might see these developments as a particular type of control strategy operating within the pre-court process (Muncie 1999). In devising the reforms, it was certainly the government's intention to impose more controls on young offenders.

With the strict limitations on pre-court disposals, and with an emphasis on the police responding to cases formally, it is perhaps inevitable that the police have not only included low level crimes, but have cast the net low and wide in terms of capturing 'social' or welfare difficulties too. Moreover, while more low level crime is being dealt with formally, there is a seeming absence of formal written justification for decisions (Evans and Puech 2001: 799).

Under the reforms, when receiving a warning, a young offender is to be referred to the YOT for an assessment in carrying out a 'rehabilitation (change) programme'. The Home Office intends that a programme will be carried out in the 'vast majority' of cases (1999b para.14). In Holdaway et al.'s (2001) study of 1,700 warnings, however, a change programme was assessed as appropriate in only 43 per cent of cases (18 per cent later had non-compliance recorded against them). A large proportion of offenders were not referred for an assessment, it seems, because the police felt that there was little risk of re-offending and so an intervention was not required (2001: 77–78). Evans and Puech produced similar findings in Liverpool where less than half of those receiving a warning were placed on a rehabilitation (change) programme (2001: 802).

How can this be explained? It is conceivable that the police may not refer all warned young offenders for an intervention either because this is perceived to be disproportionate to the offence committed, or because they are aware that the 'great majority' commit offences only once or twice in any event (Home Office 1997b: 16). Holdaway et al. are critical of such decisions because of the potential significance of the final warning intervention to address 'a range of needs – educational, medical, vocational and other needs'. At the same time, the researchers accept the apparent negative net-widening effects of responding to the needs of young offenders in cases of minor offending where officers perceive the final warning be of help rather than simple punishment (2001: 30 and 73). For Evans and Puech, early intervention means 'a classic case of using the justice system as a gateway to providing mainstream welfare and youth services' (2001: 804). What can be seen from the ground, however, is that there is no clear, shared operational philosophy. Thus past inconsistencies, and the inconsistencies of practice discovered in Northamptonshire (widely-acclaimed champions of 'good practice'), live on.

With the police and Crown Prosecution Service under pressure to deal with cases more quickly, there is a danger that the final warning scheme could encourage a routinised approach to decision-making, concentrating on the *number* of previous offences and types of disposals, rather than undertaking a thorough review of the evidence.

An important finding in the Northamptonshire case study was that the legal criteria were not always applied. This is perhaps not surprising when the police and legal advisers considered cautions to be a 'let off' and accordingly tended to disregard the weight of, or even need for, evidence. Somewhat optimistically, it now seems, Leng considered that with clear procedures and criteria for the new final warning scheme, and with responses to offending having serious consequences for the offender, such unfair practices would be consigned to history (1999: 7).

To add final criticisms to the rather depressing picture of pre-court decision-making that is emerging both from Northamptonshire and from national pilot studies of the youth justice reforms introduced since 1998, Holdaway et al. found that it was not always clear that young people had admitted guilt (2001: 73). When considering if there is sufficient evidence to prosecute, the police are also required to take into account 'any lines of defence' when assessing the evidence (Home Office 1999a: para.11(a)). Responsibility for decision-making under the final warning scheme, however, 'belongs solely to the police' (Home Office 1999a: para.6), and it seems unrealistic to expect them, having constructed a case, to then take account of a suspect's version of events when considering if there are any lines of defence (McConville et al. 1991). While defence solicitors would take account of a suspect's version of events, Evans and Puech found that only a third of the young people in their sample requested or received legal advice, despite there being occasions where the evidence was contested (2001: 800). Holdaway et al. note one 'very minor offence' where a lawyer advised the young person to admit the offence, 'because she would go to court if she did not' (2001: 73).

Within the final warning scheme, Evans and Puech found there to be 'prima facie evidence of the lack of priority given to evidence' (2001: 799); they express concern about the apparent absence of a robust internal review system or an external independent review of the evidence (2001: 800). Holdaway et al. similarly note that there should be 'stronger guidance, appropriate training and strengthening of mechanisms of accountability' (2001: 74). They also propose that there should be 'written evidence of a young person's guilt' (Holdaway et al. 2001: 74). Attractive as it seems as a way of overcoming difficulties, this proposal is problematic, not only because guilt is an emotional response (and often also involves assessment of dishonesty or intent), but because an admission of guilt could also be used as a proxy for there being sufficient evidence to prosecute. Just because an offence is admitted, this does not mean that there is also sufficient evidence to prosecute. On the contrary, detailed legal knowledge is necessary to take account of the various elements often needed to prove guilt. With a minority of young offenders receiving independent legal advice, presumably the majority would depend on advice from the police when providing written evidence of guilt. Written evidence is also likely to be readily provided by the young people whom Evans and Puech found to be under pressure to accept a warning instead of going to court, even where there were doubts about the evidence, or the offence was not fully admitted (2001: 800). Although the final warning scheme has placed constraints on police discretion, there is seemingly no effective mechanism to ensure that the legal rights of suspects are protected.

The youth justice reforms in general have come under scrutiny (Gelsthorpe and Morris 1999; Fionda 1999, for example). The findings from Northamptonshire and from early research studies on pre-court decision-making draw attention to the continued centrality of discretion within the early decision-making stages of the youth justice system, an area which, overall, has received rather less attention from critics. In theory, the increasing emphasis on formality and on restricting the number of pre-court disposals makes for fairness and consistency. In practice, a number of difficulties are revealed. As Evans and Puech warn, 'Policy makers ignore processes at their peril if their aims are not to be frustrated' (2001: 805). It is arguable that much more attention should be given to the exigencies of decision-making on the ground.

One question, of course, is whether or not the newly created national Youth Justice Board should assume a stronger regulatory role, but enough is known about previous attempts to control from the top to suggest that this may not be a fruitful course of action.

Moreover, many recent attempts to control from the 'fitted carpet land' at the top might be described as managerialist interventions which have focused on the need to drive through national policy without necessarily recognising difficulties and consequences on the ground. In this regard then, we cannot assume that increased managerial control means better justice. It may be that we should look at more and better training, supervision and accountability at a local level.

Notes

1 See Blagg et al. (1986), Davis et al. (1989) and Hughes et al. (1998).
2 Also during 1993, the Health Authority seconded two community psychiatric nurses to work with mentally disordered offenders diverted from court (Hughes et al. 1998).
3 Vicky Kemp carried out the fieldwork as part of her doctoral research.
4 The September sample comprised police forms that were *submitted* to the PNC Bureau during September 1999, and not decisions taken during that month.
5 The recording of a 'caution' in Northamptonshire, was only meant to be used in cases where an intervention had been carried out. It was evident, however, that a caution decision was sometimes recorded as an instant disposal with no intervention.
6 We discuss the applicable rules in the following pages.
7 It is not known what happened to cases following the decision to prosecute; our interpretation of custody officers' recommendations being dominant reflects the decision-making only to the police prosecution stage, but not beyond it.
8 Custody officers directly charged 315 of the 389 young offenders prosecuted.
9 Of the 193 cases referred for review, custody officers recommended 112 individuals for a 'caution plus' and 81 for prosecution. The process-markers decided to divert for a 'caution plus' 119 young offenders and to prosecute 74. Thus in very few cases (7) was there any discrepancy in recommendations.
10 There were 4,662 arrests of young offenders in 1996 and 3,855 in 2000 (Northamptonshire Police 2001).
11 For further details of police decision-making in Northamptonshire following research by NACRO, see Kemp et al. 2002.

References

Ashworth, A. (1998) *The criminal process: an evaluative study*, 2nd edn. Oxford: Oxford University Press.
Audit Commission (1996) *Misspent Youth: Young People and Crime*. London: HMSO.
Austin, J. and Krisberg, B. (1981) 'Wider, Stronger, and Different Nets: The Dialetics of Criminal Justice Reform', *Journal of Research in Crime and Delinquency*, 18(1), 165–196.
Bennett, T. (1979) 'The social distribution of criminal labels', *British Journal of Criminology*, 19, 134–145.
Blagg, H. et al. (1986) *The Final Report on the Juvenile Liaison Bureau, Corby*. Lancaster: Department of Social Administration, University of Lancaster (unpublished).

Bottoms, A. (1995) 'The Philosphy and Politics of Punishment and Sentencing' in Clarkson, C. and Morgan, R. (eds.) *The Politics of Sentencing Reform*. Oxford: Clarendon Press.

Bucke, T. and Brown, D. (1997) *In Police Custody: Police Powers and Suspects Rights Under the Revised PACE Codes of Practice*, Home Office Research Study No. 174. London: Home Office.

Cohen, S. (1985) *Visions of Social Control*. Cambridge: Polity Press.

Crown Prosecution Service (1986) *Code for Crown Prosecutors*. London: HMSO.

Crown Prosecution Service (1994) *Code for Crown Prosecutors*. London: HMSO.

Davis, G., Boucherat, J. and Watson, D. (1989) 'Pre-Court Decision-Making in Juvenile Justice', *British Journal of Criminology*, 29(3), 219–235.

Dignan, J. (1990) *Repairing the Damage: An Evaluation of an Experimental Adult Reparation Scheme in Kettering, Northamptonshire*. Sheffield: Faculty of Law, University of Sheffield.

Ditchfield, J. (1976) *Police Cautioning in England and Wales*, Home Office Research Study No. 37. London: Home Office.

Emsley, C. (1983) *Policing and its Context 1750–1870*. London: Macmillan.

Evans, R. and Puech, K. (2001) 'Reprimands and Warnings: Populist Punitveness or Restorative Justice?', *Criminal Law Review*, 794–805.

Evans, R. and Wilkinson, C. (1990) 'Variations in Police Cautioning Policy and Practice in England and Wales', *The Howard Journal*, 29(3), 155–176.

Fionda, J. (1999) 'New Labour, Old Hat: Youth Justice and the Crime and Disorder Act', *Criminal Law Review*, 36–47.

Fisher, C. and Mawby, R. (1982) 'Juvenile Delinquency and Police Discretion in an Inner-City Area', *British Journal of Criminology*, 22(1), 63–75.

Garland, D. (1996) 'The Limits of the Sovereign State: Strategies of Crime Control in Contemporary Society', *British Journal of Criminology*, 36(4), 445–471.

Gelsthorpe, L. (1989) *Sexism and the Female offender*. Aldershot: Gower.

Gelsthorpe, L. and Morris, A. (1994) 'Juvenile Justice 1945–1992' in Maguire, M., Morgan, R. and Reiner, R. (eds.), *The Oxford Handbook of Criminology*. Oxford: Clarendon Press.

Gelsthorpe, L. and Morris, A. (1999) 'Much Ado About Nothing: A Critical Comment on Key Provisions Relating to Children in the Crime and Disorder Act 1998', *Child and Family Law Quarterly*, 11, 209–21.

Hawkins, K. (1992) *The Uses of Discretion*. Oxford: Clarendon Press.

Her Majesty's Inspectorate of Constabulary (1994) *A Report of Her Majesty's Inspectorate of Constabulary: Northamptonshire Police*. London: Home Office.

Holdaway, S. et al. (2001) *New strategies to address youth offending: The national evaluation of the pilot youth offending teams*. Home Office Occasional Paper No. 69. London: Home Office.

Home Office (1927) *Report of Departmental Committee on the Treatment of Young Offenders*, Chaired by T. Molony, Cmnd 2831. London: HMSO.

Home Office (1970) *Part I of the Children and Young Persons Act 1969: A Guide to Courts and Practitioners*. London: HMSO.

Home Office (1985) *The Cautioning of Offenders*, Circular 14/1985. London: HMSO.

Home Office (1986) *Criminal Statistics for England and Wales 1985*. Cmnd 10. London: HMSO. Also, the Criminal Statistics annually.

Home Office (1990) The Cautioning of Offenders, Circular 59/1990. London: HMSO.

Home Office (1994) *The Cautioning of Offenders*, Circular 18/1994. London: HMSO.

Home Office (1997a) *Review of Delay in the Criminal Justice System: A Report*. London: Home Office.

Home Office (1997b) *No More Excuses. A New Approach to Tackling Youth Crime in England and Wales*. London: HMSO.

Home Office (1999a) 'Guide to the Final Warning Scheme', *Guides to the Crime and Disorder Act 1998*, Circular 9/1999. London: Home Office.

Home Office (1999b) *The Establishment and Operation of Rehabilitation (Change) Programmes under the Warning Scheme*. London: Home Office.

Hughes, G., Leisten, R. and Pilkington, A. (1998) 'Diversion in a Culture of Severity', *Howard Journal*, 37(1), 16–33.

Jones, R. (1984) 'Questioning the New Orthodoxy', *Community Care* (October): 15–17.

Kemp, V. (2003) Youth Justice Reform: Pre-court decision-making and multi-agency functioning. (Ph.D. thesis, University of Cambridge, in preparation)

Kemp, V. et al. (2002) *Assessing responses to youth offending in Northampshire*. Research briefing 2. London: NACRO.

Landau, S. and Nathan, G. (1983) 'Selecting delinquents for cautioning in the London Metropolitan Area', *British Journal of Criminology*, 23, 128–149.

Leng, R. (1999) 'The Crime and Disorder Act: Advising on Reprimands and Warnings' in *Police Station Practice*, March 7–8.

Littlechild, B. (1997) 'Young offenders, punitive policies and the rights of children' in *Critical Social Policy*, 53, 73–92.

McConville, M., Sanders, A. and Leng, R. (1991) *The Case for the Prosecution*. London: Routledge.

Muncie, J. (1999) *Youth and Crime: A Critical Introduction*. London: Sage.

Northamptonshire County Council (1992) *Review of Diversion of Offenders: Steering Group Report* (unpublished).

Northamptonshire Police (2001) *Unpublished Report on Police Arrests.*

Northamptonshire Police (1994) *Charging Rules and the Decision-Making Matrix* (unpublished).

Pearson, G. (1983) *Hooligan: A History of Respectable Fears*. London: Macmillan.

Piliavin, I. and Briar, S. (1964) 'Police Encounters with Juveniles', *American Journal of Sociology*, (September) 1964, 206–214.

Reiner, R. (2000) *The Politics of the Police*, 3rd edn. Hemel Hempstead: Wheatsheaf.

Sanders, A. (1988) 'The Limits to Diversion from Prosecution', *British Journal of Criminology*, 28(4), 513–532.

Smith, D. and Gray, J. (1983) *Police and People in London: The Police in Action*. London: Policy Studies Institute.

Steer, D. (1970) *Police Cautioning – a Study in the Exercise of Police Discretion*, Oxford University Penal Research Unit. Oxford: Basil Blackwell.

Wilkinson, C. and Evans, R. (1990) 'Police Cautioning of Juveniles: The Impact of Home Office Circular 14/1985', *Criminal Law Review*, 165–176.

Chapter 3

Judicial discretion in sentencing

David Thomas

The origins of judicial discretion

Seen in a historical context, the predominance of judicial discretion in sentencing is a relatively recent development. Early English common law did not allow the exercise of any discretion in sentencing for felony. The mandatory sentence provided by law in every case was death. The first inroads on this simple but severe system, in the direction of a discretionary system, may perhaps be traced to the development in the 17th century of the doctrine of 'benefit of clergy'. The rule was that any man convicted of felony who was a clerk in holy orders was entitled to be discharged from the secular court with a view to being punished by the bishop. Records were not available of who was and who was not a clerk in holy orders, and the courts developed their own instant test of literacy for this purpose, working on the assumption that any one who could read was a clerk in holy orders. If the defendant was able to read from the Bible Psalm 51, verse 1, known for obvious reasons as the 'neck verse', he was entitled to be treated as a clerk in holy orders and would escape the death penalty. The legal rules surrounding this concept were gradually elaborated, and the scope it provided to achieve some mitigation of the harshness of the law, albeit in an arbitrary and illogical manner, was extended into the 18th century.

From the late 17th century judges began to acquire discretion through a different mechanism. This was the system of transportation under conditional pardon. In a case in which the defendant was not entitled to benefit of clergy, and was liable to be sentenced to death, judges developed the practice of granting a temporary reprieve, literally a stay of execution, to allow the defendant or his friends and supporters to petition the sovereign for clemency. Clemency would be granted on condition that the defendant voluntarily submitted to being transported to what were then His Majesty's colonies in America for a stipulated period. In the early days of this practice the defendant would be required to make his own arrangements to get there. It was entirely within the judge's discretion to decide whether or not a particular defendant would be granted a reprieve for this purpose or left for execution. If the defendant was left for execution, he would normally be executed within a very short time after the completion of the court session. Although the decision to grant a pardon was not in the hands of the judges, the critical decision whether to grant a reprieve or leave the defendant for execution was. As this part of the process was not a part of the trial itself, it was not the practice for prosecutors to involve themselves in the question. This may well be the origin of the modern convention that prosecutors take little or no part in the sentencing process in this country (Radzinowicz 1948).

Even at this time, there was concern about the manner in which judges exercised this critical discretion. There was no machinery for ensuring any consistency of approach, and judges were free to follow their own notions. The system was described by Samuel Romilly in 1810 as 'the lottery of justice' (Romilly 1810).

Judicial discretion began to be recognised by statute during the course of the 18th century. Parliament steadily restricted the scope of the doctrine of benefit of clergy while at the same time giving powers to judges themselves in certain cases to sentence defendants to transportation, rather than sentence offenders to death and grant temporary reprieve in the expectation of a royal conditional pardon. The most important statute of this type was the Transportation Act 1717. Most such statutes allowed the judge to order transportation for a period fixed by statute; it was rare for Parliament to give the judge power to choose the period. The gradual statutory recognition of judicial discretion in this limited class of cases took a very long time, and by the early 19th century the fundamental structure of the system was still not greatly different from what it was 120 years earlier. Benefit of clergy had largely been abolished; the system of temporary reprieve and conditional pardon was still in operation, but in a limited range of cases judges were empowered to award sentences of transportation on their own initiative.

What can probably be described as the beginning of the modern system of judicial sentencing discretion in felony can really be traced to the period between 1820 and 1861. This was a period when the reform of the criminal law was high on the political agenda. One theme was the abolition or drastic restriction of the scope of the death penalty, which by this time applied to probably more than 200 separate offences (the exact number is difficult to calculate.) A second theme of the time was the need to consolidate and or codify the criminal law in a form in which it could be more readily understood. The achievement of both of these objectives required the construction of a new system of penalties for crime in which some penalty other than death would occupy the central position. That penalty was transportation, by now to Australia, but it was already clear that the system of transportation itself had a relatively limited future.

The task of rethinking the shape of the criminal law, and as part of the process reconstructing the system of penalties, fell to the Criminal Law Commissioners appointed in 1833, who spent 15 years on the task, producing various reports and draft codes. Their work was entirely in vain and their Draft Code was never enacted, but in the course of their work they produced some sophisticated discussions of the problems of sentencing.[1] Their proposals for a new scheme in many ways antici-pated the ideas which have become popular more recently in some of the American jurisdictions. In their view, too much judicial discretion in sentencing was not to be welcomed. Sentencing should as far as possible be regulated by rules of law in statutory form and judicial discretion should be limited to the tuning of finer details. They produced a number of reports which included a complex scheme of penalties along these lines. Their scheme was not adopted by Parliament and their proposed legislation was never actually enacted. If it had been, the role of the modern judiciary in sentencing would have been very different from what it became.

What would now be identified as judicial discretion in sentencing emerged almost by accident, as a result of the failure of the efforts of the Criminal Law Commissioners. Although their attempts to clarify the criminal law were not successful, Parliament was busy removing the death penalty from a wide range of offences. As usual this was done in a piecemeal and incoherent way. No systematic attention was given to the alternative penalty structure which was being created in its place. In some cases the death penalty was replaced by transportation for a fixed period, in others by transportation for a period fixed between upper and lower limits. In this roundabout and haphazard way, the power of the judges to fix the term of the penalty – always at this time a term of transportation – was established in the legal system and became a part of the statutory framework.

A large part of the criminal law was consolidated in 1861. By this time, the power of the judges to fix the term of a sentence had become the norm and the legislation of 1861 incorporated the principle that the court would have discretion to fix the length of a sentence, subject to a maximum fixed by Parliament.

Following the consolidation Acts of 1861, the basic foundation of the modern sentencing system was in place. Statute provided a maximum penalty for all but a handful of offences; judges had discretion within those maxima to fix the penalty in particular cases. With onec exception,[2] there were no minimum sentences. Political attention shifted to the question of securing some consistency in the exercise of discretion by the judges. There was no Court of Appeal at this time. Sentencing was carried out by a small number of High Court judges at assizes and a larger number of magistrates sitting at county quarter sessions. Different judges and different benches adopted different practices or simply followed their own idiosyncratic approaches.

The greatest controversy surrounded the treatment of persistent offenders. Persistent offenders had not been seen as a problem in earlier times. If they were not executed, they were transported to foreign parts and not seen again. With the decline first of the death penalty and later of transportation, together with the development of more accurate systems of record keeping, the problem of dealing with persistent offenders was recognised. A system of dealing with them which became popular in the late 19th century was known as the 'cumulative principle'. It was articulated most simply by a magistrate from Gloucester, Barwick Lloyd Baker.[3] The system was an early version of the 'three strikes' approach which has been adopted more recently. The rule was intended to be easily understood by those who were then described as the criminal classes. It was this: on a first conviction, the defendant would receive a very lenient punishment – this meant about six months' imprisonment; on a second conviction the penalty would be twelve months' imprisonment; but on a third conviction, irrespective of the gravity or otherwise of the offence, the sentence would be seven years' penal servitude. Some judges expanded the principle so that on further or subsequent convictions, the sentence would be 14 or 21 years. The use of this principle was extremely controversial and many judges declined to follow it. The result was massive disparity between those sentenced by adherents of the principle and those sentenced by its opponents. This conflict in particular focused attention on the need to develop some system of harmonising or rationalising the sentencing practices of different judges.

The late 19th-century literature offers many discussions of this problem.[4] Eventually it was thought that a solution could be found in the creation of an appellate court with power to review the sentences passed in the lower courts. The movement to establish a Court of Appeal was reinforced by awareness that the correction of miscarriages of justice in the form of the conviction of innocent persons was woefully deficient. Eventually, after a number of unsuccessful proposals, Parliament established the Court of Criminal Appeal by the Criminal Appeal Act 1907. The court had power to hear appeals against the sentence by defendants convicted in the assizes or quarter sessions. The power of the Court of Criminal Appeal was not restricted to reducing sentences; for almost 60 years the court had a power, which it used occasionally, to increase the sentence imposed on a person who claimed that his sentence was too severe.

At about the same time the scope of the sentencing discretion of the judge was substantially expanded by the development of alternative methods of sentencing. In the 19th century, there were few alternatives to custody. Sentencing for the most part consisted either of fixing the term of a custodial sentence, imprisonment or penal servitude, or of releasing the offender by way of a bind-over to come up for judgment, a sort of suspended sentence. The creation of new forms of sentence such as probation, borstal training and preventive detention for habitual offenders in the early years of the 20th century required judges to focus on a wider range of issues. Sentencing was no longer exclusively a matter of quantifying the punishment in the name of deterrence and retribution; it now required in addition the choice between competing penal objectives – deterrence and punishment on one hand, or rehabilitation and the prevention of crime on the other.

Judicial sentencing discretion in modern criminal law

The role of judicial sentencing discretion in modern criminal law is a function of the legislation passed by Parliament. It is clear beyond argument that Parliament by legislation may constitutionally grant or restrict the powers of judges. Until relatively recently, the style of sentencing legislation has been to confer wide discretion on the judiciary, and rely on internal judicial mechanisms to secure some consistency in the powers granted. Modern English sentencing law begins with the Criminal Justice Act 1948, which set out the statutory law of sentencing (except for maximum penalties) in 30 straightforward sections and two short schedules. The Act stated no philosophy; sentencers were left with the choice between the traditional punitive sanctions of imprisonment (which absorbed the former sentence of penal servitude) and fines on the one hand, and a variety of measures intended to influence or control the offender's future behaviour –

probation, detention in a detention centre, attendance at an attendance centre, borstal training, corrective training and preventive detention. Of these, detention in a detention centre, attendance at an attendance centre, and corrective training were new; probation, borstal training and preventive detention had been available to the courts for 40 years. Unlike most subsequent Criminal Justice Acts, the 1948 Act was not a crisis measure; it modernised a body of legislation which had been enacted piecemeal over the previous hundred years, and made a few marginal innovations. It survived, without substantial modification, for almost 20 years.

Some signs of a change in the style of sentencing legislation may be seen in the Criminal Justice Act 1961, a short Act dealing with the sentencing of young offenders, which was intended to promote the use of borstal training in preference to imprisonment. However, a more important step in the direction of greater legislative control over sentencing, at the expense of judicial discretion, was seen in the Criminal Justice Act 1967. By the early 1960s it had become clear that serious problems lay ahead for the penal system.[5] The incidence of reported crime had increased steadily since the end of the Second World War, and the prison population, which had declined sharply in the last two decades of the 19th century and remained relatively stable between the wars, had maintained a constant rate of increase since the end of the war. By 1964, it had reached the level from which it had declined in 1880, and was about double the level of 1947. A Royal Commission was appointed to inquire into the penal system, but sadly it failed to report and the chance of a clearly articulated penal strategy was lost.[6] Instead, Parliament enacted the Criminal Justice Act 1967, the first of many omnibus Criminal Justice Acts dealing with a variety of subjects. As well as sentencing, the Act dealt with committal proceedings, proof of intent in criminal cases, proof by written statements, alibi defences, majority verdicts, bail, legal aid and other matters. Its major innovations in relation to sentencing were the introduction of the suspended sentence and discretionary parole. Courts were empowered to suspend any sentence of imprisonment not exceeding two years, and required to suspend any sentence of imprisonment which did not exceed six months unless the case fell within one of a number of exceptions (offenders convicted of offences involving violence, or with a previous custodial sentence, were the most important exceptions). The parole system allowed a prisoner to be released after serving one third of his sentence or 12 months, whichever was the longer; it effectively applied to those sentenced to more than 18 months. To this extent, it removed from the judges the power to determine how long a particular offender would serve under a custodial sentence. A sentence of three years had previously meant that the offender would serve two years, the final third of the sentence being remitted automatically in all cases unless remission was denied as a sanction for misconduct in prison. After the introduction of the parole system, a sentence of three years meant that the offender would serve something between one year and two years, depending on what the Parole Board decided. The importance of the judge's decision on the length of sentence was correspondingly diminished. The experiment with mandatory suspension of short sentences did not last for long, partly because in some cases judges avoided the requirement by passing longer sentences. It was abandoned in the Criminal Justice Act 1972.

The intervals between statutes affecting sentencing became shorter. The Criminal Justice Act 1972 introduced community service orders and deferment of sentence, and empowered courts to make compensation orders. Most legislation dealing with the sentencing powers of the courts was consolidated in the Powers of Criminal Courts Act 1973; the Criminal Law Act 1977 included a provision (not brought into force until 1982) allowing a court to suspend a sentence of imprisonment in part.

The effective authority of the judiciary, and therefore the importance of the decisions which they made, was reduced by changes to the parole system made in 1983. The original parole system, introduced by the 1967 Act, applied to a relatively limited number of prisoners. Eligibility for release on licence was not achieved until the prisoner had served one third of his sentence or 12 months, whichever was the greater; all prisoners were entitled to the remission of the final third of their sentences. The shortest sentence under which a prisoner could qualify for parole under the original scheme was about 20 months; for an offender sentenced to two years imprisonment, release on licence at the earliest possible moment meant the difference between 12 months and 16 months in custody. (The difference was less if he had spent time in custody on remand, as that time would count towards the 16 months but not the 12.) The Criminal Justice Act 1982 contained a provision (section 33) allowing the Home Secretary to reduce the 12 month minimum period (the 'specified period') which an offender was required to serve before he could be considered for release on licence; this power was exercised in 1983 so as to reduce the specified period to six months. The result was that a large number of prisoners sentenced to shorter terms of imprisonment became eligible for parole, and a high proportion – approaching 80 per cent – of those who were eligible were released.

The new scheme worked in an arbitrary way. Under the revised scheme, a prisoner became eligible for release after serving one third of the sentence or six months, whichever was the greater; remission of one third of the sentence remained an entitlement. What this meant in practice (given the high rate of release) was that there was no significant difference between sentences of nine months', 12 months', 15 months', and 18 months' imprisonment – all would in most cases result in six months in custody. The effective difference between a sentence of nine months' imprisonment and two years' imprisonment was reduced to two months (nine months meant six months in custody, two years meant eight months in most cases). Despite an attempt to rationalise the system by extending the remission of sentences of up to 12 months to one half (and thereby creating further anomalies), the parole system had lost much of its credibility and the Carlisle Committee recommended a substantial reduction in its scope (Home Office 1988).

Statutory criteria

A second important development in sentencing legislation made by the Criminal Justice Act 1982 was the introduction of statutory criteria for sentencing, limited to the imposition of custodial sentences on young offenders. The Act rearranged the powers of the courts to pass custodial sentences on offenders under 21 years old, introducing a new sentence known as youth custody, to replace borstal training and imprisonment for offenders under 21. The introduction of statutory criteria for the imposition of the sentence of youth custody in what eventually became section 1(4) of the 1982 Act was not government policy. The criteria were not included in the original Bill; they were enacted as a result of a back bench initiative. They were written in very broad language. A court was prohibited from imposing a custodial sentence (youth custody or detention centre order) on an offender under 21 unless it was of the opinion that no other method of dealing with him was appropriate because it appeared to the court that 'he is unable or unwilling to respond to non-custodial penalties or because a custodial sentence is necessary for the protection of the public or because the offence was so serious that a non-custodial sentence cannot be justified'.

The enactment of the criteria had little impact on sentencing practice, and the proportionate use by the courts of custodial sentences for offenders in the relevant age group increased marginally in the years immediately following the implementation of the legislation. The Court of Appeal was rarely invited to consider the meaning of the new provisions in the first two years after they came into effect, and lay magistrates appeared to be unaware of their existence, despite a statutory obligation on magistrates' courts to identify the criterion by which a custodial sentence was justified (Burney 1985). The criteria were revised in the Criminal Justice Act 1988. To qualify for a custodial sentence on the first ground, the offender was required to have a history of failure to respond to non-custodial measures, in addition to being unwilling or unable to respond to them; the criterion of public protection was made specific to the individual offender, and the nature of the harm from which the public required protection was limited to 'serious harm'. The criterion of seriousness was restricted by an amendment whose effect was to require the court to consider one offence only for the purpose of the criterion, even though the offender had committed many others (this interpretation of the earlier version of the criterion had previously been adopted by the Court of Appeal).[7]

The effect of the enactment of the revised criteria, which came into effect in October 1988, is difficult to assess; they were followed by a noticeable downturn in the proportionate use of custodial sentences for offenders in the relevant age group, but a similar downturn occurred in the proportionate use of custodial sentences for adult offenders, which were not controlled by statutory criteria. There is no doubt that the judiciary were fully aware of the new provisions, as a result of the efforts of the Judicial Studies Board; the legal profession were more ready to use them as the basis of arguments on appeals, and cases on the meaning of the new criteria began to come before the Court of Appeal frequently within a few months.[8]

The apparent success of the statutory criteria in reducing the use of custody for young offenders persuaded various pressure groups that the way to control the growth of the prison population was to extend them to sentences of imprisonment passed on adults.[9] The assumed prerogative of the judiciary to determine sentencing policy without statutory or other forms of intervention had come increasingly under question,[10] and the respect in which the judiciary were held by the public had been damaged by particular decisions in a small number of cases. Extending the statutory criteria for the imposition of custodial sentences on young offenders to adults would suffer from one obvious drawback, as a glance at the prison statistics made clear. The vast majority of adults sentenced to imprisonment would easily satisfy the first criterion for the imposition of a custodial sentence, 'he has a history of failure to respond to non-custodial penalties and is unable or unwilling to respond to them', and applying the criteria to adults would produce no significant change in the use of custody. The only strategy which would be likely to reduce the use of custody for adults was one in which the recidivist who repeatedly committed less serious offences was not imprisoned.

The Criminal Justice Act 1991

The Criminal Justice Bill introduced in 1990 followed closely the proposals set out in the White Paper 'Crime, Justice and Protecting the Public' (Home Office 1990). A framework of rules for the imposition of custodial sentences was proposed which differentiated between cases in which the offender (necessarily over the age of 21) was convicted of an offence triable only on indictment and had previously served a sentence of imprisonment; those in which the offender was convicted of an offence triable only on indictment and had not previously served a sentence of imprisonment; those in which the offender was over 21 and was convicted of an either way offence; and those in which the offender was under 21 and was convicted of an either way offence. Previous convictions and previous sentences were to be disregarded in assessing the seriousness of an offence. The length of a custodial sentence was to be commensurate with the seriousness of the offence or offences concerned, with no scope for mitigation on the grounds of personal considerations not directly related to the offence. The question of whether a custodial sentence could be justified on the grounds of the seriousness of the offence was to be judged by reference to one offence only, or at most two offences considered in combination, however many offences had been committed. Similar provisions were made with respect to what were now to be known as community orders – probation orders, community service orders, and the new combination orders. Any community order was to be justified on the grounds of the seriousness of the offence (evaluated according to the complex rules of the Act, considering only two offences); the offender's needs were a subsidiary consideration. A new system of unit fines was proposed for the magistrates' courts.

Mercifully, major changes were made (some at a very late stage) as the Bill passed through Parliament. In particular, the complex criteria for custodial sentences, which would have been totally unworkable in practice, were simplified, and a revised set of criteria for all custodial sentences was enacted. Specific provision allowing the court to mitigate a sentence on the grounds of factors not directly related to the offence was introduced. The government refused to abandon the rule that the criterion of seriousness for the imposition of a custodial sentence or a community order (as opposed to the determination of the length of a custodial sentence, or the restrictiveness of a community order) must be judged by reference to two offences only, but made some concession to those who pointed out the difficulties that this would cause in the case of multiple offences, by allowing the court to take account of 'aggravating factors of an offence … disclosed by the circumstances of other offences committed by the offender'.

In the form in which it was enacted, the Criminal Justice Act 1991 set out criteria for the imposition of a custodial sentence, and for determining the length of a custodial sentence. A court was allowed to impose a custodial sentence only if the offence, considered in isolation or combination with one other offence for which the offender was to be sentenced at the same time, was so serious that only a custodial sentence could be justified.[11] No definition or explanation of the concept of seriousness was offered, but it was provided that a court, in assessing the seriousness of an offence, might have regard only to the circumstances of the offence[12] (as opposed to information about the offender) and in particular that previous convictions and the offender's response to previous sentences must be disregarded for this purpose.[13] A court dealing with an offender for an either way offence was required to obtain a pre-sentence report prepared by the probation service before imposing a custodial sentence, whether it considered such a report likely to be helpful or not.[14] In determining the length of a custodial sentence, the court was required to impose a sentence which was commensurate with the seriousness of all the offences for which the offender was being sentenced.[15] Again, previous convictions were to be disregarded in assessing the seriousness of the offences. In relation to the imposition of a custodial sentence, and the determination of the length of a custodial sentence, the court was allowed to take account of 'aggravating factors of an offence … disclosed by the circumstances of other offences committed by the offender'.[16] Courts were allowed to mitigate a sentence by reference to any factors which were considered relevant in mitigation.[17] Special provision was made for offenders guilty of violent or sexual offences.[18]

Corresponding rules were enacted to govern the imposition of community orders. A court was required to be satisfied that a community order was justified by the seriousness of the offence, again considered in isolation or combination with one other offence for which the offender was to be sentenced at the same time, that the proposed order was the most suitable for the offender, and that the restrictions on liberty involved in the order were commensurate with the seriousness of the offences.[19] The restrictions on considering previous convictions and response to previous sentences applied in this context as in the case of custodial sentences.

The unit fine system was enacted so as to apply only to the magistrates' courts.[20] In determining the amount of a fine in all but a few exceptional cases, the court was required to determine the number of units which was commensurate with seriousness of the offence or offences concerned, and then calculate the value of the unit in the case of the defendant.

Implementing the 1991 Act

The key sentencing provisions of the Criminal Justice Act 1991 were brought into force on October 1, 1992. For once, a relatively long period was allowed to elapse between the enactment of the legislation and its commencement, and an extensive training programme took place for magistrates and judges. Immediately before the Act came into force, the Lord Chief Justice made a practice statement drawing the attention of judges to the changes in the procedure for the release of offenders sentenced to custodial sentences, which would in many cases mean that a given sentence would involve a longer period in custody than under the earlier system, and encouraged sentencers to take this into account in determining the length of sentences. As early as was possible after the implementation of the Act, a series of cases were listed in the Court of Appeal to allow the court to determine the meaning of some of the controversial provisions of the Act.[21] Among the points decided by the Court were that there was no general definition of what constituted an offence which was 'so serious that only a custodial sentence can be justified' for the purposes of the Act; that the prevalence of an offence was a relevant factor in determining its seriousness; that the fact that an offence satisfied the criterion of seriousness did not mean that the court had to pass a custodial sentence, as it was open to the court to mitigate the sentence by reference to factors relating to the offender; and that the fact that the defendant was on bail when the current offence was committed was an aggravating feature of the current offence.

The provisions restricting the consideration of previous convictions and response to previous sentences were elucidated in detail, and it was held that the Act allowed the sentencing court to take account of deterrence, so long as the sentence was commensurate with the seriousness of the offences concerned. The Act did not permit the addition of an extra element to the sentence to make an example of the offender.

Within a short time of its commencement, the sentencing provisions of the 1991 Act began to attract adverse criticism. Judges of the Crown Court complained of the restrictive effect of the rule which limited the court to considering two offences only when deciding whether the case was sufficiently serious to warrant a custodial sentence; and the unit fine system attracted extensive media attention as a result of a series of bizarre cases in which enormous fines were imposed for trivial offences.

There was frequent criticism of the restrictions imposed on courts in considering previous convictions, some of it based on a misunderstanding of the effect of the new law. The relevant section of the 1991 Act, section 29(1), did not prohibit the court from considering previous convictions at all, merely from taking previous convictions into account when assessing the seriousness of an offence. It did not really go much further than established sentencing principle, which allowed a court to take account of previous convictions for the purpose of determining whether to mitigate the sentence justified by the seriousness of the offence, but not to justify a sentence more severe than the current offence would warrant.[22]

Criticism of the Act came to a peak in an address by the Lord Chief Justice of England, Lord Taylor, to the Law Society of Scotland.[23] Congratulating the Scottish judiciary on the fact that the Act did not apply to Scotland, Lord Taylor CJ said that parts of the Act defied common sense and that he hoped it would be reviewed and that sanity would be restored. On May 13, 1993, just over seven months after the Act came into force, the Home Secretary announced that changes would be made to the Criminal Justice Act 1991 with unprecedented speed. A further Criminal Justice Bill dealing amongst other things with aspects of sentencing (primarily the confiscation of the proceeds of drug trafficking and serious crime) was in the last stages of its consideration by Parliament. The opportunity would be taken to add provisions to this Bill which would abolish the unit fine system, repeal section 29 and do away with the rules restricting the court to the consideration of a maximum of two offences when deciding whether the threshold of seriousness for a custodial sentence or a community order had been reached. These intentions were carried out in the Criminal Justice Act 1993 which received the Royal Assent in July 1993. The Act amended the 1991 Act so as to allow a court to consider all the offender's current offences when deciding whether the seriousness threshold had been reached; section 29(1) was repealed and replaced by a provision which had the opposite effect.

More mandatory sentences

The aftermath of the 1991 Act can be seen as a reassertion by the judiciary of the principle that judicial discretion should remain the central feature of the sentencing system. Apart from the amendments made so soon after the implementation of the Act, its weakness was compounded by its failure to offer any definition of seriousness, its central concept. The judiciary were left to decide when an offence was 'so serious that only a custodial sentence was justified', and resolved the problem by deciding that just about any offence met this requirement. Despite the failure of the 1991 Act to establish statutory control of the sentencing behaviour of judges, governments had now acquired a taste for mandatory sentencing legislation, and mandatory provisions continued to feature in the criminal justice legislation which was placed on the statute book at ever decreasing intervals. The Criminal Justice and Public Order Act 1994 included a requirement that courts should take into account the stage in proceedings at which a defendant indicated the intention to plead guilty – hardly necessary when courts had been giving discounts for pleas of guilty in one shape or form for many years – but the main blow to the principle of judicial discretion came in the legislation which became the Crime (Sentences) Act 1997. This Act introduced automatic life sentences for offenders convicted on a second occasion of an offence which was listed in the Act as a 'serious offence'. In addition it provided for minimum mandatory sentences of seven years for offenders convicted on a third occasion of a class A drug dealing offence, and three years for offenders convicted on a third occasion of residential burglary.

The Act received the Royal Assent shortly before the 1997 general election, and was brought into effect by the incoming Labour administration. It represented a return to the sentencing philosophy of the 19th or some would say the 18th century. Mandatory minimum sentences had been unknown in English law, with the exception of the mandatory life sentence for murder, for over a century. The 1997 Act predictably brought about all manner of bizarre and anomalous sentences; courts found themselves obliged to impose life imprisonment on offenders who would not be considered eligible for such a sentence in the normal course of events. One example was the case of Turner [2000] 2 Cr.App.R.(S.) 472, a man who in his fifties became involved in a fight which led to his conviction for the offence of wounding with intent to cause grievous bodily harm, a 'serious offence' under the Act. He had been convicted of manslaughter 30 years earlier as a result of a street fight in which he was involved at the age of 22. The court found that it was unable to avoid imposing a life sentence.

The enactment of the Human Rights Act 1998 gave the Court of Appeal the opportunity to take a broader view of the meaning of this expression, and in the case of Offen [2001] 2 Cr.App.R.(S.) 10 (at 44) the Lord Chief Justice held that the Act must be interpreted in the light of its purposes. These were to ensure that potentially dangerous offenders were subject to the possibility of indefinite confinement. It followed that if an offender who otherwise qualified for the automatic life sentence could not be considered dangerous, there were 'exceptional circumstances' and the court was justified in not imposing a life sentence. Determining whether there were 'exceptional circumstances' in this sense was the task of the judiciary. If exceptional circumstances were found, the obligation to impose a life sentence was avoided and the sentence became again a matter for judicial discretion. Turner was among those whose life sentence was reconsidered and quashed under the revised interpretation of 'exceptional circumstances'.

Further sentencing legislation was introduced by the Labour government, and mandatory provisions ceased to be exceptional. The Crime and Disorder Act 1998 introduced new custodial sentences for young offenders, which could be awarded only in fixed portions: 4, 6, 8, 10, 12, 18 or 24 months. It became mandatory to treat 'racial aggravation' (subsequently extended to include 'religious aggravation') as an aggravating factor. The Criminal Justice and Court Services Act 2000 introduced mandatory disqualification orders, preventing those con-victed of offences against children from working in occupations relating to children. Courts are obliged to make such orders even though the offender never has, and probably never would, work in such an occupation. Mandatory 'referral orders' were provided by the Youth Justice and Criminal Evidence Act 1999 and these were implemented in April 2002.

Judicial self-regulation

Given the looseness of the statutory framework for the exercise of sentencing discretion, any hope of achieving consistent sentencing practices depended on the ability of the judiciary to regulate itself. The principal instrument was appellate review of sentences. Appellate review of sentences by a Court of Criminal Appeal was established in 1908 (since 1966, the court has been known as the Court of Appeal, Criminal Division). This court was given power to hear appeals against sentence brought by defendants (but not by the prosecution). On an appeal it could vary the sentence imposed by the trial court, and substitute any lawful sentence for that passed by the trial judge, including a more severe sentence. In its first few years, the Court of Criminal Appeal laid down a few basic sentencing principles, but its impact on sentencing in the trial courts was limited. Few offenders appealed against their sentences, as they were in danger of an increased sentence; few decisions were reported, and there was little interest among the judges who sat in the court in the idea of developing principles or guidelines on sentencing for judges in the lower courts.

Interest in the use of appellate review as a means of achieving more consistent sentencing revived in the 1960s. There were probably a number of reasons. Academic interest in the criminal law generally had developed, and in particular the Criminal Law Review (first published in 1954) provided a vehicle for the discussion of all aspects of the criminal law. Reporting of decisions of the Court of Criminal Appeal, albeit in a rudimentary form, began in the Criminal Law Review. Articles on aspects of sentencing began to appear in legal journals, and the idea that sentencing could be examined using the traditional techniques of legal scholarship began slowly to gain acceptance. The first attempt at a comprehensive analysis of the (still largely unreported) decisions of the Court of Appeal (Criminal Division) was published in 1970 (Thomas 1979, 2nd edition).

Gradually, sentencing judges became accustomed to looking to decisions of the Court of Appeal for guidance on every type of sentencing issue. Citation of sentencing decisions in argument, both in the Court of Appeal and in the trial court, which was once considered inappropriate, is now widely encouraged and practiced.

The kind of guidance offered by the Court of Appeal falls under a number of headings and takes a variety of different forms. Many decisions are concerned with the general principles of sentencing and procedural issues. A perennial problem is that of deciding the factual basis which is to be adopted as the foundation of the sentence. In some cases, the defendant has pleaded guilty to the charge in the indictment, but disputes the prosecution's account of what exactly happened. Decisions of the Court of Appeal now establish the procedures which must be followed in this situation. If the dispute is likely to affect the sentence (as it frequently will) it must be resolved by a post-conviction hearing (known as a Newton hearing after the case in which the rule was established), in which evidence is called and evaluated by the judge sitting without a jury, but otherwise following the normal rules of criminal procedure. Sometimes the prosecution and the defence agree that the defendant will plead guilty on the basis of a particular version of the facts. A recent judgment establishes that the sentencing judge is not bound by such an agreement, and can direct the prosecution to call evidence in the form of a Newton hearing if the judge considers it appropriate to do so. If so, the judge can then determine the facts on which the defendant is to be sentenced, and is not constrained by the agreement between prosecution and defence. One recent decision of great importance (Canavan and others [1998] 1 Cr.App.R.(S.) 243) concerns what are known as 'specimen charges'. It had been a common practice for many years to charge a defendant, who was in reality believed to be responsible for a large number of crimes, with a limited number of offences which were treated as specimens representing the greater number of offences. If the defendant was convicted of the specimen charges, it was open to the judge to pass sentence on the basis that he was actually guilty of the greater number of offences. This practice, which clearly offends the principle that an offender is not to be sentenced for an offence of which he has not been convicted and which he has not admitted, has now been outlawed by the Court of Appeal.

The growth of legislation on sentencing means that the Court of Appeal is frequently called on to interpret the terms of the legislation. The Drug Trafficking Offences Act 1986, subsequently replaced by the Drug Trafficking Act 1994, provides for confiscation of the assets of drug traffickers. Its provisions have been described as 'draconian' and have given rise to many cases in which convicted offenders have attempted to restrict its application – usually without success. Legislation empowering courts to impose 'longer than commensurate sentences' on offenders convicted of violent or sexual offences has produced a significant body of case law, on such questions as the definition of 'violent offence' and the principles on which the power should be used.

The main body of the work of the Court of Appeal, Criminal Division is concerned with simpler questions. For example, the appellant complains that his sentence is too long. Thousands of such cases are considered every year. An intending appellant must first obtain leave to appeal. His written application for leave to appeal, setting out the grounds of the appeal, is first considered privately by a judge of the court, who will either grant leave to appeal (usually with legal aid) or refuse leave, setting out his reasons briefly in writing. A defendant who is refused leave has the right to renew the application before a court of three judges, but the majority do not do so. The single judge procedure provides an important filter to prevent the system becoming overwhelmed by large numbers of cases which have no real chance of success. Those cases in which leave to appeal is granted are argued before a court of three judges by the appellant's counsel; the prosecution only attend if requested by the court to do so (to clear up some question of fact, or to argue some question of law). The vast majority of appeals are determined after hearing only counsel for the appellant.

The statutory authority of the Court is to substitute any sentence which the trial court could have imposed, if the Court of Appeal thinks that 'the appellant should be sentenced differently for an offence'. In exercising this power, the Court of Appeal acts on the principle that a sentence will be varied only if it is 'wrong in principle or manifestly excessive' (although these terms are given a broad interpretation and sometimes forgotten entirely). The Court may not impose a sentence on appeal which would result in the appellant being dealt with more severely than he was in the court below, taking the case as a whole. (The power to increase a sentence on an appeal by the defendant was abolished in 1966.) A sentence can be increased only on an appeal by the prosecution (known as an Attorney General's Reference).

An example of a sentence which is 'wrong in principle' would be a case where the trial judge has made no allowance for the fact that the defendant pleaded guilty to the charges. It is now a well-established principle that a defendant who pleads guilty should normally receive a reduced sentence for that reason (commonly described as the 'discount'). If a judge fails to allow a discount (the extent of the discount is in the judge's discretion) the Court of Appeal will normally reduce the sentence, unless the case is one of those exceptional cases in which no discount is allowable (for example, where the evidence against the defendant is overwhelming and he would have no realistic hope of avoiding conviction). It is common for counsel to argue that the sentence of (say) three years imposed on the appellant following a plea of guilty means that the judge would have imposed four or four and a half years following a conviction by the jury, and that sentence would have been manifestly excessive.

Where the Court is asked to find that a sentence is manifestly excessive, the test is not what the individual judges who sit in the Court would have passed if they had tried the case at first instance, but whether the sentence is outside the range or bracket of sentences which would be permissible for that offence in the circumstances in which it was committed. This approach recognises that sentencing is essentially a discretionary process and that there is no exclusively correct sentence for any given case. Some sentences are clearly manifestly excessive and others would be unduly lenient, but between the extremes there is a range where the sentencing judge can exercise discretion.

In deciding cases of this kind, the Court has over a period of years created what amounts to a database of decisions in similar cases. A judge faced with sentencing a particular offender in the Crown Court may well look at decisions of the Court of Appeal in comparable cases (set out in *Current Sentencing Practice*, see Thomas 2002) for such guidance as they offer. To take one example, a judge dealing with the offence of doing an act tending to pervert the course of justice by making a false allegation of crime against an innocent person can easily find seven examples of decisions of the Court of Appeal in similar cases over the period between 1989 and 2000, mostly dealing with false allegations of rape. A brief review of the cases shows that the bracket approved by the Court of Appeal for such cases (where the innocent party has been arrested) is between 6 and 12 months' imprisonment. None of the cases purports to lay down general guidelines, but as a series of examples of how the Court of Appeal has dealt with similar cases in the past they provide a framework of reference for the new sentence. The judge might decide to pass a longer sentence than those shown in the reported cases (if, for instance, the false allegation was maintained over a substantial period of time with the result that the innocent party was held in custody for several months). The judge might also pass a shorter sentence if he or she considered that there were exceptional mitigating circumstances. The same exercise could be repeated for virtually any kind of crime which comes before the courts with any degree of frequency.

In some contexts, the Court of Appeal has gone beyond the provision of examples and formalised more general guidance on how a particular type of crime should be dealt with. The first 'guideline judgments' were delivered in the 1970s, but the more important ones today date from the early 1980s and onwards. Many have been revised in the light of changes in the law or public attitudes. Most of the guidelines are based on the existing practice of the Court of Appeal, and are intended to provide a convenient restatement of that practice; others were intended to signal a change in the practice of the Court of Appeal, often in response to a change in the maximum sentence for the offence.

An example of a guideline case is Billam (1986) 8 Cr.App.R.(S.) 48, dealing with rape. After some general discussion of the problems of sentencing in rape cases, the judgment offers a framework for sentencing. If the offence is not marked by particular aggravating features, the starting point in a contested case is five years' imprisonment. If the rape was committed by two or more men acting together, or by a man who has broken into the victim's house, or by a man who is in a position of responsibility to the victim, or by a man who has abducted the victim, the starting point becomes eight years. An offender who has carried out a campaign of rape will qualify for 15 years. All of these figures are starting points. There is a list of aggravating factors (such as the use of violence over and above that necessary to commit the rape, or the use of a weapon to frighten or wound) which will justify enhancing the sentence (no attempt is made to indicate the extent of the enhancement). Some mitigating factors are identified – in particular, a plea of guilty. A guideline case such as this becomes the basis of a new body of case law, as later decisions elaborate or illustrate the application of various parts of the guideline. Later developments require the guideline to be extended or amended. In the context of rape, the recognition of marital rape as a crime has led to a series of decisions examining the application of the original guidelines to rape by husbands or partners.

Guideline cases such as Billam apply to a relatively small proportion of offences. Other decisions cover incest, importing and dealing in drugs, causing death by dangerous driving, theft by employees, residential burglary, unlawful possession of firearms, and social security fraud. There are numerous other cases which do not offer a comprehensive treatment of an offence, but give some general guidance on a more limited basis.

Appeal by the prosecution

For many years, a criticism of the system was that the Court of Appeal had power to control excessive severity but could do nothing to control excessive leniency, which was just as capable of producing disparity. This deficiency was remedied to a limited extent in 1988 by the introduction of a new procedure under which the Attorney General can refer a sentence to the Court of Appeal for review on the ground that it was unduly lenient. This is in effect a prosecution right of appeal against sentence. If the Court of Appeal decides that the sentence was unduly lenient, it can and does substitute a more severe sentence which the offender must serve. This can mean that a sentence of imprisonment is made longer, or a non-custodial order is replaced by a term of imprisonment. The Court of Appeal normally indicates that the sentence it has substituted is less severe than the sentence which should have been imposed at first instance, to compensate the offender for what it describes as the element of double jeopardy inherent in appearing for sentence twice. The scope of this procedure is limited to the most serious offences (offences triable only in the Crown Court, indecent assault, threatening to kill, cruelty to child and serious frauds). The procedure has recently been extended to drug dealing or importation.

The introduction of Attorney General's References has strengthened the position of the Court of Appeal and has provided opportunity for a significant number of judgments giving guidance – either in the form of guideline judgments as described earlier, or statements of general principle (one such case emphasises that racial motivation is to be treated as an aggravating factor in cases of violence). Unlike appeals against sentence, references by the Attorney General are always argued by both prosecution and defence, normally before a court presided over by the Lord Chief Justice or one of the senior Lords Justices.

It would be wrong to pretend that the system of appellate review as operated in England is the answer to all problems related to securing harmony and consistency in sentencing. It does not deal with the large number of sentences in less serious cases imposed by magistrates' courts (voluntary sentencing guidelines for magistrates' courts are published by the Magistrates' Association); most of its cases are concerned with custodial sentences, and decisions on the principles to be followed in using (for instance) community service orders are rare. A large number of judges now sit in the Court of Appeal, which may sit in up to four divisions every day, and not all decisions are easily reconcilable. However, taken as a whole, there can be no doubt that the Court of Appeal provides a powerful influence on sentencing in the Crown Court, discourages maverick sentencers from going to the extremes of either severity or leniency, and has established a substantial body of guidance on sentencing issues which is available to judges in the Crown Court.

The Sentencing Advisory Panel

The Sentencing Advisory Panel is a newcomer, created under the Crime and Disorder Act 1998. Its function is to stimulate the development of guidelines by the Court of Appeal, Criminal Division. The panel has an advisory role only; it may suggest to the Court of Appeal, Criminal Division that a guideline is needed, and make proposals for the content of the guidelines; at the same time, the Court of Appeal, Criminal Division is required by statute to consult the Panel before formulating guidelines. The Court of Appeal, Criminal Division is free to adopt or reject the proposals of the Panel. The Panel has now been in existence for several years, and is beginning to make its presence felt. It has proposed a number of guidelines, some on its own initiative, some at the request of the Court of Appeal, Criminal Division. Some have been used by the Court as the basis of a guideline judgment. (The Panel's reports and consultative documents are accessible on the Internet.)

The future of discretion in sentencing

The balance between statutory regulation and judicial regulation in the sentencing system of the future is difficult to predict. There seems little doubt that future sentencing legislation will follow the current fashion for increasingly detailed rules which must be followed in particular cases, despite the practical problems they create. Judicial self-regulation has now reached a reasonably high level of sophistication; the senior judges of the Court of Appeal, Criminal Division, by contrast to their predecessors of the period before 1960, fully accept their obligation to set standards for sentencers and give guidance, both on matters of general principle and detailed sentencing problems in particular cases. Political and public interest in sentencing is at a high level, although often public understanding of the realities of sentencing is limited, and judges are criticised for excesses of leniency and of severity, often in the same case. Total consistency in the exercise of discretion by sentencers will never be achieved so long as human beings have to make the decisions, but a mechanical appearance of consistency such as can be produced by too rigid guidelines is as capable of producing injustice. Perhaps the most realistic aim of a sentencing system was expressed by Samuel Romilly in 1810 when he expressed the hope that 'there might be, if not a perfect uniformity in the administration of justice, yet the same spirit always prevailing, and the same maxims always kept in view' (Romilly 1810: 16).

Notes

1 See in particular their Second Report (1836), Fourth Report (1839), and Seventh Report (1843).
2 Buggery: see Offences against the Person Act 1861 section 14. The minimum sentence of ten years penal servitude remained in effect until 1891.
3 See *War with Crime* (eds. Philips and Verney) 1889.
4 See for example, Crackanthorpe, *The Nineteenth Century*, (1893: 630).
5 The attitude of the day is well captured in the White Paper, *Penal Practice in a Changing Society*, (Home Office 1959).
6 The Royal Commission published a number of volumes of evidence, but no report: see Royal Commission on the Penal System in England and Wales, Written Evidence, 1967.
7 See R.v.Davison (1989) 11 Cr.App.R.(S.) 570, R.v.Scott (1990) 12 Cr.App.R.(S.) 23.
8 See for instance Littler and others (1990) 12 Cr.App.R.(S.) 143; Marsden (1990) 12 Cr.App.R.(S.) 274.
9 See, in particular, publications of the Penal Affairs Consortium, *A Joint Manifesto for Penal Reform*, and *Criteria for Imprisonment* (both 1989).
10 Principally in the writings of Andrew Ashworth: see in particular *Sentencing and Penal Policy* (1983), chs. 2 and 3.

11 Section 1(2)(a).
12 Section 3(3).
13 Section 29(1).
14 Section 3(1).
15 Section 2(2)(a).
16 Section 29(2).
17 Section 28.
18 Section 1(2)(b) and 2(2)(b).
19 Section 6.
20 Section 18.
21 The cases are R.v.Cunningham, R.v.Robinson, R.v.Okinikan, R.v.Oliver and Little, R.v.Bexley and others, R.v.Baverstock, and R.v.Cox, all reported at (1992) 14 Cr.App.R.(S.) pp.444–485.
22 See Thomas, D.A. Principles of Sentencing (1979) pp. 41–44 for a discussion of the treatment of previous convictions before the 1991 Act.
23 The full text of the address is published in the *Journal of the Law Society of Scotland*, (1993: 129–131).

References

Ashworth, A. (1983) *Sentencing and Penal Policy*. London: Wiedenfeld and Nicholson.

Burney, E. (1985) *Sentencing Young People. What Went Wrong with the Criminal Justice Act 1982?* Aldershot: Gower Publishing.

Crackanthorpe, M. (1893) 'New ways with old offenders' in *The Nineteenth Century*, 44, 614–32.

Criminal Law Commissioners (1836) *Second Report*, XXXVI, 183–314.

Criminal Law Commissioners (1839) *Fourth Report*, XIX, 235–432.

Criminal Law Commissioners (1843) *Seventh Report*, XIX, 1–288.

Home Office (1959) *Penal Practice in a Changing Society* (Cmnd 645). London: HMSO.

Home Office (1988) *The Parole System in England and Wales: Report of the Review Committee* (Chairman: Lord Carlisle of Bucklow QC) (Cmnd 532) London: HMSO.

Home Office (1990) *Crime, Justice and Protecting the Public* (Cmnd 965). London: HMSO.

Penal Affairs Consortium (1989) *A Joint Manifesto for Penal Reform*. London: Penal Affairs Consortium.

Penal Affairs Consortium (1989) *The case for statutory guidelines on the use of imprisonment for adult offenders*. London: Penal Affairs Consortium.

Philips, H. and Verney, E. (1889) (eds.) *War with crime* (written by T. Baker). London: Longmans.

Radzinowicz, L. (1948) *History of the English Criminal Law*, 1. London: Stevens and Sons.

Romilly, S. (1810) *Observations on the Criminal Law of England as it relates to capital punishments and on the mode in which it is administered*. London: Cadell and Davies.

Royal Commission on the Penal System in England and Wales (1967) *Minutes of Evidence taken before the Royal Commission*. London: HMSO.

Taylor, P. (Lord Chief Justice) (1993) *Journal of the Law Society of Scotland*, 38, 129–31.

Thomas, D.A. (1979) *Principles of Sentencing* (2nd edn). London: Heinemann.

Thomas, D.A. (2002) *Current Sentencing Practice*. London: Sweet and Maxwell.

Chapter 4

Prison officers and the use of discretion

Alison Liebling and David Price[1]

We're governed by rules, and there is a saying that exceptions prove the rule. The most important thing is to know when that exception should be used. The good prison officer will bend the rules for good reasons, for the right reasons.

(Sparks et al. 1996: 155)

[Discretion] is inevitable because the translation of rule into action, the process by which abstraction becomes actuality, involves people in interpretation and choice. Law is fundamentally an interpretative enterprise in which discretionary behaviour is compelled by … 'the vagaries of language, the diversity of circumstances, and the indeterminacy of official purposes'.

(Hawkins 1992: 11)

Introduction

In this chapter we consider the role of discretion in the work of prison officers, and the links between this essential feature of prison life and other literatures. We draw on some recent research carried out in a single maximum security prison in England (Liebling and Price 1999), on our subsequent reflections, and on material published on the role of the prison officer at earlier stages in our thinking (Liebling 2000; Liebling and Price 2001).

Rules may be the anchor in a world of uncertainty, but their flexible interpretation and application is a key feature of the best of prison work, as well as a key feature in its corruption. Norms of reciprocity exist between the enforcer and the enforced, which result in rules being suspended in the interests of long-term compliance. There may be similarities between the work of prison officers and the work of regulation inspectors, as well as between prison officers and police officers.

A policy of Incentives and Earned Privileges (IEP), introduced in prisons in England during 1995, required governors to introduce a system of encouraging and rewarding 'good' behaviour by prisoners, and deterring 'bad' behaviour. It was based on the use of three levels of privileges: basic, standard and enhanced. In a two-year evaluation of the operation and effects of this new policy, we became intrigued by marked differences in the use of formal and informal power in establishments by prison officers (see Liebling et al. 1997; also Liebling 2000). In one of the five prisons studied, very different numbers of prisoners were allocated to the basic (most restricted) level of privileges on different wings, without any clear relationship between the types of prisoners involved and the frequency with which they were being sanctioned. Prison officers on one wing (E Wing in Figure 1, below) resorted to the formal procedures at their disposal far sooner than staff on other wings. This was linked to a distinct lack of informal contact between staff and prisoners, and other features of daily life. Officers were less likely to warn prisoners before they sanctioned them (despite this being a requirement of the policy) and were less likely to engage with them about their behaviour generally, or to intervene in disciplinary situations 'brewing' on the wing. Staff spent more time in their offices and used formal disciplinary and quasi-disciplinary tools to manage prisoner behaviour. Linked to this apparent distance between staff and prisoners were higher levels of fear among prisoners, more trade (a more developed economy), higher stakes and so on. The question of relationships with staff was mixed, as many prisoners reported that staff–prisoner relationships were 'good', but on further elaboration, tended to say this was because staff 'were never there' and 'left them alone'. The wing where this 'stand-off' pattern was most marked subsequently went on to experience a major disturbance towards the end of our research (Liebling 1999). Staff were rigorously resisted by prisoners because they used too much power, of the wrong sort. They relied on the rules, and on sanctions, rather than on 'right relationships', to achieve compliance.

On E Wing, few prisoners were 'warned about their behaviour' (despite the high numbers on basic); there were greater problems of debt and 'taxing'; the number of threats were high; a core group on the wing were strongly opposed to IEP; there were low levels of trust, and large

	Basic No. %	Low Morale %	Safety (not safe) %	Relationships (fairly/ very poor) %	TOTALS
A Wing (VPU)[2]	6 (5)	50	11	17	102
B Wing (Dispersal)	11 (10)	56	38	50	106
C Wing (Lifers)	4 (5)	47	24	35	87
D Wing (VPU/ SOTP)	1 (1)	42	21	16	103
E Wing (Dispersal)	17 (18)	77	30	24	82
F Wing (Dispersal)	6 (13)	29	–	56	45

Figure 1 *The relationship between use of basic level of privileges and other aspects of prison life in a single prison*

divisions regarding perceptions of the wing; staff were seen by prisoners as divided, and their relationships with management were seen as very or fairly poor by 40 per cent prisoners. F Wing was also low on perceptions of justice, but was seen as high on safety.

What this indicated was that staff practices varied to considerable degrees, and that these variations were linked in important ways to the use of formal and informal rules, and to relationships. The links between these dimensions of prison life to order could not have been more dramatically illustrated (see further, Liebling 2000; Sparks et al. 1996). We had here an empirical demonstration of the often cited maxim that staff–prisoner relationships are at the heart of a prison.

Prison officers and the 'defects of total power'

Gresham Sykes argued, in his study of a maximum security prison in New Jersey:

> The rulers of this society of captives nominally hold in their hands the sole right of granting rewards and inflicting punishments and it would seem that no prisoner could afford to ignore their demands for conformity … The custodians have the right not only to issue and administer the orders and regulations which are to guide the life of the prisoner, but also the right to detain, try, and punish any

individual accused of disobedience – a merging of legislative, executive and judicial functions which has long been regarded as the earmark of complete domination. The officials of the prison, in short, appear to be the possessors of almost infinite power within their realm; and, at least on the surface, the bureaucratic staff should experience no great difficulty in converting their rules and regulations – their blueprint for behaviour – into a reality.

(Sykes 1958: 41–2)

Prison officers cannot enforce all the rules if they want to get to the 'end of the day' without difficulty. Despite, on the surface, having a significant amount of power at their disposal, officers cannot draw on this resource alone. Officers are well aware that the use of physical coercion has severe limits on a day-to-day basis. Our example above indicates that over-use (or even officially sanctioned use) of formal powers generates resistance amongst prisoners. Prisons vary in the balance sought and achieved between formal and informal power, and as we have illustrated above, wings (micro-climates) within prisons will also vary in this respect.

Prisons are typically regarded as places of rules, limits, uneven power and clear standards. There is a clear pyramid of authority, with prison officers 'at the coalface' responsible for the translation of policy into everyday practice. The problem is:

The objectives which the officials pursue are not completely of their own choosing and the means which they can use to achieve their objectives are far from limitless. The custodians are not total despots, able to exercise their power at whim, and thus they lack the essential mark of infinite power, the unchallenged right of being capricious in their own rule.

(Sykes 1958: 42)

In practice, despite the availability of coercion, the surveillance and the rewards and punishments available, the actual behaviour of prisoners 'differs markedly from that which is called for by official commands and decrees' (Sykes 1958: 42). Despite the fact that 'the prison' is generally regarded as the ultimate sanction (or the ultimate tool for the control of deviance), violence, theft and drug use persist in the prison, and prison staff have to manage their effects:

Far from being omnipotent rulers who have crushed all signs of rebellion against their regime, the custodians are engaged in a struggle to maintain order – and it is a struggle in which the custodians frequently fail.

(Sykes 1958: 42)

Once the use of force is rejected as a means to secure obedience (for it is inefficient as well as the least legitimate mode of power), then other means must be sought:

In short, the ability of the officials to physically coerce their captives into the path of compliance is something of an illusion as far as the day to day activities of the prison are concerned and may be of doubtful value in moments of crisis. Intrinsically inefficient as a method of making men carry out a complex task, diminished in effectiveness by the realities of the guard–inmate ratio, and always accompanied by the danger of touching off further violence, the use of physical force by the custodians has many limitations as a basis on which to found the routine operation of the prison.

(Sykes 1958: 49–50)

Rewards and punishments constitute 'a better means of persuasion', although these have to be genuinely perceived as such.

So, prison officers are operating without the moral duty of their charges, without coercion and with limited rewards and punishments which are difficult to distribute fairly. Staff may also be, paradoxically, unwilling to impose the rules:

The un-issued order, the deliberately ignored disobedience, the duty left unperformed – these are cracks in the monolith just as surely as are acts of defiance in the subject population.

(Sykes 1958: 53)

The 'un-exercise' of power in prison is significant – and may constitute both 'the best' and 'a worst' form of practice, as we shall argue later. Sykes called these practices 'corruptions'; Sparks et al. called them 'accommodations' (Sparks et al. 1996). We have argued elsewhere that, deployed in an appropriate manner, the under-use of power constitutes 'the best' form of prison officer work: what we (and others) have called 'peacekeeping' (Liebling, Elliott and Price 1999). This best work consists of the diligent and skilled use of *discretion*. Used in the wrong way, the under-use of power can be regarded as lax, unprofessional and, at worst, as a form of 'conditioning' or omission of duty.

Three structural features of the prison bring about a reluctance to use all the power at officers' disposal:

1. The close nature of the contact or 'lack of social distance' between staff and prisoners throughout the day.

2. A desire to promote reciprocity and goodwill.

3. The involvement of prisoners in some 'formal' duties (orderlies; library staff; hotplate servers, etc.).

Prison officers unlock prisoners, bear the brunt of their resentments or pass on bad news. Their working style is the subject of commentary and sometimes rebuke by prisoners on a daily basis. Staff may come to share some of the irritants of the 'unreasonableness of authority', and they may come to like and respect certain of their charges. A study by Shapira and Navon found that contrary to the picture of total institutions painted by Goffman and others after him, the apparent 'gap' between staff and prisoners is often narrow, linked as officers and prisoners are by common interests, values, experiences and deprivations (Shapira and Navon 1985). This narrowing of the gap can render officers vulnerable to corruption (for example, bribery, malign under-enforcement, yielding to unreasonable demands, or 'romantic ties') (Shapira and Navon 1985: 136–139). Staff and prisoners live in a state of mutual dependence within prison, and may share extra-institutional pressures (such as negative feelings towards managers, political or religious affiliations, neighbourhoods, family problems) which serve to moderate the 'basic split' often assumed to exist.

The second structural constraint on the use of power arises from the dependency of staff on the consent of the prisoners in order to 'get through the day'. Prisoners move from the wing to work, because they are willing to. Staff ability to 'handle' prisoners in a basically co-operative way demands goodwill.

The third arises from the presence of 'trust', as trusted prisoners ('trustees' or red bands) are given small duties and responsibilities (in other words, powers). Such positions may bring influence beyond the strict definition of their role. In this sense, the staff have 'given away' a certain degree of power, and may not be fully aware of how it is being used.

All of these practices are necessary and appropriate aspects of prison life. A certain tolerance of minor infringements is necessary so that compliance can be achieved 'where it counts' (Sykes 1958: 57). But such practices need to be self-consciously policed; they can cross important thresholds. Staff do (very occasionally) become emotionally entangled; they make deals; they often tolerate (and sometimes collude in) rule-breaking behaviours. They may fear prisoners, and under-use their power for this reason. One officer may find it difficult to exercise power in an area where another officer has given it away.

Prison officers are 'under strong pressure to compromise with their captives'. It is a paradox, Sykes argued, that 'they can ensure their dominance only by allowing it to be corrupted'. As others have argued subsequently, you have to 'lose control' in order to gain it. These 'corruptions' are rooted in flaws in the social system of the prison (Sykes 1958: 60), and mean, in practice, that 'the job requirements of the guard's position are not technical skills' but rely on 'matters of character such as courage, honesty, and so on'. Mutual understandings develop whereby staff and prisoners 'establish tactical agreements and unofficial arrangements enabling them to carry out their work'. Staff must use the largely underestimated discretion they have to do this.

What are the 'right' reasons for bending rules?

> I can normally get them to do what I want … without having to resort to putting them on report. In my opinion, you can't be doing the job that well if you're having to place them on report all the time … There are ways of getting them to do what you want. They know the rules and regulations, and we know them. If an inmate is refusing to go to work, nine times out of ten I'll be able to get him to go to work … just through communication skills. If he doesn't, then he goes on report, but normally … I just explain to them – you're being stupid here. Just because you got out of bed the wrong side this morning get yourself up, washed, dressed, go to work, then you'll be able to get your canteen on Friday. If you don't do that, you know I've got to place you on report and you'll lose your wages. It's up to you … I'll leave you to get on with it. I'll close the door, and within a few seconds the bell will go. And they do just go to work.
>
> (Prison officer)

There is an extensive literature on the use of discretion in non criminal justice contexts (see, for example, Dworkin 1977; Goodin 1986; Galligan 1986; Hawkins 1992); and in policing (Dixon 1997). The inevitability of discretion springs from three sources:

1. **The wording of rules themselves**: 'vagaries of language' mean that words can never perfectly describe a situation or action. Rules are 'open-textured' (Hart 1958; see also Twining and Miers 1991);

2. **The situations to which the rules will apply**: the diversity of circumstances – no two situations are ever exactly alike, and rules cannot be written that will cover every imaginable situation. Some interpretation will therefore be required by those whose task it is to apply the rule;

3. **The official purposes guiding an organisation**: there is often, in any organisation, a lack of clarity in organisational aims. There may be also confusion or contradiction between different aims and objectives. The governmental literature alerts us to the way in which political rationalities and political technologies are liable to subversion by interested groups and individuals (see, for example, Rose and Miller 1992; Barry et al. 1996).

Prison officers and staff–prisoner relationships

In an ethnographic (observational) study carried out in a maximum security prison in East Anglia by the authors during 1998–9, we found that relationships provided the framework through which prison officers made decisions about prisoners. Relationships were instruments of control as well as instruments of justice.[3] They were described as a sort of 'quiet power'. This was one of the reasons that staff–prisoner relationships matter: because power is fundamentally *relational*. In our shadowing of prison staff, we learned that exceptions were the rule:

> **Interviewer**: So are prisoners unlocked on here if they don't go to work?
> **Officer**: No. We don't unlock if they don't go to work. Only the cleaners.
> [We come across a prisoner as we walk the landing.]
> **Prisoner**: Hello [begins conversation, asking who I am and what the research is about ... conversation continues and is about to finish. As a parting remark:] Of course, I'm not supposed to be unlocked today ...
> **Officer**: Ah, I made an exception in his case [begins to explain what turns out to be one of several exceptions, linked to this prisoner's 'trustworthiness'.]

The observation of staff at work taught us that their verbal accounts of their behaviour are far more straightforward than the behaviour in question, which is invariably more complex and more sophisticated than the unconsciously edited account. Giddens uses the term 'practical consciousness' to describe the taken for granted unwritten rules which underlie social practices. Every day decisions are embedded in knowledges that prison officers take for granted. These knowledges are inseparable from relationships, within which judgments are made about demeanour, gestures and language. Some of the most important skills officers develop are located in this realm of practical consciousness. Like a footballer who scores a wonderful goal, an officer may have difficulty describing how he did it (a useful analogy we have borrowed from Hay and Sparks 1991). This dimension of prison life is crucial, as the translation of rules (and policies) into action is an *interpretative* exercise, where the particular case cannot be addressed by the general rule. The world of the prison is a world flowing with power, judgement and feeling.

Prisoners and staff felt that the 'decent thing' was to be reasonably sparing with the rules, unless there was a good reason not to be:

> **Interviewer**: Has there been an occasion recently where you were expecting to be placed on report and weren't?
> **Prisoner**: Yeah – I've c---ted off a few screws and thought that I'd gone a bit far, but didn't get a nicking sheet that night.
> **Interviewer**: How does something like that then change the relationship you have with that officer you swore at?
> **Prisoner**: It actually improves your attitude to that officer. The screws can earn respect. If a screw comes in and finds booze and pours it down the toilet, they've got my instant respect, because I know they're told to nick us. I've lost, because I've lost the hooch. That's enough of a punishment for me. The officer's been sensible – if I had bucket after bucket, then fair enough, nick me. But a little bit, if they ran out and nicked me for it, no respect at all. They get instant respect, they've behaved in a humane manner.[4]

Rules were *resources upon which to draw*, rather than templates to be applied. Rules were one source of power, and they ensured one sort of order, and were not always the best way of achieving order. Less coercive methods of power often achieved a more sustainable or consensual form of order.[5] It was all a question of balance. While formal punishments such as adjudications or loss of incentives status were not meaningless to prisoners, they might not have the desired impact if prisoners had 'friends who would sort them out' if privileges were lost (or if prisoners gained status amongst their peers for 'going down to basic'). Although full enforcement of the rules is impossible, prison officers are aware that a lax *under*-enforcement of rules can produce other undesirable results. Under-enforcement is justifiable when it is intended to achieve an effect or end informally, that is, without recourse to formal authority. The tone of voice used in conversation, or the use of humour, are often effective substitutes for formal 'orders'. Here, rules are still enforced, but tacitly.

The consent of prisoners (and most prisoners consciously felt that they were consenting to or granting order to the prison, rather than being controlled) was crucial to whatever type of 'order' was established. This was just like the concept of policing with consent. Animosity could quickly develop if staff took a hard line over detail, or approached prisoners with 'the wrong attitude':

> (Prison Service) college is a little bit like learning to drive a car. Once you've passed your test at the end of college, and you're put in a prison, that's when you really learn to drive. You take things a little bit further, you learn where your line is ... can I go a little bit faster round this corner? And the next day, a little bit faster ... and then you nearly lose it and you think, whoa ... I'll pull back a bit there ... I went to a YOI and I learned the job there and so it was quite difficult coming here, from a place where I was shouting and screaming ... if you holler at some of these, it doesn't get you anywhere.
>
> (Senior officer)

Different styles were required in different types of establishment. One of our most important findings concerned the reasons through which officers justified their decisions to enforce a particular rule, or to withold its application. Whilst it was widely recognised by staff and managers that rules were often bent or under-enforced, and that situations were sometimes best not handled in the strict and inflexible manner of the rule-book, there were few explicit principles guiding the exercise of discretion. Whilst senior managers confidently communicated their vision to us, this vision (about moving from 'control' to 'order', and about safely granting prisoners some agency) was not clearly understood by prison officers. Each prison officer had their own principles, their own 'bigger picture' of what prison was about and of what their particular role was in the prison. This in turn informed how they handled specific situations.

One question we asked a lot of officers during interviews was about what they would do if they came across a prisoner who was 'wired-up' during a regular cell check (drawing a wire to his stereo from the lightbulb socket to avoid having to pay for batteries). Officers gave us a range of responses, each of which was shaped by the individual's own 'bigger picture' of prison work. For example:

- Officer A (just out of the Special Security Unit, where procedures were followed 'to the letter') answered, 'Close the cell, call the Works Department to safely take down the wire, and place the prisoner on report'. His reasoning was that wiring-up was against the rules of the prison, and was also a potential safety-hazard. His 'bigger picture' centred on the enforcement of the rules as a route to safety and order. While the officer was willing to 'bend' some rules, this incident was serious enough to warrant a formal adjudication. Any repercussions for his relationship with the prisoner or with others were not considered – or were subordinated to the need to maintain the rules.

- Officer B said that he would, 'Take down the wire and confiscate it, and have a word with the prisoner when he came back on the wing'. The prisoner would be 'warned that wiring-up was a dangerous thing to do and could end up with him being placed on report or electrocuted'. This officer recognised the expense of batteries to prisoners and appreciated that some of them might resort to wiring-up. He did not want to place the prisoner on report (but would do so if the prisoner was caught again), and chose to reach the same overall result as Officer A (stopping the prisoner wiring-up) but in a less formal manner. He also felt that this method of resolution had the added bonus of granting the prisoner a favour. Strictly, the prisoner should have been placed on report. In this way, the prisoner was placed in the officer's debt, and the favour could be called in at an opportune time in the future. The 'bigger picture' of this officer was centred on long-term wing order, and the maintenance of relationships.

- Officer C said that he would take the wire down, but leave it in the prisoner's cell. He would let the prisoner know that he'd found the wire, and that he'd put the prisoner on report if he found him wired up again. ('You don't leave a wire up when an officer's coming round, do you? It's taking the piss. He should know that someone's going to get annoyed at that.') He felt that this action meant that he was granting the prisoner a favour. His reasoning was pragmatic: prisoners are going to wire-up, whether we like it or not; they have to get the wires from somewhere, so he might as well leave it in the cell. If I take this wire away, then the next time the hair clippers (or another electrical item) are signed out from the office, they'll eventually re-appear without a lead; the wing will then be without hair clippers for a week while Works fixes them. The wing runs more easily when officers are able to let prisoners have access to all the items they are entitled to. This officer's 'bigger picture' was all about keeping the flow of the wing going; ideas about enforcement, related to wider principles of rule-breaking, were subordinated to the principle of 'smooth flow'.

Each officer did 'enforce' the rule about wiring up, but in different ways, to different degrees. The decisions made by prison officers were embedded in meaning, knowledge, experience, values and relation-ships. These different ways of working were differences in the exercise of discretion – differences as to which rules would be enforced and to what extent, and in which times and places. Senior managers were aware that officers enforced or under-enforced rules for different reasons. They were concerned to ensure that the reasons for staff behaviour were the correct ones:

> **Interviewer**: This is what we are trying to get at – where the boundaries are; and these questions, 'Do you play pool, don't you play pool?'; 'Do you take a biscuit, don't you take a biscuit?' – they divide the staff.
>
> **Senior Manager**: The answer is in your head; the answer is the kind of person you are as an officer. And if you are playing pool because you feel that you need to ingratiate yourself with prisoners, then playing pool is the worst thing you should do. If playing pool is simply a vehicle for communicating at a more significant level with prisoners about issues of order, control, responsibility, ownership, drug dealing, whatever it is you want to legitimately discuss – if doing it over a game of pool is the way to do it, then that's absolutely the right way to do it.

There was a lot of talk about the boundaries of rule-bending and relationships, about where these boundaries were, and about how prison officers and prisoners knew when they were crossing them, or when they had to be 'policed'. In this sense, the job of being a prison officer was compared to the job of being a parent. It was important that staff were in charge of the boundaries, rather than prisoners. By the nature of their position, prisoners were compelled to challenge these boundaries and frequently did so. Like parents, prison officers had different personal thresholds, just as they had different 'bigger pictures'. Yet unlike parents, prison officers also had to bear their professional 'line' in mind:

> We've got quite a volatile mix at the moment, so every day you get through, you think, we've done OK there. When you get someone talk to you … Prisoner X was here two days ago and we had a confrontation on the hotplate about fruit. And he didn't get what he wanted. We then had another confrontation three days later about visits. He knew I was new on the wing, and he was really trying to see how far he could go. So I just put my official head on: 'You ain't getting nothing. They're the rules and you'll obey them'. I did that for about a fortnight. He actually approached me about a week later, said this and that, is there any chance you can sort it out? I said I'd have a go, did it, and we now get on very well.
>
> (Officer)

The use of discretion in other agencies: (i) policing, prison work and the significance of peacekeeping

> The central concept underlying police research has been *discretion*, the recognition that the police do not automatically translate law into policing practice.
>
> (Reiner 1997: 999)

There are significant similarities between the work of a police officer and that of a prison officer (Liebling 2000; and see Reiner on 'policing' as 'the whole craft of governing a social order' – Reiner 1997: 997). Prison officers 'police' the prison, as if it were a community. A certain amount of consent is required to achieve the task. Over-policing threatens this consent. Studies of the police's use of discretion have examined the significance of *non* law-enforcement, peacekeeping work and the dependence of formal upon informal modes of control (Banton 1964; Bittner 1967; and Smith 1986, for example). Underlying all police practice is the potential use of legitimate, state-granted physical force – although this potential remains unused for the vast majority of the time. Police practice has complex and often contradictory functions, and most examples of good policing rely on verbal skills rather than physical coercion. These observations are also true of prison work. Both the task of policing the wider community and the task of 'policing' prison behaviour require the use of power and authority, the use of discretion, the pursuit of order, and an opposition to lawlessness.

The policing literature suggests that officers frequently enforce their authority rather than 'the law' or 'the rules'. There are significant non-legal factors which influence decisions to enforce the rules. For example, whether an officer is treated with respect, or whether the safety of the environment is threatened, may determine whether or not a sanction is used (Sykes and Brent 1983). Sykes and Brent suggested that the police operate with an *asymmetric deference norm* – that is, that they adjust their level of deference/respect to just below that of a civilian. Police officers expect civilians to acknowledge that this asymmetric status norm governs their relations – in effect, the police assume a slightly higher status than the status of civilian (Sykes and Brent 1983: 101). Police officers are also problem solving, and often do so with long-term objectives in mind. They are not simply choosing between arrest and non-arrest, but between different typifications of the situation, of the 'situated identities' of the civilians, and between many alternatives in addition to arrest/non-arrest (calming the situation down, for example). Both police and prison officers make judgements about interactions by considering demeanour, gestures and language, whose content and tone is continually interpreted. Negative interaction can be a substitute for a formal sanction. Thus, prison officers under-enforce the rules, but may still enforce their authority. Prison officers reach a solution to the situation in front of them that does not necessarily draw upon the rules at all.

A wider interest in the use of discretion amongst law enforcement officials has often been linked to the potential abuse of power (Liebling and Price 1999), rather than its *under*-use. We found that prison officers under-used formal power more often than they over-used it. Under-enforcement, the movement from tension to peace without incident, the use of language rather than action to avert the requirement for force, was far more common. Managers did not often recognise or reward this kind of professional conduct. In practice, staff used their judgment, experience and sensitivity to the specific context of the wing:

> When you first come onto a new area, as a new officer, you basically say 'What happens here?' and they say 'It's done like this'. So you do it like that, but the regular staff do it their own way, which is the relaxed way and you say 'No it's like that' – then you get abuse. A few times I got that. I remember a con had a go at me once here, shouting, and the whole wing watched. I didn't shout back, I didn't lose my temper, and nobody got hurt.
>
> (Officer)

As an officer, what you could do was limited by your confidence, your credibility on the wing, and the relationships you had with prisoners:

> You can't walk straight in as a new officer, because the prisoners will spot you a mile away, and start calling the shots and throwing your weight around. You can legally! – but the cons don't accept that. You have to earn the respect of the prisoners. There have been quite a lot of new officers who have turned up in the past few months, and they try to copy the old officers straight away – and this doesn't really work. You must develop your own style. You can be influenced by people in a certain extent – you've got to be as you do that in any job – but you must establish your own personality within the job.
>
> (Officer)

The successful use of discretion was central to being a good prison officer. It involved not having to resort to asserting their authority formally, being willing not to use force (although that did not mean never using force), and attempting to solve situations peacefully and through talk before anything else (except in an emergency when physical force was required). Through those relationships, 'peace' could be accomplished (and re-accomplished). This routine part of prison officers' work was highly valued among officers.

David Dixon argues in *Law in Policing* (Dixon 1997) that there are three theoretical approaches to law: the legalistic, the culturalist and the structural. The **legalistic** approach takes the laws, or formal policies and rules, as the key determinant of action: the rules drive behaviour. This is largely how policy-makers view prison life. Conservative critics of prisons (like Woodcock or General Sir John Learmont; see Home Office 1994; 1995) also have this sociologically impoverished view of prison life – what the prison service should be doing, Woodcock argued, is following its own rules. The 'rule following or compliance model' of prison life and work is favoured by risk-averse officials or those who make and manage policy. But there is a 'negotiation model' actually delivered by most prison staff, except in exceptional cases. Each model has different implications for our understanding of how prisons work, how staff should be selected, trained and managed, the type of relationships prison officers develop with prisoners, and how order and security are legitimately obtained. Each model can make competing claims for legitimacy. Whilst prisons are designed and managed and prison policies conceived and evaluated under the assumptions of the rule-following model, in practice most of what goes on in prison takes place under the negotiation model, as Sykes so ably describes in *The Society of Captives*. If the use of discretion is denied, then no guidance is available on how to use it. In the current 'audit' climate, process, rules and procedures clearly matter. But this daily, complex dimension of prison life also has to be taken seriously.

Dixon is right to suggest that in practice, the rules are rather abstract. No-one on the ground sees them. As an aside, it is significant that not a single officer in our IEP evaluation had read or even seen the policy instruction. The rules are a conception, a resource, for achieving other ends, like order. Dixon's point is that we need a more sophisticated concept of just what the rules are, and how they are differentiated. We agree.

In Dixon's **culturalist** approach, rules are a resource to achieve a primary aim which in policing, and also to a large extent in prisons, is order. Order might be achieved by methods other than law-enforcement; and there may be in existence many different conceptions of order to which the rule-resources are applied. Laws in practice meet norms – working norms and broader cultural norms. Officers are not engaged in enforcing the law but in 'handling the situation'. Dixon criticises the culturalist approach for failing to take seriously the significance of legal rules in shaping police work. The naive sociologist is tempted to overlook the rules altogether. Structural approaches include the legal rules. Some practices are more amenable to legal regulation than others. What we need is an account of rules and policy in action. What specific constraints and resources exist? This requires a more elaborate theorisation of policy-making, legal frameworks and so on; of how these frameworks, structures, discourses, are translated into practice through daily social patterns; and how they resonate with occupational, establishment, and wing-level cultures and sensibilities. For this task, only high-quality observational and interview data, together with an awareness of structures and administration, will do.

Finally, we turn to the regulation industry, where other similarities can be found: compliance is secured by many means, but the rules are a last resort.

The use of discretion in other agencies: (ii) the regulation industry

> Given the vast number and kind of regulatory illegalities, it seems that some measure of discretionary enforcement ... will be inevitable.
>
> (Hawkins 1992: 461)

Links can be drawn between the task of regulation[6] and the work of prison officers due to the continuing contact between prison officers and prisoners and because regulatory regimes seek to encourage forms of activity rather than to 'punish' (see Baldwin et al. 1998; also Harding 1997 on the role of controllers in private prisons). The traditional regulatory relationship takes place between a single inspector or regulator and an organisation or company. Inspectors usually interact with or visit companies on their own rather than in a team. The same inspector is often responsible for the same company over an extended period, enabling knowledge to be acquired by each side of the expectations and actions of the other, and allowing a relationship to develop. Behind the inspector lies the larger regulatory body, itself given power by statute or legislation. The purpose of the 'policing' of the company will be to ensure that it adheres to the regulations laid down for its safe or legitimate operation.

One of the similarities between the regulatory context and rule enforcement in the prison environment is that compliance with the rules takes place within a continuous process rather than being a one-off event. The enforcement strategies inspectors adopt within an ongoing regulatory relationship may be of relevance here. Ayres and Braithwaite (1992) produced a model they termed a 'sanctions and enforcement pyramid'. Such a model recognises that the greatest amount of work done by inspectors uses the least severe methods or sanctions. The techniques of verbal persuasion or negotiation, advice and education thus form the large 'base' at the bottom of the pyramid. The more severe the sanctions employed by an inspector, the less frequently they are used – hence, each level of the pyramid becomes smaller, with criminal prosecution at the top.

Hutter (1997) re-works Braithwaite's sanctions and enforcement pyramid in her own work on regulatory inspectors (see Figure 2). At the bottom of the pyramid sits the majority of the work of inspectors, the area with the least formality and least punitive sanctions. She terms this part of the pyramid 'persuasion'. It comprises inspectors using various techniques such as the education of companies, advice on the best course of action, or shaming them into action:

> The inspectors … all spent at least part of their day helping the regulated understand what was required of them and why.
>
> (Hutter 1997: 207)

The next level of the pyramid ('warnings') consists of verbal or written warnings. From there, action moves to the issuing of written 'notices' to

Figure 2 *'Sanctions Pyramid' (Hutter 1997, after Ayres and Braithwaite 1992)*

an organisation demanding improvement in their performance. The final step, to 'criminal prosecution', is rarely used by inspectors. It is perceived as a 'last resort', should none of the other actions work.

This model does not suggest that each level of the pyramid must be deployed for each incident. Depending on the seriousness of the infraction noted by the inspector, the first course of action taken might be a written warning or notice, bypassing the 'persuasion' stage altogether. Ayres and Braithwaite (1992) acknowledge that the specific parts of each layer of the pyramid can change from context to context. Actions are mediated by relationships, institutional dynamics, the nature of the rule being broken, and the culture and values of the regulator and regulatee (see further, Baldwin et al. 1998).

There are some important differences between the work of regulatory inspectors and that of prison officers. Inspectors have a strict set of laws from which to work. The goal of inspectors is to ensure that organisations work within the standards set down by these laws, thus ensuring, for example, proper levels of health and safety within their workplaces. The situation for prison officers is subtly, but significantly, different. There is a large amount of prison rules available, and many other instructions and procedures, but these are not as prescriptive as regulatory standards (although they are arguably developing in this manner; see Baldwin et al. 1998 on the general growth of centralised regulation agencies). Most important, they are not in themselves as directly related to the organisational goals of the prison officer as regulatory laws are for an inspector.

A second difference relates to the delay often granted to organisations after action is requested or demanded by an inspector. In the regulatory context, inspectors recognise that it can take time for an organisation to make the improvements requested, and they are willing to grant them a period of grace. In that sense, there is a distinct phase to a relationship where a difference has been demanded, and where regulator and regulated are working towards, or waiting for, the results. The behavioural changes demanded in prison are generally more immediate – don't wire up again; don't swear at me again. The need for action is here and now, rather than by some point in the future (although of course, sentence planning, parole and IEP reviews could be seen in this proactive context; see Chapter 5).

The exercise of mercy

> This jail is a complex place, there are always exceptions to things, and people should be treated as individuals.
>
> (senior manager, in Liebling and Price 1999)

One of the dilemmas in this area of work is the balance between using discretion for legitimacy (that is, making valid exceptions to the rule) and the dangers of using discretion illegitimately (for example, discrimination, or arbitrary decision-making). There is a tension between the need for consistency and the need for flexibility. One way of thinking about this tension is offered by Harrison, who uses the concept of mercy. Bottoms argues, drawing on Harrison's argument, that mercy or compassion can be rationally exercised (Bottoms 1998: 67–68), that is, that exceptions can be made. Consistency does not always lead to fairness, although *parity* (treating like cases alike) might:

> Demands for mercy within a legal system especially arise when a given general rule seems likely to lead to an inappropriate (or unjust) result in a specific case; in other words, such demands 'are really often arguments about the need for flexibility' in the application of rules.
>
> (Bottoms 1998: 68)

There is an important distinction between 'the mechanical operation of rules' and 'the question of justice' in a particular case.[7] Rules are 'blunt instruments', which do not take into account the complexity or individuality of a particular person or context (Harrison 1992; also Hawkins 1992). Real differences between individuals and situations justify differential applications of a rule, provided that the application of the rule – its enforcement or suspension – would be similar in any exactly similar case. How can this sort of flexibility avoid becoming arbitrary decision-making? How can we be certain of 'what counts as a relevant consideration'? Harrison argues as follows:

> What it requires is the trained application of the reasons of law to individual cases … If justice is to be done, the decision should be taken for reasons and be rationally defensible. Such a rational defence will include emphasising all the special features of the particular case … Judgment is needed, but the best judgment is informed by, and sensitive to, reason. The best judgment is not just about one case in isolation, but is sensitive to the possible implications of that judgment on other cases.
>
> (Harrison 1992: 122)

Discretion should be 'boundaried' by guidelines which are 'flexible enough to be adaptable to meet the special circumstances of particular cases' (Bottoms 1998: 69). Such guidelines 'draw upon and yet also develop the *deep structures* of' (in this case) penological practice and thinking (in Giddens' language, the 'practical consciousness' of prison officers):[8]

> Bringing an occupation's 'practical consciousness' into the realm of formal discussion and deliberation may well be an appropriate way to begin to develop 'the trained application of reasons of law to individual cases', as Harrison puts it, precisely because the collective 'practical consciousness' often contains some extremely useful pointers to good practice. But equally, in this process of explicit articulation of previous practice, it will very likely become apparent that appropriate good practice guidelines will need to go beyond the insights of 'practical consciousness' – which insights may at crucial points be overly vague … or even, on careful reflection, actually insupportable when critically considered.
>
> (Bottoms, 1998: 70)

Open dialogue about detail – about boundaries, decision-making, and the use of power, drawing on daily practice – is crucial to the development of 'the right' deep structures, or practices. Staff (and their managers) should engage in conversations about detail, to reason about their decision-making. Right behaviour is 'conduct for which reasons could be given' (Harrison 1992: 115). Actions are not justified by their *source* (because one has the power to decide) but by their *content* (can the decision be justified?). Without this constraint, we have 'power without accountability'. Every use of power 'should be subject to review' (Harrison 1992: 118). If there are *principles*, as well as rules, then judgment is guided, and flexibility is possible.

Notes

1 We would like to thank Loraine Gelsthorpe and Nicola Padfield for arranging the seminars at which some of these ideas were discussed. We would also like to thank Tony Bottoms and Keith Hawkins for very helpful leads. We would like to thank the Prison Service Journal for kind permission to reproduce parts of a chapter originally published in *The Prison Officer*, in a revised form here.
2 Vulnerable Prisoner Unit (accommodating prisoners not doing the Sex Offender Treatment Programme).
3 Relationships were also important for normative ('it is better'; 'it is right'; 'it makes the job more satisfying') as well as instrumental reasons: ('we need them'; 'they write our reports'; 'they get things done'; 'they help with order and control'). See further Liebling and Price 2001.
4 Here, the prisoner is making a distinction between *force* and *authority*.
5 See Sparks et al. 1996 on the differences between 'situational' and 'social' approaches to order in Albany and Long Lartin in the 1980s.
6 We are grateful to Keith Hawkins and Tony Bottoms for bringing the regulation literature to our attention.
7 Carol Gilligan, Harrison and others have argued that 'justice', 'impartiality' and 'equality' may be abstract, cold virtues, and that human beings want their interests treated mercifully, not impartially (Gilligan 1986).
8 This is prison officers almost unconsciously drawing on their experience, knowledge and skills.

References

Ayres, I. and Braithwaite, J. (1992) *Responsive Regulation – Transcending the Deregulation Debate*. Oxford: Oxford University Press.

Baldwin, R., Scott, C. and Hood, C. (1998) *A Reader on Regulation*. Oxford: Oxford University Press.

Banton, M. (1964) *The Policeman in the Community*. London: Tavistock.

Barry, A., Osborne, T. and Rose, N. (1996) *Foucault and Political Reason*. London: UCL Press Ltd.

Benyon, J. and Bourne, C. (1986) (eds.) *The Police: Powers, Procedures and Proprieties*. Oxford: Pergamon Press.

Bittner, E. (1967) 'The Police on Skid Row: A Study of Peacekeeping' in *American Sociological Review* 32 (5), 699–715.

Bottoms, A.E. (1998) 'Five Puzzles in von Hirsch's Theory of Punishment' in Ashworth, A. and Wasik, M. (eds.) *Fundamentals of Sentencing Theory: Essays in Honour of Andrew von Hirsch*. Oxford: Clarendon Press.

Dixon, D. (1997) *Law in Policing: Legal Regulations and Policing Practice*. Oxford: Clarendon Press.

Dworkin, R. (1977) *Taking Rights Seriously*. Cambridge, MA: Harvard University Press.

Galligan, D. (1986) *Discretionary Powers*. Oxford: Clarendon Press.

Giddens, A. (1984) *The Constitution of Society*. Cambridge: Polity Press.

Gilbert, M. (1997) 'The Illusion of Structure: A Critique of the Classical Model of Organisation and the Discretionary Power of Correctional Officers', *Criminal Justice Review*, 22 (1), 49–64.

Gilligan, C. (1986) *In a Different Voice: Psychological Theory and Women's Development*. Cambridge, MA: Harvard University Press.

Goodin, R.E. (1986) 'Welfare, Rights, and Discretion', *Oxford Journal of Legal Studies*, 6(3), 232–261.

Harrison, R. (1992) 'The Equality of Mercy' in H. Gross and R. Harrison, (eds.) *Jurisprudence: Cambridge Essays*. Oxford: Clarendon Press.

Harding, R. (1997) *Private Prisons and Public Accountability*. Buckingham: Open University Press.

Hart, H.L.A. (1958) 'Dias and Hughes on Jurisprudence' in *Society of Public Teachers of Law*, 4, 144–145.

Hay, W. and Sparks, R. (1991) 'What is a Prison Officer?' in *Prison Service Journal*. Spring, 2–7.

Hawkins, K. (1984) *Environment and Enforcement*. Oxford: Clarendon Press.

Hawkins, K. (1992) *The Uses of Discretion*. Oxford: Clarendon Press.

Hepburn, J.R. (1985) 'The Exercise of Power in Coercive Organisations: A Study of Prison Guards', *Criminology* 23 (1), 145–164.

Home Office (1991) *Prison Disturbances 1990 (The Woolf Report)*. London: HMSO.

Home Office (1994) *Report of the enquiry into the escape of six prisoners from the special security unit at Whitemoor Prison (The Woodcock Report)*. London: HMSO.

Home Office (1995) *Review of prison service security in England and Wales and the escape from Parkhurst Prison on Tuesday 3rd January 1995 (The Learmont Report)*. London: HMSO.

Hutter, B. (1997) *Compliance, Regulation and Environment*. Oxford: Clarendon Press.

Liebling, A. (1997) (ed.) *Security, Justice and Order in Prison*. Proceedings of a Cropwood Conference, Institute of Criminology: Cambridge.

Liebling, A. (1999) 'Doing Prison Research: Breaking the Silence', *Theoretical Criminology*, 3 (2), 147–173.

Liebling, A. (2000) 'Prison officers, policing, and the use of discretion' in *Theoretical Criminology*, 4 (3), 333–357.

Liebling, A. et al. (1997) *An Evaluation of Incentives and Earned Privileges: Final Report to the Prison Service*. Cambridge: Institute of Criminology.

Liebling, A. and Price, D. (1998) Staff–Prisoner Relationships: A Summary of Research. *Prison Service Journal* No. 120, 3–6.

Liebling, A. and Price, D. (1999) *An Exploration of Staff–Prisoner Relationships at HMP Whitemoor*. Prison Service Research Report No.6.

Liebling, A. and Price, D. (2001) *The Prison Officer*. Leyhill: Prison Service and Waterside Press.

Liebling, A., Elliott, C. and Price, D. (1999) 'Appreciative Inquiry and Relationships in Prison'. *Punishment and Society: The International Journal of Penology* I.

Muir, W. K. (1977) *Police: Streetcorner Politicians*. Chicago: University of Chicago Press.

Price, D. and Liebling, A. (1998) *Staff–Prisoner Relationships: A Review of the Literature*. Report submitted to the Home Office: London.

Reiner, R. (1997) 'Policing and the Police' in M. Maguire, R. Morgan and R. Reiner (1997) *The Oxford Handbook of Criminology*. Oxford: Oxford University Press.

Rose, N. and Miller, P. (1992) 'Political Power Beyond the State: Problematics of Government' in *British Journal of Sociology*, 43, 173–205.

Smith, D. (1986) 'The Framework of Law and Policing Practice' in J. Benyon and C. Bourne (eds.) *The Police*. Oxford: Pergamon.

Shapira, R. and Navon, D. (1985) 'Staff–Inmate Co-operation in Israeli Prisons: Towards a Non-functionalist Theory of Total Institutions' in *International Review of Modern Sociology*, 15, 131–146.

Sparks, R., Bottoms, A. E. and Hay, W. (1996) *Prisons and the Problem of Order*. Oxford: Clarendon Press.

Sykes, G. (1958) *The Society of Captives*. Princeton, NJ: Princeton University Press.

Sykes, G. and Brent, E. (1983) *Policing: A Social Behaviourist Perspective*. New Jersey: Rutgers University Press.

Twining, W. and Miers, D. (1991) *How to Do Things With Rules*. London: Butterworths.

Chapter 5

Discretion and the release of life sentence prisoners

Nicola Padfield and Alison Liebling,
with Helen Arnold

… [T]he best way to protect you from committing such an attack
and to ensure that you will not be at liberty until the risk of such an
attack has gone – is to pass a sentence of life imprisonment, not, of
course … with the intent that you should stay in prison for the rest
of your life, but with the intent that you should not be released until
those responsible for the supervision of your case are satisfied that
it is safe.

(Sentencing Judge, Case 201)

It's all about *people*, isn't it? It's all about the quality of the
psychiatrist and the judge and the independent member.

(Judge)

Given the importance of decision-making in the operation of law,
the lack of research explicitly focused on the question of how
decisions are made is surprising. Furthermore, a great deal of work
which has been carried out has relied upon quantitative
methodologies which, in conjunction with an artificial conception
of human judgment, have tended to do violence to the inherent
complexities involved in making decisions in legal settings …
There is little conception, in the first place, of decision-making as
process, a highly subtle, shifting, dynamic matter. Second, there is
little conception of the problematic nature of the information which
is the raw material for the decision. There is, third, little conception
of the broader constraints within which decision-makers operate:
ideological, symbolic, socio-political, economic, organisational and

interactional. Finally, there is little conception of the interpretative work in which decision-makers engage and the meaning of matters defined as relevant.

(Hawkins 1983: 8)

This chapter arises from our research into the release of life sentence prisoners carried out in 1999.[1] The research constituted an observational study of the nature and quality of decision-making at Discretionary Lifer Panels [DLPs]. Discretionary Lifer Panels of the Parole Board have been given the responsibility by Parliament to give a direction to the Home Secretary to release a life sentence prisoner only if they are 'satisfied that it is no longer necessary for the protection of the public that the prisoner should be confined'.[2] Panels can direct release or recommend a move to open conditions. The decision is taken at an oral hearing at which the prisoner can be legally represented. Panels also convene to confirm a released prisoner's recall to prison, if there are concerns about risk to the public. The decision-making process we observed was primarily about risk and its assessment, with an extremely difficult (and arguably high-risk) population. Approximately 200 cases are considered each year. In only about ten per cent of cases are prisoners directed for release (a declining proportion since its inception in 1992 – 20 and 27 per cent of cases considered resulted in a decision to release in 1992 and 1994 respectively). A further 20 per cent of prisoners may be recommended for transfer to open conditions. There are currently around 900 prisoners serving discretionary life sentences – over a third have been convicted of manslaughter or other serious violence, a third have committed sexual offences (often of an extremely violent nature), and others have been convicted of arson or other serious offences.

How were decisions made? How was 'the knowledge that is treated as the raw material for decision' socially organised (see Hawkins 1983). What forms of negotiation and interaction occurred? What techniques of simplification, presumption, characterisation and patterning took place? Were decision-makers sceptical about some participants' accounts and not about others? How was credibility judged? We concluded that panels spent considerable time considering 'extra curricular' items, for example, whether or not a prisoner should undertake a specified course. In general, the type of decision being made was about *outcomes*, rather than about the nature and level of risk, per se (in so far as these are separable). Hearings were divided into four key stages: the pre-hearing discussion; the hearing; the deliberation; and the drafting of the reasons for the decision. We outline in more detail what happens at each stage in our full report (Padfield and Liebling 2000). The average length of time

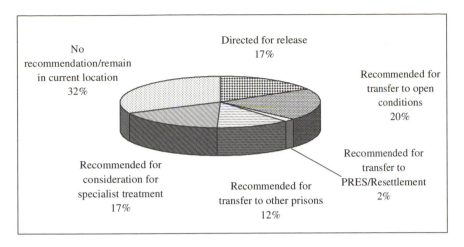

Figure 1 *Outcomes of DLP hearings 1992–1999*

of a panel hearing was one hour and 20 minutes. The assessment of risk really began prior to the hearing as each panel member received and read the dossier. Whilst the Parole Board's decision-making process was of a generally high and consistent quality, it was nonetheless cautious. Panels were hampered by a lack of structural clarity about the framework within which their decisions were being taken, and by a risk-averse culture. Panels were severely constrained by decisions taken elsewhere, particularly by the Prison Service. This chapter seeks to explore the nature of these decisions, as well as those of the DLP, that have to be taken before a discretionary life sentence prisoner is released from, or recalled into, prison. It questions the relationship between the decisions taken by the key 'players' within the system and the culture of caution in which all players operate. Considerable decision-making power lies outside the formal DLP hearing and we consider some of the broader constraints within which the Parole Board operates.

The research

The formal aims of the research were to explore and consider how DLPs operate; whether the process is fair; the effectiveness and consistency of the process; the effectiveness of panel members in performing their role; how panels assess risk (including an assessment of what information has most impact); the level of user-friendliness of panels; and the extent to which they represent value for money. The research was carried out between March and December 1999; 52 cases (DLP's) were observed (49 including the deliberations, which were normally held in private[3]). The dossiers for 69 cases were received: 13 of these cases were deferred before the date of the hearing, and three were not observed because prisoners objected to a research presence. One case was adjourned but was later observed in full. The hearings were held at a total of 22 different prisons. An observation checklist or analytic guide was devised during the pilot stage to aid systematic note-taking on relevant issues. 40 formal tape-recorded interviews were carried out with participants in the process and these interviews were transcribed in full. Less formal discussions, during which notes were taken, were held with others. The observation and interview data were systematically coded and analysed using a qualitative computer-aided data management programme.

Decisions to be taken before a lifer is released

We look next at the decisions made before a prisoner can expect to be released. We begin with the 'key' decision: the decision by the Parole Board. We then return to the beginning of the DLP process, starting with the sentencing judge, and try to illustrate how complex and subject to discretion the release process can be. Our primary task is to identify *where discretion lies*.

Decisions taken by the Parole Board

DLPs were introduced in 1992 following a decision of the European Court of Human Rights establishing the right of those subject to discretionary life sentences to regular and independent review once the tariff (punishment) part of their sentence had ended. Continuing detention, once the 'relevant' (tariff) part of the sentence has been served, can only be justified on the grounds that an individual's release poses an unacceptable risk to the public. This decision-making task was given to the Parole Board in section 34 of the Criminal Justice Act 1991.

The formal role of the Parole Board in this process is now prescribed by sections 28 and 32 of the Crime (Sentences) Act 1997. Section 28 (5) provides that:

As soon as, in the case of a life sentence prisoner to whom this section applies –

(a) he has served the part of his sentence specified in the order or direction ('the relevant part'); and
(b) the Parole Board has directed his release under this section, it shall be the duty of the Secretary of State to release him on license;

and section 28(6) that:

The Parole Board shall not give a direction under subsection (5) above with respect to a life prisoner to whom this section applies unless –

(a) the Secretary of State has referred the prisoner's case to the Board; and
(b) the Board is satisfied that it is no longer necessary for the protection of the public that the prisoner should be confined.

Thus, the Parole Board may not direct the release of a discretionary lifer 'unless it is satisfied that it is no longer necessary for the protection of the public that the prisoner should be confined'. How does it so satisfy itself? The Parole Board sits in panels of three members in the prison where the prisoner is held and, having considered a parole dossier compiled by the Prison Service, may hear oral evidence before making its decision. Between 1992 and June 1999 there were 1,271 DLP hearings, which resulted in the release of 216 prisoners (17 per cent of cases). As mentioned above, the proportion of prisoners released has been declining: from 20 per cent in 1993 to 9 per cent in 1998–9.

The Parole Board's key decision is whether to direct the prisoner's release (or whether to recommend a transfer to open conditions). This decision depends on a prior decision taken often rather implicitly about risk, which turns, of course, on the Panel's decisions about the 'true facts' of the case. The Parole Board does not use any actuarial predictors of risk for this population, but makes a clinical decision based on the dossier, and the evidence presented at the oral hearing. The Parole Board formally reaches its decision during what is normally a swift deliberation. During our observations, deliberations lasted from a matter of seconds to 20 minutes (with the average length of deliberations being just under six minutes). However, this emphasis on the formal deliberation stage is misleading: the 'moment' of decision-making may begin long before the panel hearing and continue through the deliberations and the drafting of the decision letter, which is sent to the prisoner within seven days of the hearing.

Panel members arrived at each hearing having pored over, and taken considerable notes from, detailed dossiers. They each identified 'areas of concern' which informed the questions asked at the oral hearing. What the Parole Board were looking for, in the dossiers and at the hearing, was evidence of *change*. Some insight into the offence, evidence of offending behaviour work successfully undertaken and realistic release plans were the primary factors considered throughout the hearing. A realistic release plan would usually entail some stable living arrangement and employment plans. After these primary factors, the quality of supervision was significant. Relationships with family were not always significant, as many of the prisoners whose cases we observed had lost contact with families, or their offence had involved a family member. Occasionally, 'unsuitable', 'turbulent' or newly formed relationships were scrutinised in order to assess risk and the potential contribution to risk made by relationship patterns. Some contact with a family member was usually seen as a positive indication.

Behaviour in prison was seen as significant in fairly specific ways: a co-operative attitude was taken to be an indication of maturity, as was a willingness to take responsibility for the offence (accept the punishment) and take positive steps to live a more law-abiding life. Engagement in education (particularly leading to qualifications) and in work was often regarded as a good indicator of risk reduction, but successful completion of offending behaviour courses was seen as more important (and was more commonly raised during panel hearings).

Attitude and behaviour were crucial factors in the assessment of risk. If prisoners' attitudes were regarded as anti-social or their behaviour uncontrolled, they were often judged to pose an unacceptable risk. Involvement in serious disciplinary offences or drug use were regarded as poor indicators. Evidence of behaviour reflecting the index offence (usually indicating violence) was carefully considered, often with some speculation. Where the index offence was extremely violent or, for example, sexual violence, or what some judges referred to as 'nasty killings' as opposed to outburst killings, considerable time was spent during the hearings on these features of a prisoner's behaviour. This would often include detailed interrogation about insight, fantasies, impulses and strategies for control.

'Other factors' considered by panels included judgments about 'stability' and habitual behaviour, some of which were open to subjective interpretation. The following example is taken from the DLP hearing of a recalled lifer:

[pre-hearing discussion]

Psychiatrist: Mrs X is not very stable, is she? And his attitude to work is not very good.

Judge: The kids are probably a bit out of control too, reading between the lines. This is my provisional view, and it's unfair to judge before the hearing.

Psychiatrist: His failure to turn up to probation appointments is compatible with the behaviour of a drinker; she seems a bit of a victim, she quickly backed down about the violence.

Judge: She is described as self-reliant and independent, but she has a drink problem – what does that mask?

[They discuss the case, and the various reports – they have all read the papers very well. Later, during the hearing, when the home probation officer is called as a witness:]

Legal representative: He has co-operated with probation in the past; he has been less co-operative with you?

Home probation officer: I supervised him in 1997, and now I have taken him on again. This time he was more unsettled. He was in limbo. He was doing casual work, so he didn't keep to his appointments as agreed. When he did come, it was unannounced. I could see he had been drinking, and I couldn't do any relevant work with him. He came in the evenings; we just couldn't look at the issues I was concerned about.

Legal representative: Would you say he has the capacity to co-operate?

Home probation officer: Yes.

Legal representative: You have heard that he would like more involvement? He has asked for better supervisory arrangements?

Home probation officer: According to 'national standards' he should be seen weekly and then fortnightly. It is important that it is at an agreed appointment time. Home visits are unlikely in the current resource and workload climate.

In this case there were clear indications that the prisoner had developed a very good relationship with his previous probation officer, who had visited him in his home, and worked with his family and with him on many aspects of his behaviour. He had moved area, and was now faced with a probation officer with whom he did not get on and who he did not see as helpful. The panel were not convinced that he could be released safely. His compliance with the requirements of supervision shortly before his recall had been variable. With a different relationship with his probation officer, he may have been a much better prospect (the same medium level of risk, but an effectively managed level). There were serious concerns about his drinking, which both he and his wife failed to appreciate. He drank four cans of Guinness regularly, and there was evidence that he fought with his wife (sometimes leading to minor violence) under the influence of alcohol. The panel and the prisoner were unable to reconcile their very different perceptions of what constituted an acceptable amount of alcohol (and of what sort) to drink, as well as what was an acceptable level and manifestation of conflict within a relationship. This failure to agree was interpreted by the panel as 'a poor attitude to alcohol, which incorporates minimisation and resistance to advice from others'. Financial difficulties, step-children and working for cash were seen as 'adding to the risk'. Cultural and class differences made this dialogue impossible to resolve. How far the ordinary problems of living could or should be included in risk assessments was a question which taxed us as observers.

We have considered the roles played by each panel member, the type of negotiations over 'the evidence' and the style of questioning at hearings in our full report (Padfield and Liebling 2000). Before a prisoner reaches the hearing, there are clearly other important decisions being taken. We were surprised, given the relatively heavyweight process we were invited to observe, and its generally high standard, that the real 'decision-making power' lay elsewhere. We return to the beginning of the discretionary lifer process here, setting out and exploring, where we can, these stages in what is a complex and power-laden decision-making process.

Decisions taken by the sentencing judge

When imposing a discretionary life sentence, the judge states in open court 'a tariff': the period that the prisoner should serve for 'punishment and deterrence', taking into account the seriousness of the offence.[4] This decision will have been influenced by what the probation officer may have written in a Pre-Sentence Report, or by psychiatrists' reports (many of which remain on the parole file decades later). A life sentence is a possible (that is, discretionary) sentence for a number of offences such as: attempted murder; manslaughter; rape; robbery; arson; criminal damage with intent to endanger life; aggravated burglary; kidnapping; incest; sexual intercourse with a girl under the age of 13; infanticide; possessing a Class A drug for supply; unlawful abortion; and forgery of births, deaths or marriage certificates. A judge may choose to impose a life sentence in such cases only where:

- the offence is in itself grave enough to require a very long sentence

- the offender is a person of mental instability who, if at liberty, will probably re-offend and present a grave danger to the public

- it appears that the offender will remain unstable and a potential danger for a long or uncertain time.[5]

Lord Lane CJ explained the position in *Wilkinson* (1983) 5 Cr App R (S) 105:[6]

> It seems to us that a sentence of life imprisonment, other than for an offence when the sentence is obligatory, is really appropriate and must only be passed in the most exceptional circumstances. With a few exceptions … it is reserved, broadly speaking, for offenders who for one reason or another cannot be dealt with under the Mental Health Act, yet who are in a mental state which makes them dangerous to the life or limb of members of the public. It is sometimes impossible to say when that danger will subside, and therefore an indeterminate sentence is required, so that the prisoner's progress may be monitored by those who have him under their supervision.

Since the enactment of section 34 of the Criminal Justice Act 1991, passed as a result of the decision of the European Court of Human Rights in *Thynne, Wilson and Gunnell* (1990) 13 EHRR 666, a discretionary life sentence is divided into two parts: first, the 'tariff' period, a period which should be between a half and two thirds of what would have been the appropriate sentence for a determinate case, given the early provisions applicable in determinate cases. The remaining part of the sentence is governed by considerations of risk.

It was beyond the scope of our research to consider whether judges do impose as tariff periods the equivalent period to that imposed in determinate cases. The tariffs of the prisoners in our sample ranged from two to 17 years. The length of time that prisoners spent post-tariff was significant: the majority of our sample had already served an average of five years since tariff expiry. Judges (like the general public) appeared to misunderstand the nature of the sentence and believed that the offender would be released soon after tariff.[7]

A life sentence can even be perceived as a 'lenient' sentence, where the judge imposes a short tariff. Thus, in the case of an arsonist sentenced to a life sentence with a two-year tariff, the judge said on sentencing that he hoped it would soon be possible to release him. At the time of our research, this lifer had already served nearly four years, and was probably many years from release, since the Panel did not recommend release, nor a move to open conditions, nor an early review. Other sentencing judges had expressly stated at trial that since an offender's 'dangerousness' was difficult to assess, he, the judge, was therefore handing over the task of predicting and assessing risk to a panel of experts, the Parole Board.

Decisions taken by the Prison Service

(a) Categorisation and allocation   As soon as a lifer is received into prison, their progress is 'managed' by the Lifer Management Unit [LMU] of the Sentence Management Group in the Directorate of Regimes (although Category A lifers remain the responsibility of the Category A Section within the High Security Directorate). From a local prison, all life sentence prisoners are allocated to one of five main lifer centres, although 'governors pointed out that the system for moving lifers in and out of the main centres was in danger of grinding to a halt'.[8] There are two poorly integrated parallel systems for the sentence planning of lifers: the Life Sentence Plan, kept under review in the prison where the prisoner is held, and the LMU dossier and F75s.[9] A Joint Thematic Review of Lifers carried out by HM Chief Inspectors of Prison and Probation was highly critical of the initial risk assessment within the Life Sentence Plan, suggesting that the overlap of LSPs and F75s detracts from their quality and effectiveness.[10]

One early decision is the security categorisation of the newly sentenced prisoner. In our study, nearly half of the lifers were still in either dispersal (high security) or Category B conditions, although some were many years post-tariff (see Figure 2 below). The prisoner's security classification seemed to be the key to release: no prisoner in our study was released unless they were already in a Category D prison (in open conditions). On only one occasion did we witness a full panel hearing at an open prison at which the panel made the decision not to release the prisoner. A lifer is thus normally expected to move systematically through the categorisation system before being seriously considered for release. It seemed ironic that great emphasis has been given to creating due process rights for prisoners before a DLP, yet their 'rights' in the categorisation process are minimal. Interestingly, panels did not always understand the categorisation process, and it remains remarkably obscure for such a key process.[11]

It is well known that prisons differ (Liebling 2000; Sparks et al. 1996). The Joint Thematic Review of Life Sentence Prisoners noted that there

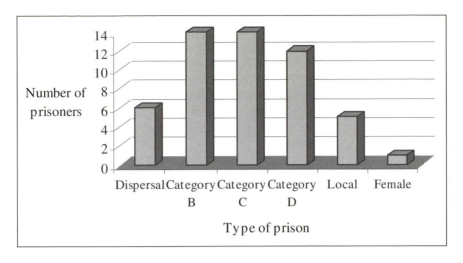

Figure 2 *Prisoners location at observed DLP hearing*

were considerable delays in achieving a transfer to a second stage prison, and that there was considerable variation in accommodation and regimes for lifers mid-sentence.[12] A prisoner's parole chances are likely to be affected by his experience of prison. Thus, where a prisoner moves, whether within the Category A, B, C or D estate, may have an important impact on his chances of release. Some prisoners seemed to get 'stuck in the system', or were held back by a breakdown in their relationship with a particular establishment. We witnessed several such 'negative spirals' in which progress had ceased.

(b) Provision of suitable courses　The Parole Board attributed huge significance to offending behaviour courses completed by prisoners. It is important therefore that prisoners should have the opportunity to participate in such courses; however, few such courses are widely available. The Joint Thematic Review found that 27 per cent of lifer prisons ran the Sex Offender Treatment Programme (SOTP), 31 per cent offered the Enhanced Thinking Skills course and 53 per cent offered either the Enhanced Thinking Skills or the Reasoning and Rehabilitation programme. Other courses had become the casualties of the diversion of resources into only accredited offending behaviour programmes. Paul Boateng reported, in a Parliamentary Answer in the House of Commons on 19 December 2000, that in 1999–2000, 669 prisoners had completed the SOTP, out of a total population of 4,946 sentenced sex offenders. The minister stated that it is not possible to calculate what percentage of all convicted sex offenders have completed the SOTP.

Year	Number of prisoners completing SOTP	Sentenced sex offenders in custody (as at 30 June)
1996–7	680 (17.2 % of then sentenced population of sex offenders)	3,951
1997–8	736 (18%)	4,077
1998–9	664 (13.8%)	4,795
1999–2000	669 (13.5%)	4,946

Figure 3   *Number of prisoners completing SOTP 1996–2000.*

Prisoners were slowed in their progress through the system by the shortage of courses available, sometimes choosing to defer their biannual DLP in order to wait until they had managed to get onto (and complete) a particular course. We concluded that post-tariff lifers have a 'right' to be released as soon as they are 'safe', which means that they should have at least equal access to opportunities for recategorisation, taking part in offending behaviour courses, and opportunities to work in the community. In other words, they should have maximum opportunity to demonstrate that they no longer pose an unacceptable risk to the public.

(c) Preparations for the Parole Board, including the construction of the dossier   Parole Board dossiers are composed of a large number of documents. A dossier would normally include: the formal referral document from the Home Secretary to the Parole Board; a proforma case summary; offence-related papers; the Life Sentence Plan; a summary of previous DLP reports; current reports from prison and probation staff (perhaps the lifer liaison officer, the personal (case) officer, prison probation officer, medical officer, psychologist, psychiatrist); the prisoner's representations and, perhaps, the Secretary of State's representations. There are surprising omissions: dossiers do not contain details of adjudications, for example. Reports written by individuals with limited contact with or knowledge of the prisoner were considered 'a waste of everyone's time' by prisoners but were often treated with more weight by the panel. Some individual report writers were not aware of how much weight was given to their report and their recommendations, nor of how important it was that reports directly addressed the question of risk, and provided evidence. Some panel

members thought it was difficult to distinguish between 'old' and 'new' or 'irrelevant' and 'relevant' information, and felt that dossiers should be compiled with these distinctions in mind. Inevitably the management and delivery of external reports was often harder to achieve than the management of internal reports. Prisoners observed that reasons for (especially positive) recommendations were important, in order to make the reports useful to the panel.

Coker and Martin (1985: 47) identified five overlapping concerns about the use of official documentation when making risk decisions in their study of parole decision-making:

1. Reports tend to be subjective and judgmental rather than objective, and reflect staff perception of the interaction between themselves and the prisoner.

2. There are dangers that opinions are formed early in a prisoner's career and then subsequent information is used to support that view.

3. There are dangers that out-of-date material is reused, and that negative labels may stick.

4. The material may be organised to suit standardised forms rather than an individual's case.

5. The prisoner does not see these reports and cannot correct inaccuracies.

The last of these objections has been largely addressed by open reporting, but the first four remain a concern. Unlike most official records used in research, DLP dossiers were compiled and used for a single purpose: they were intended to assist in the process of risk assessment. But like many official records, they could be contradictory, unreliable, selective and biased.[13] Files tended to present a grimmer picture of a prisoner than other sources based on contact, and they could not tell 'the whole story'. Valuable contextual information might be missing. Sometimes information contained in reports was attributed a significance it might not possess.[14] There are clear parallels with the way police files are constructed in the prosecution process:

> ... constructing the case is not simply an exercise in collecting together and marshalling all relevant material. Rather, the selection, creation and presentation of the evidence is geared towards the objective which the police seek to achieve, and

effectively dominates later review procedures ... Construction by omission is equally significant ... Case construction may also be a means of co-opting non-police reviewers into police ideology and values or may convey a more general message about local policing imperatives ...

The rhetoric of prosecution decision-making emphasises objectivity, impartiality and individualisation ... The reality is a system of routinised decision-making embodying an overwhelming propensity to prosecute, bolstered by a presumption that earlier decisions were properly made and should not be overturned. The system is dominated throughout its stages by the interests and values of the police, with the CPS playing an essentially subordinate and reactive role (126).

(McConville, Saunders and Leng 1991)

By substituting the 'Prison Service' for the 'police', and the 'Parole Board' for the 'CPS' in the final sentence, the authors' account is a fitting description of the roles of the players in the discretionary lifer release process. Research into the construction of parole dossiers would be valuable, as would greater feedback from the Parole Board to the Prison Service on the adequacy or usefulness of dossiers.[15]

Other practical problems with dossiers were the time lag between the preparation of dossiers and the oral hearing, and the lateness of reports. Panel members received dossiers about two or three weeks before a hearing, but they were invariably supplemented with (often crucial) late reports at, or shortly before, the hearing. This resulted in time spent reading before the hearing could begin, and sometimes major changes in direction and strategy when new information came to light. The other problem with timeliness was the inclusion in the dossier of out-of-date reports: the balance between achieving fully up-to-date material and providing information ahead of the hearing was a difficult one. In our study, six (9 per cent) of the scheduled panel hearings were deferred due to the lateness of reports. The Secretary of State's view, which was dependent on complete reports, often arrived at or on the morning of the hearing. This made the panel's task (and the roles of Lifer Governor and legal representative) particularly difficult.

The responsibility for the production of timely reports was unclear, as the 'blame' was placed on establishments, on the Lifer Review Unit, and on panel secretaries, whose job was to ensure timely delivery. Late reports were mostly psychiatric or psychological reports, including post-treatment psychological assessments. The late arrival of reports made it very difficult for the prisoner or his representative to prepare their case. Late reports sometimes led to deferral of cases (for about six months), either before, or sometimes at the hearing, wasting public money and risking considerable unfairness to the prisoner. Chasing these reports was an administrative burden. We were informed that in 60 per cent of DLP cases in 1998, disclosure of full dossiers was achieved before the hearing. We were also encouraged to learn that an auditable standard on the timeliness of submitting reports has recently been introduced.

(d) Vetoing recommendations   In many cases where the Parole Board did not direct the release of prisoners, they did make some recommendation, built on the recommendations which emerged in the reports or at the hearing. These recommendations have no legal force. The most important recommendation was a transfer to open conditions. Of the 12 prisoners in our study who the panel recommended for a transfer to open conditions, only two had moved at the time the research report was written; in a further five cases the Secretary of State had agreed to the prisoner's transfer. Fewer than half of the other recommendations (such as a transfer to another prison within the same security categorisation) had been acted upon. Unless the Home Secretary rejects a DLP recommendation within a given time, such recommendations should in our view create a 'legitimate expectation', which should allow the prisoner to seek judicial review.[16]

Decisions taken by the prisoner

The prisoner is obviously partly responsible for his or her own release: those who co-operate and comply with the system are likely to progress more swiftly through the 'system' than those who do not. Those who show remorse or 'victim empathy' are more likely to be released. Of particular concern are those who continue to deny their offence.[17] More articulate prisoners were sometimes at an advantage compared to less articulate (or non-English speaking) colleagues, in terms of their 'performance' at the oral hearing.

Decisions taken by the prisoner's legal representatives

The life sentence prisoners in our study had served from between three to 29 and a half years in prison by the time we came to observe their DLP hearing. The majority were unsuccessful in gaining release. The lawyers who represented them at their DLPs were unlikely to be those who had represented them at their original trial. There are a number of firms of solicitors who appear to be recognised 'specialists' in this field. Solicitors themselves have to make key decisions: whether, for example, to attempt to persuade their client to be less ambitious and more realistic in what they seek to achieve from the panel. Eight of our sample were represented by Counsel; we did not explore whether this was always at the suggestion of the solicitor. It was not obvious to us that Counsel necessarily improved the chances of success from a prisoner's point of view. The most influential legal representatives appeared to be those who contributed least to the proceedings, those who simply helped their prisoner do the talking. The role, quality and influence of legal representatives were significant variables in decision-making.

Decisions taken by the Probation Service

All those prisoners who were successful in convincing the DLP to direct release had the support of their home probation officer. In other words, if a prisoner did not have the support of their home probation officer, they could be almost certain that they would not be released. The importance of a good release plan and a convincing and effective home probation officer were undeniable.

The vast majority of lifers achieve stability in their lives after release.[18] The influence of the Probation Service is especially important when things go wrong in the community: prisoners may be recalled to prison where it appears to the Home Secretary that 'it is expedient in the public interest' to recall the prisoner before it is practicable to get a recommendation from the Parole Board to do so (section 32 of the Crime (Sentences) Act 1997). In all five recall cases in our sample, the prisoner had been taken into custody without prior warning at the request of the Probation Service, and the first full DLP to consider this recall took place several months thereafter (between five and 12 months). During this period, the local prison to which the prisoner had been recalled did little by way of assessment or working with the prisoner, and in all cases, the recall decision was confirmed. The panel accepted the Probation Service's version of the facts even when heavily contested by the prisoner. Given that an earlier DLP had directed the release of the prisoner it is surprising that there is not a clear obligation on the Probation Service to 'prove' dangerousness. All the recalls were confirmed because at the recall hearing no adequate release plan had been prepared.

We were surprised by the extent to which prisoners seemed to be held back by the ordinary, practical problems they might encounter on release. This was particularly clear in the recall cases. Issues such as financial problems, relationship tensions and small-scale alcohol abuse encouraged panels to confirm recalls, when these 'ordinary' and fairly common problems of living might have been exaggerated in the minds of the panel as a result of class and cultural differences. For example, does four cans of Guinness drunk regularly pose a drink 'problem'? This tension was also apparent at 'ordinary' DLPs: risk assessment was not a science, but also involved a 'gut feeling' or 'common sense'. For this reason, it seemed essential that the panel should consist of at least three members.

We concluded that it was appropriate that a panel should be chaired by a judge: the 'court-like' nature of the panel needs to be emphasised. It was also appropriate in most cases, given the type of offenders whose release was being considered, that the second member of the panel was a psychiatrist. It is interesting to note that in 1992 it had been envisaged that where there was conclusive medical evidence that no serious concern existed about a prisoner's state of mind at the time of the offence or subsequently during imprisonment, a psychologist or probation officer could be appointed as the second panel member, but in reality this has never been the practice. The third member is an 'independent member',[19] who may be a criminologist, probation officer or a genuinely 'lay' member (who come from a variety of backgrounds). When the Parole Board was established in 1967, to consider determinate sentence cases, it convened in panels usually consisting of six members, to include a judge, psychiatrist, probation officer, criminologist and independent member. Panels were later reduced to four members and now sit in panels of three, with a majority of panellists in determinate cases being independent members.[20] The Carlisle Committee was concerned to preserve the inter-disciplinary nature of panels and feared that this would be impaired if they were reduced from four to three members.[21]

There was a lack of structural clarity about the framework in which decisions were taken: concerning, for example, the extent to which the Parole Board acts as a 'court';[22] the Parole Board's relationship with the Prison Service and Home Office; the onus of proof (who has the burden of proving what is put before the panel); and whether the process should be inquisitorial or adversarial. These uncertainties should be explored further in order that the process can develop more fairly and effectively, especially in relation to the DLP's responsibility to recognise the human rights of the prisoners whose cases are being reviewed.

Reflecting on the decision-making process

We were struck by the cautiousness of the decision-making and in this section we discuss some of the factors which lead to this caution. It is worth stressing that the decision taken by the Parole Board here is very different from that taken in determinate cases: whilst the protection of the public is a key factor in both cases, in determinate cases the prisoner is having time 'deducted' from their sentence; in DLP cases, the prisoner is having time 'added'. In a determinate case, the court fixes the length of time that a prisoner should serve for 'punishment', and it is the Parole Board's role to decide when, and if, the prisoner should be released before that date. In the case of lifers, all prisoners will serve the complete 'punitive' period before their lawful release is even a possibility. For this reason, our research conclusions sought to underline the significance of the prisoner being post-tariff and to give proper recognition to the prisoner's rights. The Parole Board's responsibility to 'protect the public' too easily swamps the rights of the individual prisoner, whereas it is part of their 'core function' to test whether the prison and probation services are respecting the rights of the prisoner.[23]

In this second part of the chapter we reflect on certain themes emerging from our research, which may help to explain why the emphasis of the Parole Board seems to lean much more towards the 'rights' of the public to be protected than towards the 'rights' of the prisoner to be released. We consider the difficulty and ethics of predicting dangerousness, as well as the risk-averse culture in which the Parole Board is working. We conclude with some thoughts on the need for greater openness and accountability within this blame culture.

The difficulty of predicting dangerousness

Can degrees of risk of re-offending be measured and predicted? For the purposes of discretionary conditional release, a risk of re-offending predictor has been devised. The main tools used for parole decisions were devised by Copas, Marshall and Tarling (1996), and are constantly reassessed. Yet by the time of Hood and Shute's research no actuarial predictor was being used.[24] The problem of predicting dangerousness for discretionary lifers is, of course, very much more difficult. Walker (1996) identified four particular problems:

1. The less frequent the outcome which has to be predicted, the less accurately will samples predict (to which it is worth adding that re-

conviction rates are a very blunt instrument for measuring re-offending).

2. It is impossible to establish scientific conditions (i.e. releasing violent offenders after short periods of incarceration) for discriminating between those who repeat their offences and those who do not.

3. Most follow-up studies are far too short.

4. Violent offenders being followed-up may commit minor offences which result in custody and have to be discarded from the sample.

Many lifers have committed a very serious one-off offence. Genders and Morrison (1996) carried out a study of violent crime in the West Midlands between 1989 and 1991 and highlight the social-situational correlates of violent crime: both circumstances and the victim play a part. As Bowden (1996) says, 'We are not explaining outcomes which are highly probable; what we are looking for is something which will explain why unexpected behaviour is not as improbable as it seemed'. Can the risk of serious re-offending by the kinds of offenders within the discretionary lifer population be effectively predicted?

It needs to be stressed that assessing risks which may appear in the community whilst a prisoner is in prison adds to the difficulties of prediction, and may add to the risk of over-prediction. Prison may be part of the problem – as one prisoner put it:

I don't feel that I am as mature at thirty-[something] as a thirty-[something] year old is outside, and that's true of many people in prison; it kinds of stunts your maturity.

To this may be added problems to do with the physical environment, the isolation from the community, the widespread availability of illegal drugs and the impossibility of walking away from difficult situations. There is inherent difficulty in predicting and assessing a person's future behaviour at liberty whilst they are in captivity.

Some of the beliefs on which the decision-making process was based were unfounded. Some validated risk factors (such as age, experience of local authority care, number of convictions at an early age) were not discussed during the decision-making process; others (such as the experience of violence and abuse, absence of a positive role model, disrupted educational history, susceptibility to peer pressure, low self-esteem) were considered haphazardly. Whether what panels did during a hearing could accurately be called 'risk assessment' without more standardised and validated techniques at their disposal, was a question which troubled us throughout the research process. Without standardised risk assessment tools, there was a danger that assumptions could be mistaken for assessments. Panels should more clearly distinguish the risk of re-offending from the level of harm risked. This trend towards risk management, actuarial justice and the 'commercialisation of crime control' (Christie 1993) or the management of offenders and the targeting of resources rather than the moral engagement with the individual assumes a reliable knowledge base, a mechanical solution to crime risk and a complete break with what might once have been called 'social work' approaches to offending (see Kemshall 1998; and Sparks 1997 and Nash 1999 on the 'new risk industry').

Hawkins argues that decision-makers operate with master codes or decision-frames in mind. Possible 'master frames' may be moral, organisational, professional or operational, and these constitute ideological frameworks which emphasise some values (for example, rehabilitation, efficiency, 'covering oneself', etc.) over others (such as fairness). Master frames are 'subtle, shifting and interacting things' and may change over time (Hawkins 1983: 22). Sometimes shifts (for example in perceptions of what is an acceptable risk) become institutionalised, for instance, in a redefinition of what sorts of decisions panels are making and to what end. We found this analysis helpful, and return to it in the section below.

The ethics of predicting dangerousness

The judge, when sentencing, had specified the tariff, the length of sentence which he thought the prisoner should serve 'for punishment and deterrence'. This is therefore arguably the 'just' sentence for the offence, and this is why the European Court of Human Rights imposed on the British government an obligation to improve the due process rights of those being detained post-tariff, purely for the protection of the public. Any period in prison post-tariff is justified simply because of the risk of future serious offending. Motivated, presumably, by the danger of false predictions ('false positives'), Stuart-Smith LJ (in *R v Parole Board, ex p Bradley* [1991] 1 WLR 134) suggested that the Parole Board should recognise that a prisoner is paying a 'progressively higher price' the longer that he serves beyond the tariff period. If anything, our research suggested the opposite: that the longer a prisoner was in prison, the more wary the Board would be of releasing him. Those who remain in prison a long time beyond tariff are seen as those who 'lack insight' or who have failed to take courses. Being a 'failure' in prison may become a self-fulfilling prophecy.

Tonry (1998: 139) identifies four areas of difficulty with predictions: simple injustice; past and future crimes; false positives and the 'convictions of innocents' analogy; and inappropriate predictors. He concludes that:

> Whether the ethical and policy criticism of predictive sentencing summarised here are regarded as devastating depends largely on the premises that shape one's views of punishment. Retributivists tend strongly to disapprove of predictive sentencing; utilitarians tend to accept it. However, almost every analyst of predictive sentencing is uncomfortable with some of its features.
>
> (Tonry 1998)

In our study, panel members stated that they were confident, or reasonably confident, in the decisions they made. Our research did not explore their views on the ethical problems attached to their decisions.

A risk-averse culture

Hawkins (1983: 8) discusses the 'broader constraints within which decision-makers operate: ideological, symbolic, socio-political, economic, organisational and interactional'. All these constraints can be developed in the context of DLP decision-making:

- **Ideological**: the Parole Board may deliberately select 'cautious' members. Panel members interviewed identified themselves as cautious people. They worried about under-sentencing as much as over-sentencing. Being cautious was seen as appropriate, given the ideological 'master-frame' of protecting the public.

- **Symbolic**: the symbolic role of the Parole Board, particularly as representatives of the public deciding on the level of risk which should be accepted, was clear. Panels were conscious, for example, of how they might be 'seen' on the front page of the local newspaper. The symbolic function of the judge as chair was significant, reminding participants of the court-like nature of the panel. Several panellists regretted that the Parole Board was housed within the Prison Service headquarters: they recognised a need for greater symbolic independence to underline what they perceived as their 'real' independence.

- **Socio-political**: the Parole Board cannot exist in a vacuum, and individual members were aware of the increasingly intolerant political agenda around them. The new risk-averse culture and political climate has exerted a marked influence on the way in which the Parole Board operate (Hood and Shute 2000; see also Beck 1992; Giddens 1991, 1999; Sparks 1997).

- **Economic**: issues relating to value for money and resource constraints were clearly of concern, particularly given the likely extension of DLP-like procedures to increasing numbers of prisoners in the future.[25] The DLP process costs £1,286 per case. Whether the process is cost-effective is unclear and depends on the outcomes being sought. Releasing people less cautiously might save money. It is difficult to weigh up the costs of prison (at an average of approximately £25,000 per prisoner per year) against the possible cost of violent crime. It is difficult to place a monetary value on due process for prisoners reaching the end of the tariff stage of their sentence.

- **Organisational**: the inter-play between the different agencies involved in the management of life sentence prisoners could slow down a prisoner's release. Prisoners were not moved from one prison to another pending their DLP; others said they had not started a course because they were waiting for their DLP. One, having started a SOTP, decided to defer his DLP hearing. Another prisoner who thought that the fact he had now started one-to-one counselling was a positive fact which might move him forwards, was informed at his hearing that this was the reason for not moving him forwards.

- **Interactional**: for example, the consideration of wider social and political pressures; the relationship between the Prison Service and the Parole Board.

The Parole Board may be over-cautious. The DLP has to consider a wide variety of cases: the 'true' discretionary lifer may be particularly difficult to assess. The DLP process also applies to those who committed murder when under the age of 18 (these offenders may not have a significant criminal record before the offence which led to their indeterminate sentence); to recalled lifers; and to those who receive an automatic life sentence for a repeat serious crime. These 'automatic' sentences were only introduced in 1997, but it would appear, particularly from the very short tariffs which trial judges are fixing, that the offenders are frequently not perceived, at least by the trial judge, to be particularly dangerous. It is important to remember that all recalled lifers have at one stage been deemed safe to be released by the Parole Board, and may not have committed any subsequent criminal or 'prisonable' offence. Many of these offenders will not be as 'unpredictable' and 'dangerous' as the lifer whom the trial judge chooses to give an indeterminate sentence. Yet these different groups are not clearly distinguished either at the hearings, or in the statistics on recall and re-offending.

Accountability in a blame culture

Kemshall (1996, 1998) argues for 'defensible' rather than 'defensive' decisions. Defensive practice is reliant on the precautionary principle which focuses on 'worst case' scenarios and low tolerance of errors. Many Parole Board members spoke to us of the high recall rate for lifers (31 per cent), and this was always presented as a measure of failure: these people should never have been released. However, from what we witnessed, the majority of recalled lifers were recalled not because they had committed another serious offence, but because the supervising Probation Service was concerned that the offender's lifestyle was moving him unacceptably close to committing a serious offence. The offender was proving a risk to manage. These judgments were perhaps the most subjective, the least amenable to 'evidence', the least visible or protected by due process checks, and the most difficult of all those we encountered.

Recalls to prison were never regarded as a measure of success (in that increasing risk had been detected) rather than failure. Several Parole Board members were concerned about 'setting people up to fail' – that is, about taking a risk. We had some sympathy for this view: it would clearly be unfair to release someone in order to prove that they could not survive 'safely' in the community. However, there was insufficient effort expended on managing risk in the community. As one psychiatrist reminded his reluctant panel, 'This woman's risk will never be lower. If we are to release her at all, we have to do so today'. Post-tariff discretionary lifers should have the 'right' and the opportunity to prove themselves in open conditions, and then in the community, with all the management difficulties this poses.

It was difficult to identify where overall accountability lay when things went wrong in the release process. Players tended to see faults in other parts of the system. Increasing liaison between the Probation Service and the Prison Service may lead to greater consultation and policy development, but will it lead to a less defensive process? Multi-agency management of high-risk offenders may be useful, so that probation, police and other services may increasingly share information about dangerous people. But there are important issues of accountability in this area. The participation of the prisoner in the discretionary lifer release process at the DLP was intended to provide a real procedural safeguard against the unwarranted detention of an already punished prisoner. However, the Parole Board is only one player amongst many who may influence the release of a life sentence prisoner, and there are many more hidden stages of the process. Greater openness and accountability at these other stages in the release process is equally important.

Notes

1 See Padfield, N. and Liebling, A. with Arnold, H. (2000), *An Exploration of decision-making at Discretionary Lifer Panels*, Home Office Research Study No 213; and Padfield, N. and Liebling, A. with Arnold, H. (2000) *Discretionary Lifer Panels – An Exploration of Decision-Making*, Home Office Research Findings No 132. See also Padfield (2002).

2 Section 28(6) of the Crime (Sentences) Act 1997.

3 In three of these cases the deliberations were not observed at the request of the panel Chair.

4 See Practice Direction (Imposition of Discretionary Life Sentence) [1993] 1 WLR 223 and numerous judgments of the Court of Appeal: see note 5 below. Adult murderers, who are sentenced to a mandatory life sentence, do not benefit from the DLP process, but murderers under the age of 18, who are sentenced to be detained during Her Majesty's pleasure, do (and were within our study). As a result of the decision of the European Court of Human Rights in *T and V* (16 December 1999), the law has been amended so that juvenile murderers not only come within the DLP process, but their tariffs are also now fixed by the sentencing judge: see section 60 of the Criminal Justice and Courts Services Act 2000. A third category of lifer, those who receive an 'automatic' life sentence having been convicted of a second serious offence (see section 109 of the Powers of the Criminal Court (Sentencing) Act 2000), also come within the DLP process.

5 *Hodgson* (1967) 52 Cr App R 113.

6 See also *Attorney-General's Reference (No 32 of 1996) (R v Whittaker)* [1997] 1 Cr App R (S) 261; Chapman [2000] 1 Cr App R (S) 199; Simmonds [2001] Crim LR 326.

7 The Lord Chief Justice's Practice Statement issued on 27 July 2000, issued as a response to the decision of the European Court of Human Rights in *Venables and Thompson* (16 December 1999), states that the tariff is 'the amount of time actually to be served by a person convicted of murder in order to meet the requirements of retribution and general deterrence'. It would be useful if such statements were followed by an acknowledgement

that lifers actually spend much longer inside. For example, in *Black* [2000] 1 Cr App R (S) 41, the Court of Appeal had to criticise a trial judge who had imposed a disproportionate sentence on a life sentence prisoner in order to ensure that the prisoner remained in custody beyond the date his 'tariff' expired. It would appear that the trial judge was unaware that the Parole Board is highly unlikely to release a prisoner deemed to be dangerous, and that it was unnecessary as well as inappropriate for him to 'bend' the sentencing law in this way.

8 *Lifers: A Joint Thematic Review by Her Majesty's Inspectorates of Prison and Probation* (Home Office, 1999), para 6.5.

9 F75 reports are named after the number on the form which is required to be completed by prison staff for LMU for the Parole Board dossier.

10 See note 8 above, para 6.61.

11 The role and operation of categorisation has been studied in detail recently by Price, D. (2000) *Security Categorisation in the English prison system* (unpublished Ph. D. thesis). The Court of Appeal has recently recognised that the recategorisation of prisoners significantly affects their prospects of release, and granted a declaration that they should be given a reasonable opportunity to make representations on retrogressive recategorisation: see *R v Secretary of State for the Home Department, ex parte Hirst* [2001] EWCA Civ 378.

12 See para 8.19.

13 Kitsuse and Cicourel (1963); Liebling (1992: 91–3).

14 Hawkins (1983) uses the example of B's sex play with a six-year old when he was a boy, which might be regarded in another setting as 'normal' behaviour, but in a prison record, especially the record of a rapist, it can be made to appear ominous. More striking, perhaps, is the fact that it was considered significant to record that B's *mother* had a traumatic incident at the age of *seven* when she was in a car accident and saw her mother decapitated. This displays not only the salience of history and the almost infinite capacity of pieces of supposedly 'relevant' data to survive in files, but also the kind of theorising which deems such material to be relevant. The decision-maker may be led into speculating that the traumatic incident may have affected the way in which B's mother later brought him up, which in turn had some (unspecified) link with his subsequent sexual misconduct. Or he may be able to deduce a different meaning from the information. At the very least it is likely that the board member will be led to believe that its very presence in the file *must mean something* (Hawkins 1983: 123). In one of our dossiers, the prisoner had early in his prison career told a psychiatrist about his fantasies about killing people in a wood at the moment of ejaculation. Although he has long admitted that 'I was taking the piss, I made it up', the fantasy finds itself repeated in the dossier and in the prisoner's words, 'I think it's probably the stupidest lie I've ever told in my life. It comes back and haunts me'.

15 Our original tender included a component which would have explored the quality of parole dossiers. It was clear that the research sponsors felt that the quality of the dossiers was very good and not in need of critical analysis.

More could be learned about the relationship between the Parole Board and the Prison Service by a detailed study of the composition and role of parole dossiers, and whether reports provide sufficient information of the right type to enable a risk assessment to be made.

16 Recent cases on 'legitimate expectation' include *R v Secretary of State for the Home Department, ex p Simms* [1999] 3 WLR 328; *R v Secretary of State for Education and Employment, ex p Begbie* [2000] 1 WLR 1115; *R v North and East Devon Health Authority, ex p Coughlan* [2000] 2 WLR 622.

17 The link between denial and risk has recently been addressed by the Court of Appeal in *R v Parole Board, ex p Oyston* (17 April, 2000), where the Parole Board's decision was held to be flawed.

18 It is interesting to note from the Joint Thematic Review (para 11.50) that probation services believe that applications to cancel supervision arrangements (for those who are felt no longer to present a significant risk) produce an over-cautious response from LRU.

19 All members of the Parole Board are, of course, meant to be 'independent'. However, we adopt this as the term used in the Parole Board to describe the non-judge, non-psychiatrist, third member of the panel.

20 See Hood and Shute (2000: 21–2) for a fuller discussion of the historical background to panel membership.

21 Carlisle (1988), para 367.

22 We were struck by the paradox that, whilst DLPs were created specifically in response to the ECHR's recognition of the special status of 'post-tariff' lifers, this special status plays almost no part in the thinking of panels as they discharge their central tasks.

23 It is interesting to note parallels with the proposals in the Halliday Report (Making Punishments Work: a report of a review of the sentencing framework for England and Wales, July 2001) for the courts to develop a 'sentence review' capacity: a court would decide whether to endorse proposals developed jointly by Prison and Probation Service, or whether to commission advice on further options.

24 Hood and Shute (2000) explored the system of parole for determinate sentence prisoners serving four years and over, introduced in 1991 (Discretionary Conditional Release). Here 'risk to the public' is the primary consideration. The proportion of prisoners granted parole under the new scheme fell from 70 per cent to 48 per cent, with far more of those prisoners granted release having conditions attached to their licence. Half of the prisoners in the sample (437 cases) studied had a low actuarial risk of reconviction for a serious offence during the parole period (using the Risk of Reconviction Score developed by Copas et al. 1996), yet only half of this number were granted parole. Parole Board members often estimated the risk to be much higher than that predicted by actuarial methods and their decision-making is described by the authors as 'risk-averse'. Hood and Shute conclude that the parole rate could be substantially increased without increasing the proportion of prisoners who would be reconvicted of a serious offence on parole and that panel members made 'unduly pessimistic

"clinical" estimations of risk when compared with actuarial risk calculation". In fact, by releasing more low risk prisoners, the average rate of reconviction on parole would decline. Reasons for denying parole included: lack of progress, previous failure to respond to supervision, the seriousness of the offence and unsatisfactory release plans. More than 89 per cent of those prisoners refused parole said that the reasons they had been given were 'unfair'. Three quarters said that the reasons given had not made them change their behaviour and many said they had responded negatively to the 'knockback'. Conversely, prisoners who had undertaken a Sex Offender Treatment Programme were more likely to be granted parole, whatever their level of risk.

25 It is worth noting that it was part of our terms of reference to explore cost-effectiveness.

References

Beck, U. (1992) *Risk Society: towards a new modernity*. London: Sage.

Bowden, P. (1996) 'Violence and Mental Disorder' in N. Walker (ed.) *Dangerous People*. London: Blackstone Press.

Carlisle, Lord (1988) *The parole system in England and Wales: report of the Review Committee*. London: HMSO.

Chapman, T. and Hough, M. (1999) *Evidence Based Practice: a guide to effective practice*. London: HMSO.

Christie, N. (1993) *Crime Control as Industry: towards gulags, Western style*. London: Routledge.

Coker, J. B. and Martin, J. P. (1985) *Licensed to Live*. Oxford: Basil Blackwell.

Copas, J.B., Marshall, P. and Tarling, R. (1996) *Predicting Reoffending for Discretionary Conditional Release*. Home Office Research Study No. 150. London: Home Office.

Genders, E. and Morrison, S. (1996) 'When violence is the norm' in N. Walker (ed.) *Dangerous People*, London: Blackstone Press.

Giddens, A. (1991) *Modernity and self-identity: self and society in the late modern age*. Oxford: Polity Press.

Giddens, A. (1999) *Runaway World*. London: Profile Books.

Hawkins, K. (1983) 'Thinking About Legal Decision-Making' in J. Shapland, (ed.) *Decision-Making in the Legal System*. Issues in Criminological and Legal Psychology No. 5. British Psychological Society.

Home Office (1999) *Lifers: A Joint Thematic Review by Her Majesty's Inspectorates of Prison and Probation*. London: Home Office.

Hood, R. and Shute, S. (2000) *The Parole System at work: a study of risk based decision-making*, Home Office Research Study No. 202. London: Home Office.

Kemshall, H. (1996) *Reviewing Risk: A review of research on the assessment and management of risk and dangerousness: Implications for policy and practice in the*

Probation Service. A report for the Home Office Research and Statistics Directorate, London: Home Office.

Kemshall, H. (1998) 'Defensible Decisions for Risk: or It's the Doers Wot Get The Blame', *Probation Journal*, 45, 67–72.

Kemshall, H. (1998) *Risk in Probation Practice*. Aldershot: Ashgate Press.

Kitsuse, J. and Cicourel, A. (1963) 'A Note on the Uses of Official Statistics', *Social Problems*, 11, 131–139.

Liebling, A. (1992) *Suicides in Prison*. London: Routledge.

Liebling, A. (2000) 'Prison officers, policing, and the use of discretion' in *Theoretical Criminology*, 4 (3), 333–357.

McConville, M., Saunders, A. and Leng, R. (1991) *The case for the prosecution*. London: Routledge.

Nash, M. (1999) *Police, Probation and Protecting the Public*. London: Blackstone.

Padfield, N. (2002) *Beyond the Tariff: Human Rights and the Life Sentence Prisoner*. Cullompton: Willan.

Padfield, N. and Liebling, A. with Arnold, H. (2000) *An Exploration of decision-making at Discretionary Lifer Panels*. Home Office Research Study No. 213. London: Home Office.

Prins, H.A. (1999) *Will they do it again?: Risk assessment and management in criminal justice and psychiatry*. London: Routledge.

Sparks, R. (1997) 'Recent social theory and the study of crime and punishment' in M. Maguire, R. Morgan and R. Reiner, (eds.) *The Oxford Handbook of Criminology* (second edition). Oxford: Clarendon Press.

Sparks, R., Bottoms, A.E. and Hay, W. (1996) *Prisons and the problem of order*. Oxford: Clarendon Press.

Tonry, M. (1998) 'Selective Incapacitation: The debate over its ethics' in A. von Hirsch and A. Ashworth (eds.) *Principled Sentencing: Readings on Theory and Policy*, second edition. Oxford: Hart.

Walker, N. (1996) 'Ethical and Other Problems' in N. Walker (ed.) *Dangerous People*. London: Blackstone Press.

Chapter 6

Discretion in access to forensic psychiatric units

Adrian Grounds, Marie Howes and Loraine Gelsthorpe

Introduction

Secure psychiatric hospital facilities play an important role for both mental health services and the criminal justice system. Local mental health services need access to secure in-patient beds for patients whose behaviour is particularly hazardous and difficult to manage. The police, criminal courts and prisons also commonly deal with arrestees and offenders with mental disorder who need hospital care in secure conditions. The security may be needed for safe clinical management, for reasons of public safety and for public confidence.

Secure psychiatric units therefore have to meet a range of potentially conflicting expectations. In the UK they are an integral part of the health service rather than of the criminal justice system. They are funded, commissioned and managed as part of the health system, and staffed by clinical professionals whose primary adherence is to clinical values and ethics. At the same time the units take patients detained by virtue of criminal court orders or Home Office directed transfers of prisoners. In many of these cases the patient must remain detained unless the Home Office or a mental health review tribunal directs otherwise. Both as a matter of mental health policy (Department of Health 1998) and because secure units detain offenders who would otherwise be in the criminal justice system, the units are expected to meet expectations of public protection and reduced recidivism risk.

In the UK there are different levels of secure psychiatric provision. The three high security hospitals (Broadmoor, Ashworth and Rampton) provide a national service for patients needing maximum security. Medium secure units provide an intermediate level of security, historically for their NHS regions. Local psychiatric services have a variable amount of locked ward provision (variously described as 'low secure' or 'intensive care' units).

The development of regional secure units was proposed by the Butler Committee in 1974 because of the urgent need to provide medium secure hospital care for mentally disordered offenders who did not need maximum security but whose needs could not be met in local services (Home Office and Department of Social Security 1974). The suggested time of stay for treatment was two years. The medium secure services have developed and expanded since that time, both in the NHS and the independent sector, but bed numbers to date have always been insufficient in relation to demand and perceived needs (Gunn et al. 1991; Department of Health and Home Office 1992; Maden et al. 1993; 1996; Fryers et al. 1998; House of Commons 2000). Thus the units not only have to meet the varied expectations of mental health and criminal justice agencies, but they have to select and prioritise between competing referrals to their limited capacity. The referrals come from local mental health services unable to cope with violent patients; from the prison service in respect of mentally disordered prisoners needing assessment or treatment; from criminal courts seeking pre-trial assessments or medical disposals; and from the high secure hospitals in respect of patients needing transfer to lesser security and eventual resettlement in the community (Murray 1996).

In 1998 the Department of Health commissioned a national study of access to medium secure psychiatric care in order to inform policy development and planning (Melzer et al. 2000). Summary papers from the study are currently in preparation. The main component of the study was a substantive survey of a national cohort of assessments for admission during a six-month period.

We recognised that in order to understand the admission practices it would be necessary to combine two kinds of study: an analysis of the factors associated with outcome in a large sample of cases, and a qualitative study designed to elucidate the beliefs, assumptions and modes of thinking that shaped the judgments made by clinicians.

Quantitative analysis of the data was carried out with regard to the hospital units, the reasons for referral, the features of the assessed patients, and the outcomes of the assessments. A separate component of the research was a qualitative study of admission decision-making, and this aspect of the research is the subject of this chapter.

As Hawkins (1983) notes, in order to understand decision-making there needs to be recognition of the context of constraints in which decision-makers operate, and the ways in which they interpret what is before them, determine what is of relevance, and make choices. Underlying the assessment decisions are processes of human judgment. Decision-makers are often concerned with the implications of particular courses of action, their possible harms, and how they may affect the decision-maker's future relationships. Past experience and considerations of precedent may be influential, and there may be intricate negotiations before decisions are finalised. The need to maintain inter-organisational relationships may also be an important constraint. Overall, it is important to have an understanding of the 'decision frame', namely, 'the structure of values and meanings which the decision-maker as a human being brings to any choice' (Hawkins 1983: 12).

At the time of the fieldwork (1999) there were 29 purpose-built NHS medium secure units and eight independent sector hospital units providing medium security in England and Wales, together comprising about 2,600 beds. Admissions were thought to number two to three thousand per year. Thirty six of the units participated in the qualitative study.

The qualitative study was based on interviews with a purposive sample of lead clinicians. Thus a representative spread was sought of male/female, newly appointed and long-experienced clinicians and urban/rural, large/small, and older/newer units. Letters were sent to each of the units, inviting one or two lead clinicians to participate in this component of the research by way of a semi-structured interview lasting about one hour. An interview schedule was drawn up and piloted. The interview schedule was informed by initial group meetings with medium secure unit representatives, and focused on six broad topic areas of potential relevance to the decision-making process. These were: the unit (history, ethos, regime, morale); the tasks and roles involved in the assessment process; relations with referrers and sources of referral; judgments relating to patients; organisational and processual issues; and the clinician's own background and training. Prior to interview, each clinician was sent a copy of a prepared case vignette to facilitate discussion. This was a composite fictitious case drawn from several sources.

Interviews were conducted with 55 clinicians (53 consultants and two nurse managers). On the understanding of complete anonymity and confidentiality, interviews were audiotaped and later transcribed. A thematic content analysis of the anonymised transcripts was undertaken.

Patient selection

Four basic conditions necessary for admission into medium secure care became clear in all interviews: that the patient is mentally ill, has committed some serious act linked with the illness, needs conditions of security and their illness can be treated in a medium secure unit. However, the discussions about the case vignette led to the emergence of a range of other issues that could be taken into account in assessing the individual case. These included specific aspects of the prospective patient's past behaviour and psychiatric history, the presence of co-morbid psychiatric conditions, and the views of the referring psychiatrist. Additional factors to be weighed up in considering admission included the skills of staff in the unit; the current patient mix; whether successful treatment within two years could be achieved; and the availability of a bed. Factors such as these were not considered in a formulaic fashion: the weighting and nuances given by clinicians to particular items was complex and varied. When a specific factor was mentioned, it was not necessarily something that would sway the decision to admit but it was a matter to be taken into account.

In discussing their admission practices more generally, most interviewees described an inter-disciplinary approach to decision-making: they strongly believed that those involved in the care of patients should also be involved in the decision-making process. This was generally done through a weekly referral meeting, a format that helped promote peer review, consistency and consensus:

> [The meeting] ... has an enormous impact on first of all transparency; everybody from the most junior staff nurse if they are free can attend; certainly all ... the trainees in each discipline, all the senior clinicians and psychologists, social workers are there or have access to being there and can take part in that discussion.

> ... To me, ... the most important meeting in this unit is the referrals/admissions meeting, because that's what determines what the unit is like. It's the patients you admit here that set the tone of the whole place and how we work. So that's why it's so important to get that right.

However, the central influence that the consultant could have was also noted:

... I think you could direct it one way or another. I mean, I could ... in quite an influential way, because of the position that I have, not because of *who* I am but of *what* I am, I suppose. And that's a kind of burden, really, in a way ... I've a feeling people are actually looking to me for kind of signals, you know.

The case vignette led to discussion about the ease or difficulty of deciding whether a patient was appropriate for medium secure care. In addition to the range of issues noted above, the location of the referred individual was important, and there were particular concerns for those in prison:

I think the prison has most impact ... Because that's where the volume is. That's where the need is. Busy remand prisons get a lot of mentally disordered offenders ... And I think if you don't go there, then you don't find them ... If you're a mentally disordered prisoner who's harming yourself or whatever, you end up in a segregation unit more often than not, which is completely inappropriate ... I think that's probably why they take priority billing.

Decisions were more difficult in cases where there was insufficient relevant information about the patient; cases in which mental illness was unclear, associated with substance abuse and personality disorder, or unresponsive to treatment; and in cases that would have a detrimental effect on other patients or staff.

More than three-quarters of interviewees admitted to decisions that in retrospect they wished had been made differently. Sometimes they had gone against their clinical instincts or had been persuaded to accept patients against their better judgment. Some decisions concerned patients with a degree of mental illness that disguised or overlay an untreatable personality disorder, resulting in extended time in medium secure care and adverse effects on others. Such cases could affect staff efficiency, resulting in 'burn out' or, in the phrase of one consultant, 'creeping therapeutic nihilism'. Other decisions had involved choice of an inappropriate level of security: sometimes patients did better than expected but had to remain in medium secure care because the clinicians did not have the authority to transfer or release them. One or two clinicians who did not report regretted decisions acknowledged that their units could 'cherry pick' cases, and therefore they were less likely to take the more problematic ones.

Some groups of patients were seen as unsuitable for admission by virtue of general features or vulnerabilities. These included particularly young or old patients, those with learning disabilities or physical disabilities, and sometimes women when there was concern about their being at risk from other patients. Other groups considered for exclusion included serious sex offenders and those who posed a high escape risk:

> We don't on the whole take people who are capable of organising outside help in some way, terrorist groups, organised criminal gangs; those are very rare problems anyway.

Patients with primary diagnoses of personality disorder were regarded as generally unsuitable by almost half the interviewees, although exceptions would be made for patients needing transfer from high secure hospitals. However, it was also noted that diagnoses of personality disorder amongst referred patients could be misapplied:

> We've seen lots of problems with really quite ill and disturbed patients that have been re-diagnosed as personality disorder or something to exclude them from various services.

When patients with personality disorder were being considered for admission, the patient's attitude towards co-operation with psychological treatment was crucial. Resources were too scarce to admit those whose stays would be unproductive.

> We've generally found that we don't have much success with people with personality disorder. They don't integrate well in the unit, which has mostly psychotic patients. So we tend to try and avoid admitting them. I think if you were going to manage people with personality disorder, then it's necessary to have a specialist unit with staff who really like to work with that sort of patient and see it as a challenge.

There could be sharp idiosyncratic differences between clinicians. For example, one clinician regarded asylum seekers as an excluded group, but another saw them as a group needing particular attention:

> I try to keep [a bed] so that I can at least bring one in when I need to … They don't need medium security but nobody else will offer them a bed … I guess it's because they don't feel like offenders and you can see that in many ways they're like you or I, but they're

caught in a system that has no limits, no ends, no rights – it's extraordinary. All our patients here – we can detain them for a certain amount of time and they've a right to appeal. The immigration detainees don't, they can sit in [detention] for two years. And I always think I could have done a pretty good crime to get two years … All they have done is enter illegally.

Clinicians faced hard decisions when choosing which patient to prioritise for a vacant bed. Those in prison or the community were generally seen as more urgent cases than those waiting in high or medium secure hospitals for transfer. Probity was an essential part of decision-making. When rejecting a patient for admission, clinicians said they would generally be 'up front' with their colleagues in explaining their decision. They could be 'walking a tightrope', because neither the patient's illness nor public protection could be ignored, but resources to meet those needs were limited.

The interviews with clinicians indicated that they did not make admission decisions in terms of a 'checklist' or 'scoring' approach in relation to patient characteristics. Several referred to a 'gut feeling' or 'sixth sense' about patients which comes through experience and the long 'apprenticeship' of training.

I know no theorem at the moment that would lead me to put in … information and get an answer out. So there is a subjective process. That is based on my experience and a bit of gut feeling supplemented by reviews of the other members of the clinical teams.

I suppose intuition becomes part of your clinical skills in a way.

The context of the unit

Clinicians tended to adopt a pragmatic rather than narrow conception of what constituted medium security. Most saw their units as providing a service for patients who did not need maximum security (on account of grave and immediate danger to others), but who on the other hand were too dangerous or difficult to manage in local locked wards. The point was frequently emphasised that security relates not to buildings but the quality of staff, although it was also recognised that physical conditions of security were important.

Medium secure units were seen by all interviewees as providing a service for *patients*, (not 'inmates', 'prisoners' or 'clients'). The clinicians also had clear notions of what distinguished units that functioned well from those that functioned poorly. The former were characterised by good relationships between staff, multi-disciplinary working, a teaching and research ethos, and a central emphasis on patients' needs. It was stressed that clinical teams needed a clear and shared view of what they were trying to do.

When asked to assess their own services, the majority of interviewees assessed their units as functioning fairly well, but some thought their units still had some way to improve:

> I think the unit is actually not too bad. I think the people who work here perhaps don't feel as isolated, as demoralised now as they did a few years ago.

> I want the place to provide more continuity of care so that people who are deemed dangerous, who are discharged from the unit ... can be followed up by me and my service ... I wouldn't want to be involved in a unit that didn't have sort of academic ethos, that has a too custodial ethos, that didn't have any close link with prison and probation service, where we don't respect people we are working with, where the team-working was dysfunctional (because we are dealing with dysfunctional patients that cause particular problems) ... I wouldn't want to work in a unit that was within a trust that didn't understand what forensic mental health was about.

> We are happy stressed unit, probably. We have been an unhappy unit but we are sort of happy stressed unit at the moment.

The emergent picture of medium secure care was of a service that is inherently dynamic, responding to a variety of internal and external factors, some positive and some negative. Units experienced changes over time, in physical plant, staff, nursing practices and treatment approaches. Many of the changes in units were indicators of the ethos, beliefs and values of the clinicians, particularly concerning the perceived needs of patients. The concept of a well-run unit entailed a collaborative vision amongst staff. The 'dysfunctional' unit, on the other hand, was seen as characterised by internal conflict. Multi-disciplinary team working was regarded as essential, and the maintenance of a shared view of the purpose of the unit was a strong structuring influence on decisions about who should be admitted.

The context of services

The clinicians described substantial pressure on beds, resulting in waiting lists and in suitable patients being placed elsewhere. Several units had either a 'bed-management' meeting or a special 'bed manager' for the task. Admissions could be restricted by difficulties and delays in discharging patients, and in this regard 'bed-blocking' by patients transferred from high security who needed long-term medium secure care was particularly cited. Beds could also be blocked by patients with personality disorders. Bed-blocking not only affected prospective patients, but staff too, because they had to deal with the same patients with little prospect of change.

> ... At the moment there are absolute blocks and great delays in patients moving, when they are clinically ready to move. And that is frustrating. I think it is frustrating to all levels of security if they feel they are holding onto patients who should be on another level.

Interviewees who worked in independent sector units noted that one of the advantages of that sector is the possibility of finding the financial resources to develop new services to meet 'gaps' in the market and in the range of NHS provision.

> There are certain advantages we have over some of the other units. The advantages we have are of size – both in the number of patients we've got and in the physical space. And because of the size we've been able to develop specialist units which take people who would usually be excluded from mainstream regional secure units, particularly people with mild disability and challenging behaviour, and people with personality disorder because they don't tend to fit into RSUs [regional secure units] who are over-burdened with people with mental illness.

However, the independent sector tends to provide exclusively in-patient beds, and although these units may be able to expand their range of in-patient services, they cannot extend easily into community work and continuity of patient care.

Access to medium secure provision is mediated through the relationships between the unit clinicians and referrers. These relationships are important, complex, and influence dispositions to accept or reject referred patients. The decision about whether or not to admit is often set in a wider context of negotiation about the patient's longer-term management, and the admitting clinicians perceive the willingness and availability of local services to provide subsequent care as an important consideration.

In summary, the high level of demand in relation to supply of medium secure provision brings into play a range of important influences on selection for admission. Patients from the criminal justice system often have to be prioritised over those referred from high secure hospitals and local psychiatric units. The attitudes of the admitting clinicians to local psychiatric services assume importance in this context, and the interviews indicated the importance of good relationships and confidence in the ability and willingness of local services to provide for patients ready to leave medium security.

The high demand for limited beds also means that there is concern to avoid the risk of excessively long lengths of stay and the patients who might give rise to them. The blocks and delays in movement between levels of security are perceived as a major problem. Although in-dependent sector units played a major role in providing medium secure care for special clinical groups, they were similarly dependent on local services to provide continuing psychiatric care.

The context of policy

The clinicians recognised that they were making decisions about patients in a constantly changing context of policy and expectations.

> New ideas, clinical governance, changes in purchasing arrangements, all sorts of changes that are happening outside. Forensic psychiatry and people working in the specialty are dealing in a high profile area. There's a lot more criticism now if things go wrong, therefore, people are much more careful, at times over-defensive.

> Public protection is something that was never even mentioned ten years ago ... There's been a big growth industry in general psychiatry asking for forensic risk assessments on patients who, perhaps, behave violently in the community ... A buzz word, everybody must have a risk assessment.

Clinicians spoke of the importance of autonomy and of having support rather than control from their trusts and commissioning health authorities:

The other factor that allows good morale is if the managers ... are supportive – that's crucial – and don't interfere ... Places that don't seem to work very well are those where the people working there don't seem to have a say in what happens.

What the trust wants is loyalty. It is not that I feel disloyal, ... [but] they can never be my top loyalty because I also work as a doctor ... Whatever it is, you can't separate it from the autonomy of freedom of action. If you remove the freedom, you also remove something essential about what makes doctors to be doctors; it has got a lot to do with making decisions and taking risks in situations when you've only got incomplete information.

However, many clinicians also saw themselves as carrying out multi-faceted roles, including managerial ones, in partnership with team colleagues.

I would ... not say, 'Because we've got no beds this week I'm going in there to do all I can not to admit someone' ... I would hope that ... my recommendation as a clinician is going to appear in the report, 'this person needs treatment in a particular environment'. And then the next step is where I take off the hat of a clinician and then become manager ... and say, right, in the system as it exists today it is appropriate either that the patient goes on a waiting list to find out if another unit has a bed sooner ... [or] to say I feel very unsure [about] this patient ... he's on the borderline between what we can provide and what high security can provide and I'm going to get another opinion.

Although the concept of risk is central to the work of the forensic psychiatrist, very few interviewees discussed it explicitly. Instead, it was referred to indirectly:

If you talk about mentally disordered offenders in forensic psychiatry, you're talking about risk management all the way through, risk to others all the way through. You might not use the word 'risk', you might use the word 'dangerousness', or 'security', or 'management', or something, but you are talking about risk all the time. It's not a separate activity.

There was a strong awareness that risk could not be eliminated:

You are always taking risks anyway, but this is a reasonable risk to take; and of course if it goes wrong then you will be told it was an unreasonable one.

We also feel that we ourselves are at risk in trying to supervise [patients] ... You are always trying to cover your back. If something goes wrong, you know, there's a blame culture ... This Michael Stone case. And there's always that feeling that we are juggling balls in the air. Sooner or later, one of them is going to fall, and explode, and there'll be questions asked. I don't think there is an answer ... It's a risky profession. I think that puts people off psychiatry. And I think the general public doesn't tolerate any risk amongst psychiatrists.

It's a ... complex process and I suppose I find it hard to articulate how one regards that, because really the truth is that you're often taking risks once you've admitted patients, and as you give them increasing amounts of freedom, ... you're exposing the community to the risks posed by those patients; and that's the long and short of it really – you're exposing yourself to the risks that might blow up in your face. It's a very complex exercise in risk assessment and management, the short answer is that I don't really know how you do it.

Clinicians spoke of their limited influence over the voluntary behaviour of patients. There was a clinical role in relation to predicting and managing risk arising from mental illness, but harmful behaviour arising from personality factors, voluntary drug-taking and social influences was different and outside the sphere of influence of clinical treatment.

Can we say something about this person's dangerousness with sufficient confidence that we can make an estimate of risk? And, for the most part ... for a psychosis, you can, to a degree. You can say that if somebody is not complying with their medication, [they] are likely to become ill again, and when ill in the past they have done terrible things; then I think that they are risky. But we're miles away from that in personality disorder.

Mental health practitioners have dual roles to safeguard and look after individuals and to protect the society from certain members. I think there is a tension in so far as our duty is to look after our patients and protect their interests but one can't ignore one has a duty for the wider public interest as well … I don't think you do the patients any favours if you say you recognise there is a serious risk if your mental symptoms are not controlled, [but] it is up to you whatever you do. You are not doing them any favours, and certainly not to the next victim. There is a balance there.

Overall, the clinicians were strongly aware of the current climate of policy and public expectation in which their services operated. The interviews indicated both a basic assumption that risk assessment and management were central in forensic psychiatry practice, but also realism and apprehension about the limitations of medium secure care in controlling risk of serious re-offending.

The gate-keeping role in admission to medium secure care entailed managing expectations of referrers and managers, and the level of risk taken on by the medium secure service. In addition, there was primary adherence to seeking clinical benefit to patients, and it was only in this context that restrictive measures and risk containment by clinicians were seen as justified. The emphasis on protecting clinical autonomy in admission decision-making exemplified the central commitment to a medical, therapeutic purpose.

Conclusion

The study showed that a complex range of internal and external contextual pressures impinged on admission decisions. Within the medium secure units, the needs to maintain a shared, collective view amongst staff, and patient turnover, were important factors. Externally, relationships with referrers and perceptions of local services were influential. In addition, the clinicians' primary adherence to the values they associated with a clinical role both defined and limited their sense of what they can and should properly do. They therefore tended to prioritise the care of the mentally ill and the pursuit of therapeutic benefit for patients, and they saw their contribution to risk management as mainly limited to risk arising from potentially treatable mental disorder.

Findings such as these are of potential importance in the wider context of policy and service planning. From a policy and planning point of view it is likely to be assumed that in principle the level of need for medium secure services can be measured by better identification and characterisation of patient groups; this in turn should facilitate rational allocation of patients to different levels of security on the basis of defined clinical criteria. However, secure psychiatric provision does not work in this manner. The use of these services is unlikely to bear a straight-forward relationship to patient characteristics. Admission patterns will reflect decisions that are highly discretionary, and shaped by complex appraisals of context and professional values.

References

Department of Health and Home Office (1992) *Review of Health and Social Services for Mentally Disordered Offenders and Others Requiring Similar Services. Final Summary Report* (The Reed Report). Cmnd. 2088. London: HMSO.

Department of Health (1998) *Modernising Mental Health Services: safe, sound and supportive.* London: Department of Health.

Fryers, T. et al. (1998) 'Severe mental illness in prisoners' (editorial) *British Medical Journal* 317, 1025–1026.

Gunn, J., Maden, A. and Swinton, M. (1991) *Mentally Disordered Prisoners.* London: Home Office.

Hawkins, K. (1983) 'Thinking about legal decision making' in J. Shapland, (ed.) *Decision Making in the Legal System.* Issues in Criminological and Legal Psychology No. 5. Leicester: British Psychological Society.

Home Office and Department of Social Security (1974) *Interim Report of the Committee on Mentally Abnormal Offenders.* Cmnd. 6244. London: HMSO.

House of Commons (2000) *Health Committee Fourth Report – Provision of NHS Mental Health Services.* HC 373-I. London: Stationery Office.

Maden, A. et al. (1993) 'The treatment and security needs of patients in special hospitals', *Criminal Behaviour and Mental Health*, 3, 290–306.

Maden, A. et al. (1996) *Mental Disorder in Remand Prisoners.* London: Home Office Research and Statistics Directorate.

Melzer, D., Tom, B., The Mental Health Policy Research Group (2000) *Pathways into medium secure psychiatric provision in England and Wales.* Report to the Department of Health. Cambridge: The Epidemiology Policy Group, Department of Public Health and Primary Care, University of Cambridge.

Murray, K. (1996) 'The use of beds in NHS medium secure units in England,' *Journal of Forensic Psychiatry* 7, 504–524.

Chapter 7

Discretion and the release of mentally disordered offenders

Katy Holloway and Adrian Grounds

Introduction

This chapter explores discretionary decision-making in another part of the mental health system. It focuses on Mental Health Review Tribunals and on their powers to release patients who are detained in hospital under restriction orders because of their propensity to inflict serious harm on others. The first part of the chapter further addresses the general concept of discretionary decision-making and the use of discretion in the arenas of criminal justice and mental health. The second section provides background information about the Mental Health Review Tribunal system and factual information about the procedures and powers of Tribunals in restricted cases. The third section presents the results of a recent empirical study of Tribunal decision-making conducted in the Trent region in the late 1990s. The fourth part of this chapter moves on to discuss the results of this empirical research in light of discretionary decision-making research in analogous contexts. With reference to the research findings, the fifth and final section of this chapter discusses the proposals for reform of the Mental Health Act 1983.

Discretionary decision-making

Close adherence to written rules has historically been equated with procedural justice. But rules do not translate straightforwardly into practice. Discretion influences both the interpretation of the 'facts' on which decisions are based, and the selection and interpretation of the rules which are intended to guide decision-making. Socio-legal researchers today recognise discretion to be inherent in all rule-governed systems, and to have the positive potential to deliver 'individualised' justice by taking into account the circumstances of particular cases. From an organisational viewpoint, allowing a wide margin of discretion to decision-makers can provide operational flexibility. However, this must be balanced against a certain level of monitoring and consistency to ensure that individual decisions are not arbitrary, inconsistent or unfair.

(Weber and Gelsthorpe 2000)

The use of discretion in decision-making is of particular concern when the decisions being made involve loss of liberty and other serious interventions in people's lives. As Weber and Gelsthorpe (2000) point out, discretion can lead to arbitrary, inconsistent or unfair decision-making. The possibility that similar cases will be dealt with in different ways, resulting in, for example, detention for some and release for others, is a great worry to civil libertarians. Such concerns have resulted in a number of studies exploring decision-making within the criminal justice system, a system in which decisions concerning people's liberty are made every day.

Civil liberty issues are of concern also in the mental health system where decisions to detain patients under civil sections of the Mental Health Act 1983 are taken by mental health professionals and not by lawyers. An application can be made to detain a person in hospital for up to six months upon the written recommendation of two registered medical practitioners (s.3(3)).

Civil liberty issues are of particular concern for offender patients detained in hospitals under restriction orders (ss.37/41). A restriction order is imposed by the Crown Court in cases where it is thought necessary in order to protect the public from serious harm. The restriction order may be made either with or without limit of time; most are of unlimited duration. The purpose of the 'restriction' is to restrict the patient's avenues for release. Restricted patients can only be released by the Home Secretary or by a specially constituted Mental Health Review Tribunal. Considering the responsibility of discharging a patient who has been detained on account of potential to inflict serious harm on others, it is of little surprise to discover that only a small proportion of restricted patients are released each year[1]. Some restricted patients are detained for considerably longer than would have been the case if they had been given a prison sentence.

With a few notable exceptions,[2] research on decision-making in psychiatry and law in the UK has a less developed tradition than in the United States.[3] There has also been relatively little research on the decision-making of Mental Health Review Tribunals, compared with research investigating the decision-making of judges, magistrates and parole boards. Since the substantive study in the 1980s by Peay (1989), more recent studies of Mental Health Review Tribunals[4] have had methodological shortcomings (e.g. small samples, incomplete approaches, absence of sophisticated statistical analyses), resulting in contradictory findings. In addition, they have not focused on decision-making in restricted cases.

Mental Health Review Tribunals

Mental Health Review Tribunals were introduced in the Mental Health Act 1959 on the recommendation of the Percy Commission[5]. Their primary role as a judicial body independent of the detaining authority was to safeguard patients from unjustified detention in hospital. If detention was unjustified, the Tribunals were empowered to authorise the discharge of patients. This power of discharge, however, did not originally apply to all detained patients: those held under restriction orders on account of their potential risk to the public (restricted patients) could only be released on the decision of the Home Secretary.

In 1981 the Tribunals' inability to authorise the discharge of restricted patients was ruled to be in contravention of the European Convention on Human Rights.[6] The United Kingdom undertook to adhere to this ruling and bring domestic law into line with the Convention. Thus, under the Mental Health Act 1983, Tribunals were given the 'formidable responsibility' of discharging restricted patients (Lord Belstead, Hansard HL, 25 January 1982, col. 761). The Mental Health Act 1983 remains the principal Act governing the admission and discharge of mentally disordered persons, although it is currently under review.[7]

The Tribunal Panel

A Mental Health Review Tribunal is comprised of three members: a legal member (the president), a medical member (a psychiatrist) and a lay member. In recognition of the responsibility of discharging restricted patients, the Tribunal president in restricted cases must be a lawyer with substantial judicial experience in the criminal courts (i.e. a circuit judge or recorder). There is no requirement that either the medical or lay member should have specific forensic experience.

The Tribunal Process

Under section 70 of the Mental Health Act 1983, restricted patients are entitled to apply for a review of their case once in every 12-month period. If, for whatever reason, a restricted patient fails to apply for a review for three consecutive years, the Home Secretary is obliged, under section 71(2), to refer the patient's case for a hearing. In addition, the Home Secretary has a general discretionary power to refer the case of a restricted patient at any time 'he thinks fit' (section 72(1)).

Once an application or reference has been lodged with the Tribunal office, reports are prepared, including a mandatory up-to-date medical report from the patient's responsible medical officer and a statement from the Home Secretary.[8] Reports may also be received from social workers, psychologists and independent psychiatrists. Under rule 12 a copy of every document relevant to the application must be sent to the patient, the responsible authority and the Home Secretary.

At any time before the Tribunal hearing the medical member is required to interview and make an assessment of the patient's mental condition. All three members then meet before the hearing to discuss the written evidence and set an agenda. After the hearing, at which the patient may be legally represented, the Tribunal members deliberate in private and decide whether or not the patient satisfies the statutory criteria for release. The Tribunal may decide to grant an absolute or a conditional discharge. A conditional discharge can be deferred until the specified conditions have been satisfied. If more information is required before a decision can be made, the Tribunal may adjourn the case. In non-restricted cases Tribunals have the power to recommend that a patient be transferred to another hospital, and can reconvene if the recommendations are not enacted. In restricted cases, the Tribunals have no such powers.

The discharge criteria

Under section 72(1)(b) of the Mental Health Act 1983, Tribunals are required to discharge non-restricted and civil patients if they are no longer suffering from a mental disorder of a nature or degree warranting detention in hospital for medical treatment, *or* if they are no longer in need of detention for either their own health or safety or for the protection of others. Section 72 also provides Tribunals with a 'general discretion' to discharge patients in any case (Jones 1996: 254). Under section 73 of the 1983 Act, which applies to restricted patients, Tribunals are obliged to discharge patients if they satisfy either of the criteria stipulated in section 73(1)(a) (which refers to section 72(1)(b)). In restricted cases the Tribunals have no additional discretionary power to release patients in any case. Hoggett (1996: 198) describes this as a 'surprising' situation given the 'exalted membership of Tribunals' in restricted cases.

Eastman and Peay (1999: 10) note that in theory, the language of the discharge criteria 'limits the decision-makers' options and enhances for patients the substantive value of the Tribunal as a safeguard against unjustified detention'. In practice, however, the protection offered by the statute is only of 'face-value'. Indeed, under section 73 restricted patients must prove a negative (i.e. that they are no longer suffering from a mental disorder or that they are no longer a risk to themselves or others) in order to qualify for discharge. Proving a negative, Eastman and Peay (1999: 10) observe, is a 'sufficiently problematic, if not impossible' task to achieve. This difficulty is intensified by the complexity of the concepts of mental disorder and risk, which 'are rarely susceptible to precise quantification' (Richardson 1993: 295). The discharge criteria are, consequently, open to 'wide interpretation' (Richardson and Thorold 1999: 116).

Thus, the very wording of the discharge criteria raises doubts about the efficacy of the Tribunal as a safeguard against unjustified detention. Indeed, Richardson and Thorold (1999) warn of:

> ... a very real danger that the breadth of discretion contained within the criteria coupled to their negative formulation, serve merely to encourage an understandable predisposition towards caution and a consequential diminution of the Tribunal's strength as a protector of the patient's right to liberty
>
> (Richardson and Thorold 1999: 177)

This predisposition towards caution is widely reported within the Tribunal literature.[9] The Tribunals observed in the study (described in this chapter) were also observed to act cautiously and in several cases they utilised the 'double negative' to justify decisions not to discharge. In one observed case, the medical member expressed 'very grave doubts' that the patient continued to suffer from a mental disorder but was satisfied that the patient was a danger to others.[10] The judge commented: 'The double negative can cover all sorts of things – we're not satisfied that he's not suffering. He *was* psychotic at some time.'

Since the research was completed there has been a significant development in relation to the negative formulation of the discharge criteria. In a recent case (28 March 2001) the Court of Appeal made a declaration of incompatibility with the European Convention on

Human Rights with respect to sections 72 and 73 of the Mental Health Act 1983.[11] The Court concluded that it was contrary to the Convention to detain a patient compulsorily unless it could be reliably shown that the patient was suffering from a mental disorder that warranted detention. Inasmuch as sections 72 and 73 did not require the Tribunal to discharge a patient where it could not be shown that he was suffering from a mental disorder that warranted detention, the provisions were incompatible with Articles 5(1) and 5(4) of the Convention.[12] The Court noted, however, that once it was demonstrated that the patient was of unsound mind, the Convention did not require additional criteria of treatability and treatment availability to be met.

Empirical research on Tribunal decision-making in restricted cases

Aims and objectives

The objectives of the current study were to investigate the decision-making process of Tribunals in restricted cases and to analyse the process by which such patients were being released. The aim was to examine how effectively Tribunals are currently fulfilling their role as a safeguard for patients' liberty.

Methods

To achieve these aims and objectives a combination of qualitative and quantitative analysis methods was employed. First, a retrospective file study of restricted cases was conducted to explore what factors influenced Tribunals to discharge patients or to recommend their transfer to lesser security.[13] Data was collected in respect of 1,765 restricted cases heard by Tribunals in the Trent region in the nine-year period from 1 January 1990. Secondly, a questionnaire study was carried out to explore how Tribunal members used the evidence and applied the discharge criteria when making their decisions. A total of 341 members completed questionnaires in respect of 119 restricted cases heard in Trent in 1998. The third method was qualitative in nature and involved the observation of 165 consecutive restricted cases heard by Tribunal panels in Trent in 1998. These observations enabled the researcher to examine how the Tribunals operated in practice and supplemented the other more quantitative approaches.

The retrospective file study

In the retrospective file study the aim was to explore the factors predictive of Tribunal decisions. Five factors were found to be independently associated with the decision to discharge and four with the decision to recommend transfer.

The variable with the greatest influence on both the Tribunals' decisions and recommendations was the written opinion of the patients' responsible medical officer (RMO). This was in line with previous research findings (e.g. Peay 1989). The Tribunals generally endorsed the course of action recommended by the RMO; and when the Tribunals did reject the RMOs' advice this was usually so that a more cautious route could be followed. Indeed, only four per cent of patients were discharged against the RMOs' advice.

The observational study suggested that the Tribunals' rejection or acceptance of the RMOs' written advice was influenced by factors such as the reputation or experience of the RMO. In one case the medical member explained to his colleagues that the RMO was 'very new' and of 'little experience'. In another case the medical member described the RMO as 'a very competent doctor' and explained that 'if he's unsure' then the Tribunal should be too. Another influential factor was the RMOs' ability, or inability, to communicate effectively when English was not their first language. In some cases the Tribunal members were unable to comprehend what course of action the RMO was advocating. One RMO was described as 'incredibly confusing' and another as 'not the easiest man to understand'.

The type of hospital in which the patient was detained at the time of the hearing was one of the four other factors associated with the decision to discharge. There was one maximum security hospital in the region covered by the study (Rampton Hospital) and patients detained there were less likely to be discharged than patients detained in medium or lower security. The small proportion of discharges among the Rampton Hospital patients would appear to reflect a perception of special hospital patients as more dangerous than those in other hospitals. However, the index offences committed by the Rampton Hospital patients in this sample were no more serious than those committed by patients detained in medium or lower security. Furthermore, the patients detained in maximum security were no more likely to have had previous convictions than patients in medium security. The small proportion of discharges amongst Rampton Hospital patients therefore raise questions about whether the general perception of their dangerousness is valid.

The observational research suggested that long waiting lists for therapy and the frequent changes of clinical responsibility in Rampton Hospital may have prevented patients detained there from progressing towards discharge.[14] Eastman (1994) argues that society has no right to detain patients for the purposes of treatment if the resources for that treatment are inadequate. Tribunals observed deficiencies in resources at Rampton Hospital but in the absence of authoritative powers in relation to treatment and resource issues they could not adequately fulfil their role as a safeguard against unjustified detention.

The presence of an independent psychiatrist (IP) at hearings was a third factor influencing Tribunal decisions to discharge.[15] Hearings where IPs were present were significantly more likely to result in discharge than hearings where no IP was present. The observational research suggested that when IPs offer to supervise patients on discharge this could be crucial assurance to Tribunals that patients were ready to leave hospital. The IPs' offer of supervision was also influential in assuring Tribunals that patients were ready for transfer. The fact that the IPs were confident enough to assume responsibility for the patient seemed to reassure the Tribunals that the patients could leave their current hospital. As one judge explained, 'he's got to carry the can and he's prepared to say it'. Similarly the medical member in another case sought confirmation that '... you're happy to act as RMO, that's the vital question'.

The reputation of the IP also seemed to be influential. When asked by the judge about the patient's propensity to commit arson, the medical member in one case remarked, 'That won't happen. [The IP] is a superb psychiatrist. It just won't happen'. The value attributed to the IPs' views was also evident in the questionnaire study. Not one member rated the IPs' oral reports 'of no assistance' and only two members rated their written reports in a negative way.

The marital status of the patients was the fourth factor associated with the decision to discharge. Single patients were less likely to be discharged than patients in any other marital groups. Whether a patient is divorced, separated, married, cohabiting or widowed, they have at some point formed and maintained an intimate relationship with another person. Single patients, however, have not demonstrated such ability to form lasting attachments. Perhaps, Tribunals considered this might affect the patients' ability to cope in the community. It is likely that hidden assumptions were at work here: there was rarely any discussion between the members about this factor. The observational data, therefore, shed little light on the relationship between marital status and the decision to discharge.

With regard to transfer into lesser security it is of note that cases in which the Home Secretary agreed with the recommendation were significantly more likely to result in transfer than cases in which the Home Secretary opposed such a move. However, from the questionnaire and observational studies it was evident that Tribunal members often had sceptical views about the usefulness of the Home Secretary's statement. The finding may, therefore, reflect the 'safe' nature of the cases rather than any deference to the Home Secretary's views.

The Tribunals' recommendations for transfer were also influenced by the type of hospital in which the patient was initially detained. Patients detained initially in Rampton Hospital were significantly more likely to be recommended for transfer than patients detained initially in medium or lower security. The Tribunals preferred to move the special hospital patients forward gradually, by testing them out in conditions of less than maximum security before discharging them. The fact that Tribunals had no power to direct such transfers was a source of considerable dissatisfaction among members, particularly in cases where patients had been waiting years for transfers. Without this the Tribunals were powerless to protect patients from detention in conditions of security inappropriate to their needs.

In one case the inability to transfer a patient from Rampton to a less secure hospital was a factor in the Tribunal's decision to grant a conditional discharge. The medical member said, 'I have shifted from transfer, which was in my mind at the start, to a conditional discharge because I'm afraid nothing is going to happen ... the whole process is ridiculous if we make recommendations that are never going to be made'.

According to Richardson and Thorold (1999: 122) the Tribunal's inability to authorise transfers 'severely limits its efficacy as a rights protector'. The Tribunals, they argue, 'must be given the power to order a transfer' to amend this situation (*ibid.* p.130). The Tribunals' inability to order transfer was, according to Wood (1993: 20), 'the most intractable problem hampering the work of the Tribunals'. The situation continues, and the recent White Paper[16] outlining proposals for reform of the Mental Health Act 1983 does not envisage a change in this regard.

The identity of Tribunal members was not related to the nature of the Tribunals' decisions. The converse was found in previous research (see Peay 1981, 1989). Although some judges were significantly more likely than others to discharge patients, this reflected the type of hospital in which the case was heard rather than any idiosyncrasy of the Tribunal president. Some judges were more likely to deal with special hospital cases, for example. In the observational study, however, it was noted that certain members had an attributed reputation for granting, or not granting, discharges. After one 'no discharge' case the patient's solicitor approached the researcher and expressed dissatisfaction with the outcome. He said he wished that Judge 3 (who had one of the highest discharge rates) had been presiding and not Judge 13 (who had one of the lowest discharge rates). In another case where a hearing was adjourned and rearranged for a date when Judge 13 would be sitting, Judge 5 remarked, 'That makes the decision even more inevitable, doesn't it?!' One Tribunal booking clerk reported to the researcher that certain legal representatives endeavoured to avoid hearings presided over by certain judges: they would suddenly become unavailable to attend hearings upon discovering that a particular judge would be presiding.

The observational study

The observational study focused on the process by which the Tribunals made their decisions. The general aim was to collect data that would provide depth to the quantitative findings of the retrospective file study and the questionnaire survey. The observational study highlighted the personal judgment aspects of the decision-making process, and raised further questions about the Tribunals' adequacy as a safeguard against unjustified detention.

Of particular note was the influence that the number of cases heard per day had on Tribunal members. On days when two or more cases were heard, there was sometimes confusion as members tried to remember which report corresponded with which patient. One judge was heard saying, 'I spent so much time reading this afternoon's case that I have forgotten what this one is all about.' Comments such as, 'I think three in one day is a bit too many' and, 'the trouble with having three in one day is that they all telescope' were frequently heard. More troubling was one member's tendency to fall asleep during the last hearing of the day.

The day of the week also had an effect on the conduct and outcome of hearings. As the weekend approached the evidence was not always examined as scrupulously as it might have been. In the post-hearing deliberations of one case the Tribunal president explained to his colleagues, 'I don't know if it's just because it was the last case in the week but I couldn't work up much enthusiasm to investigate things'. The Tribunal members were clearly susceptible to the strains of working life and they tired as the week progressed. This was, undoubtedly, intensified by the age of Tribunal members, a large proportion of whom were retired and in their sixties or seventies.

The Tribunals' use of adjournments was a third area of concern. Problems were mainly observed in cases where the Home Secretary had not seen or commented on all of the written evidence (see Rule 12 of the Mental Health Review Tribunal Rules 1983).[17] Some Tribunals employed various tactics to avoid the costs of adjourning. One such method was to ask the authors of reports (if present) to present their reports orally. The judge in one case explained, '… if we see that, the Home Office have to see it too. We can sit within the rules if we hear it orally.' An alternative strategy to evade adjournment was to avoid mentioning the reports at all. In one case the judge questioned whether the Home Secretary had seen a letter submitted by the patient's sister. The clerk said 'no' whereupon the judge stated, 'well, we won't refer to it then'.

As Peay (1989) had found in the 1980s there was considerable divergence in the application of Rule 12. Whilst some Tribunals circumvented the rule, other Tribunal panels applied it rigorously and adjourned cases in which the Home Office had not seen certain reports. Given that the Tribunals rarely considered the Home Secretary's views in any depth, the requirement that they adjourn solely for the Home Secretary to provide comments could entail a waste of valuable resources.

Tribunals are not legally required to adjourn cases in which a member has had previous contact with a patient. The adjudicating body, McNeill J explained, 'is the corporate Tribunal not any single member'.[18] Although this may be true in theory, in practice prior knowledge of a patient could have a profound effect on the conduct of the hearing. In the case of one patient who had been recalled to hospital whilst on a conditional discharge, the Tribunal president's previous contact with the patient appeared to affect his impartiality (the judge had been involved in the patient's conditional discharge). The judge explained to his colleagues during the pre-hearing deliberations, 'This was a conditional discharge and [I] was a party to it. Let's see the reasons for it … It's beyond me now – how could we have been so deceived? What I write today is that it failed and that he's back here and he's going to stay here.' And later during a short recess, 'I'm quite determined that he's going to stay in – making a mockery of the system!'.

The questionnaire study

The objective of the questionnaire study was to investigate how the Tribunal members weighed the evidence and applied the discharge criteria when making their decisions.

As the retrospective file study indicated, the questionnaire responses highlighted the importance of the medical evidence in the decision-making process. The questionnaire study revealed the important finding that the oral reports of the Tribunal medical members (presented to their Tribunal colleagues in private during the pre-hearing discussions) were of greater influence than the RMOs' oral reports. The fact that decisions were being affected strongly by evidence not open to challenge has serious implications for natural justice. Recent proposals for reform of the Mental Health Act 1983 have recognised the unfairness of this situation and have recommended that the medical members' preliminary examination of patients be discontinued. The results of this study lend support to this proposal.

The questionnaire responses revealed a generally negative perception of the Home Secretary's statements to Tribunals in restricted cases. The Home Secretary's statements were only rarely considered to be of any assistance to the decision-makers and were frequently criticised as cautious, predictable and lacking in detailed information. Proposals for reform of the Mental Health Act 1983 have recommended that the Home Secretary provide much more detailed reports to the Tribunals.[19] The results of this project also lend support to this recommendation.

Perhaps, the most troubling result of the questionnaire study was the discovery that five patients had not been discharged in spite of majority or unanimous agreement that the discharge criteria had been satisfied. Observations of the Tribunal hearings and deliberations suggested that these no-discharge decisions arose from a failure of communication between the members. Of concern was the observation that lay members were regularly ignored or were non-active participants in the deliberations. This clearly defies the purpose of the 'tri-bunal' system.

Of particular interest was one observed case in which a patient was not released even though he was no longer mentally disordered. The patient was an elderly man whose case had been referred for review by the Home Secretary (because the patient had not made an application himself within three years). In the weeks before the hearing the patient had reported auditory hallucinations. These voices, the nurse and RMO explained to the Tribunal, were 'put on' to justify the need for continued detention. The Tribunal was in a difficult position as the patient was no longer suffering from a mental disorder, but after 34 years of institutional life he was clearly in need of detention for his own health or safety. The Tribunal president joked with his colleagues, 'He's not mentally ill at all – absolute discharge'. The lay member replied, 'Can you imagine what would happen if we did … he stays where he is, doesn't he?' The medical member agreed and said, 'Absolutely, he would be a risk'. Although the Tribunal had circumvented the law it had acted conscientiously in an attempt to protect the patient (see Grounds 1989). The Tribunal acted more like a 'welfare assessment panel' than a judicial body obliged to order discharge when the statutory criteria for it were met (Fennell 1977: 219).

The questionnaire study demonstrated that members' opinions on discharge rarely changed after the written evidence had been read – the observational research confirmed this finding. Indeed, one judge would arrive at hearings with a draft decision, and reasons for that decision, already prepared. In the pre-hearing deliberations about one case this judge explained, 'I have already reached a natural introduction to our decision' and in another case, advised a colleague that they might be 'shocked' to learn that he had prepared a preliminary reason based solely on the written evidence. Other judges were observed writing the reasons for a decision whilst the oral evidence was still being presented. Such incidents gave the distinct impression that the decision was not based on a joint evaluation of all the evidence.

The questionnaire responses also showed that without written evidence in favour of discharge, patients stood little chance of being discharged after the hearing. Peay (1981) suggested that a written report outlining the case in favour of discharge might help to curtail reliance on the RMOs' views. The results of this project lend support to this suggestion.

Discretionary decision-making in other contexts

The decisions made by judges and magistrates, and the severity of penalties imposed by them, have been of particular interest to researchers (Kapardis 1985). The decisions made by parole boards have also been investigated, but there are fewer studies focusing on the decision to grant or deny parole (Feder 1994). Tribunals, like courts and parole boards, make decisions about an individual's liberty and each of these judicial bodies has considerable discretion in the decision-making.

Court studies

Research in the courts has explored the effect of both legal variables (e.g. the nature of the index offence and the defendant's previous criminal record) and extra-legal variables (e.g. the gender and race of the defendant) on the decisions made by the judiciary. Investigations have also examined the impact of variables associated with the decision-makers themselves (e.g. their age, sex and religion).

a) Legal factors   The seriousness of the crime committed by the offender and the offender's previous criminal record have the greatest impact on custody decisions (Flood-Page and Mackie 1998). In the current study, index offence and criminal history were associated with the Tribunals' decisions to discharge. However, when the competing effects of other variables were controlled for, the significance of these two variables disappeared. This was of interest given that the patient's index offence and criminal history are fundamental to the determination of risk and, therefore, to the determination of fitness for discharge. The factors of most significance to the Tribunals were the RMOs' written opinion and the type of hospital in which the patient was being detained.

b) Extra-legal factors   Whilst legal variables refer to factors related to the determination of guilt, 'extra-legal' variables are, according to MacCoun (1990), based on factors logically irrelevant to this determination. The idea that a person's liberty may be deprived on the grounds of factors unrelated to their offending is troubling from a civil rights perspective and contrary to natural justice. Considerable attention has, therefore, been devoted to assessing the effect of extra-legal variables on sentencing decisions. Particular attention has been paid to a defendant's race and gender although investigations have also explored the impact of the defendant's employment status, financial circumstances, social status, marital status and even their physical appearance.

Hood (1992) conducted a large-scale statistical study of sentencing in the Crown Court focusing on racial issues. After controlling for legally relevant variables he found that black offenders had a five to eight per cent higher probability of receiving custodial sentences than white offenders. Asians, in contrast, had a four per cent lower probability. There was, however, 'no evidence of a 'blanket' race or colour discrimination against all ethnic minority defendants, male or female' (Hood 1992: 183).

In general, research exploring racial differences has provided 'little evidence' of racial bias in either the decision to imprison or in the length of imprisonment imposed (Farrington 1996: 256). Moxon (1998: 60), for example, found 'no significant differences in the use of custody for different racial groups sentenced at the Crown Court' whilst Kapardis (1987) found that the race of the offender had no significant effect on the severity of the sentence imposed by magistrates. The issue of race was not explored in the current study as the Tribunal files contained little, and often no, information pertaining to ethnicity. The very absence of this information from the medical reports invites two alternative inferences: either the RMOs considered race to be an irrelevant issue or they were avoiding the issue in the interests of equality. As Tribunal records had no consistent data on race, there is no means of monitoring whether there is fairness or racial bias in decision-making.

Studies investigating gender differences in sentencing have yielded contradictory findings. In the Crown Court, Moxon (1988) found that women were treated more leniently than men. Similarly, in magistrates' courts, Hedderman and Gelsthorpe (1997) identified major differences in the use of non-custodial penalties for men and women, and found that women did not stand an equal chance of imprisonment in all circumstances. Farrington and Morris (1983), in contrast, found no significant gender differences while Daly (1994), who combined qualitative and quantitative methods in a study of American courts, found that gender differences were 'negligible' (p.258).

In the current study female patients were significantly more likely to be discharged than male patients. Further analysis demonstrated, however, that this relationship did not exist independently of the RMO's written opinion, the type of hospital in which the patient was being detained, or the patient's marital status. Of these three variables only marital status was found to be significantly associated with patient gender – male patients were significantly more likely to be single than female patients.

Hedderman and Gelsthorpe (1997) discovered that being married was regarded by magistrates as a sign of stability. Cohabiting was also viewed favourably and was seen as providing a degree of 'social control' (p.48). Single people, in contrast, were viewed as 'more of a risk than others because of the perceived lack of supervision or stability in their lives' (p.48). Perhaps then, the fact that single patients were the least likely to be discharged by Tribunals in the current study reflects the perception of a partner as a controlling and stabilising influence.

In the US, Daly (1987) also found a relationship between marital status and judicial decision-making. Familied men and women, she noted, received more lenient treatment in the criminal courts than non-familied men and women. The factor of crucial importance, however, was 'having dependents' (p.167). Information pertaining to dependents was not readily available from the Tribunal files and this variable was not analysed in the current study. Further analysis could be conducted to explore this relationship in the context of Tribunal hearings.

Research investigating the effect of the defendant's employment status on judicial decision-making indicates that judges and magistrates are reluctant to pass sentences that will result in a defendant losing a job (Ashworth 1995). Crow and Simon (1987) (cited in Ashworth 1995) examined six magistrates' courts and found that employment status had only a small effect on sentencing decisions. Employed offenders, they found, were more likely to be fined whereas unemployed offenders were more likely to be given probation orders and other sentences. Moxon (1988) identified a similar pattern of sentencing in the Crown Court.

Hedderman and Gelsthorpe (1997: 50) discovered that being employed was viewed 'very positively' by magistrates. Employment ensured that offenders were occupied and, therefore, had less time in which to offend. The limited information in the reports submitted to the Tribunals made it impossible to analyse statistically the impact of 'employment status' in the current study. The results of the observational study, however, lend support to Hedderman and Gelsthorpe's findings. Indeed, members were anxious to ensure that discharged patients were kept occupied and in some cases where patients did not have employment, attendance at a day centre was made a condition of discharge.

The effect of an offender's social status and attractiveness on sentencing and custody decisions has been the subject of much less scrutiny than the variables described above. Fitzmaurice and Pease (1986: 11) report, however, that there is some evidence that social class is 'at least associated with sentence severity but the issue is finely balanced'. These authors also suggest that a defendant's attractiveness is associated with more lenient sentencing, except where the attractiveness enabled the offence. Although physical attractiveness was not explored statistically in the current study, the researcher did observe that the physical appearance of patients influenced perceptions of risk. In one case, for example, the lay member commented that the patient was a 'very tall chap'. The judge agreed and pointed out that, 'if [the patient] was wielding a knife I would expect that he could achieve his aim. He has a very long reach.' Similarly, in another case the Tribunal president described the patient as a 'great, big, strapping, murderous brute'.

c) Factors associated with the decision-makers 'Since external variables may not satisfactorily explain disparity, researchers have paid attention to the sentencers themselves as a source of variation, (Ewart and Pennington 1987: 181). Indeed, as long ago as 1919 Everson claimed that, 'Justice is a very personal thing, reflecting the temperament, the personality, the education, the environment and personal traits of +the magistrate' (cited in Kapardis 1987: 194). Similarly, Hogarth (1971) observed, 'One can explain more about sentencing by knowing a few things about the judge than by knowing a great deal about the facts of the case' (cited in Ewart and Pennington 1987: 181).

Moxon (1988) investigated the impact of 'judicial experience' on sentencing decisions in the Crown Court. The results highlighted 'marked differences between circuit judges and recorders in terms of the proportionate use of custody and average sentence length' (p.58). Circuit judges were more likely than the recorders to sentence offenders to unsuspended custody and were less likely to give community service orders. Furthermore, the average length of imprisonment ordered by the judges was approximately double the length imposed by the recorders. Although it was not possible to analyse statistically the impact of judicial experience in the current study it is interesting to note that there was variation in the discharge rates of different presidents.

Fitzmaurice and Pease (1986) reviewed some of the literature exploring sentencer variables and described how the judiciary's social class, political allegiance and internal value systems have been correlated with sentencing decisions. In the current study, it was possible to examine the impact of gender on Tribunal decision-making. Neither the gender of the individual members nor the composition (in terms of gender) of the Tribunal panel had a significant effect upon the decisions made.

According to Baldwin (1976) (cited in Kapardis 1987) a 'raison d'etre' of the magistracy is that the idiosyncrasies and prejudices of individual members can be neutralised and absorbed in the delibera-tions of people from different backgrounds. Peay (1981) points out, however, that the very process of making decisions in groups can introduce factors that are absent when individuals make decisions alone. Issues such as conformity, obedience and majority/minority influence are especially pertinent in the context of group decision-making.

Kapardis (1985: 2) noted that a large proportion of magistrates interviewed were concerned that, 'very often an individual justice, especially if he is a chairman, dominates the discussion in the retiring room and 'imposes' his opinion on others'. In the current study the researcher also observed a tendency for the Tribunal president to dominate the hearings and deliberations. The personality of the lay member seemed to play a significant role in determining their level of involvement in the decision-making. Quiet and unassuming lay members were often excluded from the discussions by judges who directed their attention towards the medical members. The more reserved medical members were also excluded on occasion but the need for the medical input guaranteed them at least some involvement in the process.

Parole board studies

Like magistrates and judges, parole boards have been subject to 'much criticism for alleged arbitrary and capricious decision-making, for disparity in the granting or denial of parole, and for ineffectiveness' (Gottfredson and Gottfredson 1988: p.x). It is interesting to note, therefore, that 'few research efforts have been directed at understanding the parole board decision-making processes' and that prior work in this area is 'sparse and has become dated' (Burns et al. 1999: 17). Nevertheless, there are several pieces of research in this area that merit comparison with the findings of the current study.

Heinz et al. (1976) evaluated the sentencing practices of the Illinois Parole Board. In line with the court studies Heinz et al. found that the nature of the prisoner's index offence and their criminal history were significantly associated with decisions to grant parole. Furthermore, the inmate's participation in educational programmes whilst in prison, record of infractions of the prison's rules, prospects for employment after release and level of intelligence were also influential. The prisoner's gender, however, was not found to affect the Board's decisions and little evidence of racial discrimination was identified.

When the Board members were interviewed a large proportion reported that marital status played a 'relatively insignificant' role in their decision-making (p.10). The data, however, presented a different picture, as the inmate's marital status and the number of dependents both had a significant effect on the Parole Board's decisions. Family commitments and 'stable' living arrangements appeared to be the influential factors. These findings reflect those of both the court studies and the current study.

Heinz et al.'s most striking finding was 'the very strong association between the Parole Board's decision and the official predictions or 'prognoses' about an inmate's future behaviour that were recorded by correctional sociologists within the institutions' (p.18). This relationship, the researchers concluded, highlighted the power of institutional officials to determine the length of time offenders spent in prison. This is also true of Tribunal decision-making, as the views of the RMOs had the strongest influence on the Tribunals' decisions in the current study. Such endorsement of the RMOs' recommendations 'casts considerable doubt on the assumption that Tribunals fulfil a truly adjudicatory role' (Richardson 1993: 297).

In a more recent investigation of decisions made by parole boards, Feder (1994) discovered that psychiatric hospitalisation during incarceration, prior imprisonment, violence in the current offence, conviction for a drug offence, educational attainment, area of conviction and prison behaviour were all significant in explaining the decision to grant or deny parole. The factor with the strongest impact on the decision to give parole, however, was the incidence of psychiatric hospitalisation during incarceration. Prisoners without this history were 30 times more likely to be granted parole. Feder (1994) points out that this relationship does not necessarily reflect concern for reoffending but might, instead, reflect the lack of programmes available for the mentally disordered offender in the community.

In the current study patients without a history of previous psychiatric inpatient treatment were no more likely to be discharged than patients with such a history. They were, however, significantly more likely to have their cases adjourned. As adjournments are usually motivated by a need for further information, the greater proportion of adjournments among patients with no previous recorded inpatient treatment may suggest that their cases were more difficult to review because of the absence of a long comparative history.

In keeping with previous research on parole boards, Burns et al. (1999) found that the factors of most importance to board members were the inmate's prior criminal record and the nature and circumstances of the index offence. The inmate's institutional adjustment, attitude towards the victim, psychological health, insight into the causes of their criminal conduct, and the adequacy of the parole were equally influential. To a lesser extent the inmate's support in the community and their attitude towards authority were also important factors considered by the parole board.

It is of note that an inmate's insight into their offending and attitude towards their victim were important to board members in Burns et al.'s study. These factors were also of importance to the Tribunals observed in the current study. Indeed, a patient's failure to appreciate the wrong-fulness of their offending behaviour and the absence of remorse for that behaviour were viewed by members as a sign of 'danger'. In the words of the medical member in one case, 'The problem with this patient is that he does not express any remorse … He has a lack of understanding and sympathy, which is very dangerous.' A patient's appreciation of, or insight into, their own mental state and the need for treatment were also important considerations in the decisions made by Tribunals.

Depriving a person of their liberty on the grounds of 'lack of remorse' or 'absence of insight' is difficult to justify. Insight and remorse are subjective concepts that are not easily quantifiable. How can one tell if remorse is sincere or if insight is real? It is notable that Tribunals referred to the concept of insight in 326 (19 per cent) of the reasons recorded in the retrospective file study. In 272 of these cases 'lack of insight' was referred to as a reason for not discharging.

Discretionary Life Panels (DLPs)

Padfield and Liebling's (2000) research on DLPs shares some interesting findings with the current study. Of particular note is the fact that the DLPs felt constrained by their inability to transfer prisoners to different security categorisations. The Tribunals felt similarly constrained by their inability to transfer patients to lower security establishments.

A further similarity concerns the style of risk assessment employed. Padfield and Liebling report that the DLPs' style of risk assessment was 'more clinical than actuarial, and seemed cautious'. They go on to explain that DLPs 'needed to weigh both seriousness and certainty of risk, yet seemed to avoid discussing levels of risk'. Tribunal assessments of risk were similarly cautious and lacked any formal structure. In some observed cases the level of risk presented by patients was not even discussed. As Padfield and Liebling (2000) recommend, more training and procedural guidance is needed for those involved in making decisions that require an assessment of risk.

Conclusions and proposals for reform

The results of this research raise questions about the quality of Mental Health Review Tribunal decision-making in restricted cases and suggest that Tribunals are failing in their fundamental duty to safeguard some patients from unjustified detention in hospital. This failure, however, is not solely a response to the current climate of heightened concern for public safety. The majority of problems were observed in the decision-making *process*, but problems were also noted with the Tribunals' powers, the rules governing the Tribunal process, and the evidence upon which their decisions were to be based.

Although many doubtful practices were evident, the broad approach to decision-making was generally highly conscientious. Tribunal panels could spend hours ensuring that reasons were accurately and appropriately phrased. Medical members were heard persuading patients to try new courses of treatment in an effort to help them make progress. Annoyance and frustration were observed because of Tribunals' inability to transfer patients out of maximum security and efforts were regularly made to help improve the patient's situation. It was notable that the Tribunal members experienced real pleasure when granting discharges. Successful patients were usually invited back to the hearing room to be told the good news in person and to be congratulated on their success. In cases where no discharge was authorised the Tribunals endeavoured to emphasise progress that had been made rather than highlighting problems and failures. The members were anxious not to damage a patient's future chances of discharge or transfer.

In September 1998 the government appointed an Expert Committee to conduct a review of the Mental Health Act 1983. The Committee, chaired by Professor Genevra Richardson, was commissioned to inquire into 'how much mental health legislation should be shaped to reflect contemporary patterns of care within a framework which balances the need to protect the rights of individual patients and the need to ensure public safety' (Department of Health 1999a). In response to the Expert Committee's report a Green Paper was issued outlining the government's initial proposals for reform of the Mental Health Act (Department of Health 1999b). Following a consultation period the government published a White Paper in December 2000 (Department of Health 2000) These proposals have important and far-reaching implications, particularly for the Mental Health Review Tribunal system.

One of the main recommendations is to establish a new Tribunal system. This would extend the Tribunals' function to include the task of confirming an initial compulsory treatment order[20] and for renewing that order at regular intervals.[21] Patients would also be entitled to apply to the new Tribunals for a review of their case once during the currency of each order. The new system would, therefore, require Tribunals to review the need for a compulsory order that in some cases they themselves had confirmed.

As noted above, the White Paper does not remedy the lack of Tribunal powers to effect hospital transfers in restricted cases. It also appears possible that the influence of Tribunals will be further restricted by limitations in their ability to order deferred conditional discharges. Whilst a Tribunal would be able to order discharge from hospital that is conditional on co-operation with a community care plan, such an order could only be made if the necessary forms of care are available.

In addition to the change in the Tribunals' fundamental role, proposals are also made for an alteration in the composition of the Tribunal panel. The medical member's role as both an expert adviser and a decision-maker is viewed as incompatible and contrary to natural justice. Recommendations have therefore been made to separate these roles, so that the patient is assessed by a medical member of an independently appointed expert panel. The White Paper does not make clear, however, whether the patient would have access to this assessment. The Tribunal would have a clinical member (not necessarily medical). The loss of medical members from the Tribunal panels may have serious consequences for the quality of Tribunal decision-making. The observational research demonstrated that the medical members were crucial in the deliberations of Tribunals: they guided the members through the medical evidence, they explained key concepts and terms, and helped in the formulation of reasons that accurately described patients' conditions. It is likely, therefore, that the absence of a medical member would result in even greater reliance on the views of the patient's consultant or clinical supervisor, thereby compromising the 'independence' of the Tribunal system still further.

Notes

1 Eleven per cent of restricted patients were discharged in 1999 (Home Office 2000).
2 See Richardson (1993), and Eastman and Peay (1999).
3 See Gutheil et al. (1991), and Gutheil and Appelbaum (2000).
4 See Saad and Sashidharan (1992), O'Dwyer and Neville (1991), and Spencer (1989).
5 The Royal Commission on the law relating to mental illness and mental deficiency (1957–1959).
6 See X v United Kingdom (1982) 4 EHRR 88.
7 See Department of Health (1999a; 1999b; 2000).
8 See Rule 6 of the Mental Health Review Tribunal Rules 1983.
9 See Greenland (1970), and Peay (1989).
10 Patients who no longer suffer from a mental disorder of a nature or degree warranting detention in hospital for treatment are entitled to be discharged even if they are considered to be 'dangerous'.
11 See R v (1) Mental Health Review Tribunal, North & East London Region (2) Secretary of State for Health, ex parte H [2001] 3 WLR 512.
12 To bring the law into line with this ruling, the Mental Health Act 1983 (Remedial) Order 2001 was passed. This order amends the discharge criteria stipulated in ss. 72 and 73 of the Mental Health Act 1983. Under the revised legislation, patients are no longer required to prove a negative.
13 Although Tribunals have no statutory power to make recommendations in restricted cases, they consistently make them nevertheless.
14 Under s.72(1)(b)(i) Tribunals are obliged to discharge patients who are no longer suffering from a mental disorder of a nature or degree warranting detention in hospital for treatment, even if they remain 'dangerous'.
15 Patients are entitled to legal representation at hearings. Some legal representatives will seek an independent psychiatric opinion on behalf of the patient. The independent psychiatrists will provide the representative

with a written report which may or may not be submitted as evidence. The legal representative can request that the IP attend the hearing to provide oral evidence to support the patient's case.

16 See Department of Health (2000).

17 Under Rule 12 of the Mental Health Review Tribunal Rules, the Home Secretary must receive a copy of every document the Tribunal receives which is relevant to the application.

18 See R v Oxford Regional Mental Health Tribunal, ex parte Mackman (Queen's Bench Division, 22 May 1986) The Times Law Report, 2 June 1986.

19 The Expert Committee, appointed to review the Mental Health Act 1983, proposed that this report should explain in detail why the Home Secretary is opposed to discharge and that it be supplemented by oral evidence, where necessary (Department of Health 1999a).

20 Offender patients would be subject to compulsory care and treatment on the decision of the court rather than the new Tribunal.

21 The new Tribunals would be required to renew orders after six months, after a second six months and thereafter annually.

References

Ashworth, A. (1995) *Sentencing and Criminal Justice* (2nd edn). London: Butterworths.

Burns, R. et al. (1999) 'Perspectives on parole: the board members' viewpoint', *Federal Probation*, 63 (1), 16–21.

Daly, K. (1987) 'Discrimination in the criminal courts: family, gender and the problem of equal treatment', *Social Forces*, 66 (1), 152–175.

Daly, K. (1994) *Gender, Crime and Punishment*. London: Yale University Press.

Department of Health (1999a) *Report of the Expert Committee: Review of the Mental Health Act 1983*. London: Department of Health.

Department of Health (1999b) *Reform of the Mental Health Act 1983: Proposals for Consultation*, Cmnd. 4480. London: Stationery Office.

Department of Health (2000) *Reforming the Mental Health Act*. Cm 5016-I & II. London: Stationery Office.

Eastman, N. (1994) 'Mental health law: civil liberties and the principle of reciprocity', *British Medical Journal*, 308, 43–45.

Eastman, N. and Peay, J. (1999) *Law Without Enforcement: Integrating Mental Health and Justice*. Oxford: Hart.

Ewart, B. and Pennington, D. (1987) 'An attributional approach to explaining sentencing disparity' in D.C. Pennington and S. Lloyd-Bostock, (eds.) *The Psychology of Sentencing: Approaches to Consistency and Disparity*, Oxford: Centre for Socio-legal Studies.

Farrington, D. (1996) 'Quantitative criminology in the United Kingdom in the 1990s: a brief overview', *Journal of Quantitative Criminology*, 12 (3), 249–263.

Farrington, D. and Morris, A. (1983) 'Sex, sentencing and reconviction', *British*

Journal of Criminology, 23, 229–248.

Feder, L. (1994) 'Psychiatric hospitalization history and parole decisions', *Law and Human Behavior*, 18 (4), 395–410.

Fennell, P. (1977) 'Mental Health Review Tribunals: A question of imbalance', *British Journal of Law and Society*, 2, 186–219.

Fitzmaurice, C. and Pease, K. (1986) *The Psychology of Judicial Sentencing*. Manchester: Manchester University Press.

Flood-Page, C. and Mackie, A. (1998) *Sentencing Practice: an Examination of Decisions in Magistrates' Courts and the Crown Courts in the mid-1990s*, Home Office Research Study 180. London: HMSO.

Gottfredson, M. and Gottfredson, D. (1988) *Decision Making in Criminal Justice: Toward the Rational Exercise of Discretion* (2nd edn). London: Plenum.

Greenland, C. (1970) *Mental Illness and Civil Liberty*, Occasional Papers on Social Administration No. 38. London: G. Bell & Sons.

Grounds, A. (1989) 'A new appraisal of Mental Health Review Tribunals', *Psychiatric Bulletin*, 13, 299–300.

Gutheil, T. and Appelbaum, P.S. (2000) *Clinical Handbook of Psychiatry and the Law* (3rd edn). Philadelphia: Lippincott, Williams and Wilkins.

Gutheil, T. et al. (1991) *Decision Making in Psychiatry and the Law*. Baltimore: Williams and Wilkins.

Hedderman, C. and Gelsthorpe, L. (1997) *Understanding the Sentencing of Women*, Home Office Research Study 170. London: HMSO.

Heinz, A. et al. (1976) 'Sentencing by parole board: an evaluation', *The Journal of Criminal Law and Criminology*, 67 (1), 1–31.

Hepworth, D. (1983) 'The decision process of the Mental Health Review Tribunal – 2. Analysis of research findings', *Medicine, Science and the Law*, 23 (3), 171–182.

Hoggett, B. (1996) *Mental Health Law*. London: Sweet & Maxwell.

Home Office (2000) *Statistics of mentally disordered offenders in England and Wales 1999*, Home Office Statistical Bulletin 21/00. London: GSS.

Hood, R. (1992) *Race and Sentencing*. Oxford: Oxford University Press.

Jones, R. (ed.) (1996) *Mental Health Act Manual*, London: Sweet and Maxwell.

Kapardis, A. (1985) *Sentencing by English Magistrates as a Human Process*. Cyprus: Asselia Publishers.

Kapardis, A. (1987) 'Sentencing by English Magistrates as a human process' in D. Pennington and S. Lloyd-Bostock (eds.) *The Psychology of Sentencing: Approaches to Consistency and Disparity*. Oxford: Centre for Socio-legal Studies, 193–203.

MacCoun (1990) 'The emergence of extralegal bias during jury deliberations', *Criminal Justice and Behavior*, 17 (3), 303–314.

Mental Health Review Tribunal Rules, S.I. 1983 No. 942 as amended by S.I. 1996 No. 314 as amended by S.I. 1998 No. 1189.

Moxon, D. (1988) *Sentencing Practice in the Crown Court*, Home Office Research Study 103, London: HMSO.

O'Dwyer, J. and Neville, P. (1991) 'Appeals against Section 2 of the Mental Health Act 1983', *Psychiatric Bulletin*, 15, 225–226.

Padfield, N. and Liebling, A. (2000) *An Exploration of Decision-Making at Discretionary Lifer Panels*. London: Home Office.

Peay, J. (1981) 'Mental Health Review Tribunals: just or efficacious safeguards?' *Law and Human Behavior*, 5 (2), 161–186.

Peay, J. (1989) *Tribunals on Trial*. Oxford: Oxford University Press.

Percy Report (1957) *Royal Commission on the Law Relating to Mental Illness and Mental Deficiency 1954–57: Report and Minutes of Evidence*, Cmnd. 169. London: HMSO.

Richardson, G. (1993) *Law, Process and Custody: Prisoners and Patients*. London: Weidenfeld & Nicolson.

Richardson, G. and Thorold, O. (1999) 'Law as a rights protector: assessing the Mental Health Act 1983' in N. Eastman, and J. Peay, (eds.) *Law Without Enforcement: Integrating Mental Health and Justice*, Oxford: Hart.

Saad, K. and Sashidharan, S. (1992) 'Mental Health Review Tribunals', *Psychiatric Bulletin*, 16, 470–472.

Spencer, D. (1989) 'A medical member's analysis of 50 patients at the Mental Health Review Tribunal', *Psychiatric Bulletin*, 13, 249–250.

Weber, L. and Gelsthorpe, L. (2000) *Deciding to Detain: How Discretion to Detain Asylum Seekers is Exercised at Ports of Entry*. Cambridge: University of Cambridge, Institute of Criminology.

Wood, J. (1993) 'Reform of the Mental Health Act 1983: an effective Tribunal system', *British Journal of Psychiatry*, 162 (1), 14–22.

Chapter 8

Decisions to detain asylum seekers – routine, duty or individual choice?

Leanne Weber

Introduction

The detention of asylum seekers in the United Kingdom takes place in a context of wide and largely unrestrained discretion. The majority of asylum applicants are granted temporary admission into the UK while their claims for refugee status are being considered. However, some are detained in prisons or detention centres from the time of their arrival. The lack of effective external review and the frequent failure by the Immigration Service to disclose the specific reasons for individual decisions have reinforced the view of human rights groups that detention practices are arbitrary (Amnesty International 1995; 1996). This chapter draws on interview-based research conducted with Loraine Gelsthorpe (Weber and Gelsthorpe 2000), which provides the first systematic account of how 'immigration officers'[1] at ports make these discretionary decisions. The main aim of the discussion is to explain the wide variation between immigration officers in their reported use of detention, with reference to the work of Herbert Kelman and Lee Hamilton on 'crimes of obedience' (Kelman and Hamilton 1989).

The decision-making context at ports

Decisions to detain asylum seekers are made in the course of day-to-day operations at busy ports – or, 'on the hoof', as one immigration officer described it. Immigration officers have the power to refuse entry to would-be tourists, students or business visitors either for technical reasons (e.g. insufficient funds or lack of an appropriate visa) or on 'credibility' grounds (e.g. where the officer believes an individual is likely to breach the terms of entry by working or overstaying their leave). In response to rapidly growing numbers of arrivals, changes in policy intended to improve efficiency at ports have altered what many immigration officers perceive to be their core function. The free movement of EU passport holders into the UK and the increasing emphasis on pre-entry clearance (i.e. reliance on visas issued at the point of embarkation) are considered by many officers to have eroded their decision-making responsibilities and weakened border controls.

Viewed from this perspective, asylum seekers fit uneasily into an already threatened paradigm of immigration control. Their eligibility to enter is not assessed on the spot by immigration officers applying the standard Immigration Rules. Instead, initial decisions about their entitlement to stay are made by Home Office officials based in Croydon exercising discretionary powers on behalf of the Home Secretary.[2] This approach, which deals with asylum seekers as exceptions operating outside the normal constraints of immigration law, means that individuals who are not readily recognised by immigration officers to be genuine refugees may be seen to be abusing asylum procedures in order to evade normal controls.

Once an asylum application is made, an immigration officer's role switches from decision-maker to information-gatherer. This is a time-consuming exercise which many officers, accustomed to seeing a short-term result in terms of their entry decisions, find frustrating or even demeaning, since it does not require the exercise of the statutory powers which denote their status. On the other hand, immigration officers retain responsibility for formally granting leave to remain to successful applicants and removing from the country those whose applications ultimately fail. This fragmented approach has considerable implications for the one significant area of decision-making which remains in the hands of immigration officers at ports – the decision about whether to detain or grant temporary admission on arrival.

Immigration officers were given powers of detention under the Immigration Act in 1971, to enable them to question arriving passengers about their eligibility to enter, and to effect the removal of those who are refused entry.[3] The power to detain for removal is triggered by a refusal decision, although temporary admission may be granted for a short period while removal is arranged. Base-grade immigration officers (IOs) hold the power in law to detain, but chief immigration officers (CIOs) are required to authorise detention as a matter of policy.[4] Decisions to detain in non-asylum cases are therefore part of a cycle of decision-making which is entirely within the control of immigration officers at ports. Any resulting detentions generally last no longer than a few hours, pending removal on the earliest available flight, train departure or sailing.

However, the prolonged procedures for assessing asylum applications have the effect of breaking this 'refuse-detain-remove cycle', creating a speculative and contradictory decision-making environment at ports. For example, in recent years immigration officers have been encouraged to distance themselves from the determination process, and asylum interview forms no longer invite their subjective comments on the applicant's credibility. At the same time, they are required under official guidelines to consider an individual's 'removability' when deciding whether to detain or grant temporary admission.[5] Since asylum applicants are never removable at the time of arrival, this creates an incentive to second-guess the outcome of the determination process, and the likely time span involved, in order to identify *potentially* removable individuals. This exercise in second-guessing has resulted in long periods of detention for many asylum seekers – including some who have ultimately obtained refugee status after many months in detention.

The experience of lengthy detentions has created some pressure against detaining asylum seekers on arrival, both on the pragmatic grounds that accommodation is costly and scarce, and because of the public criticism which prolonged detention has attracted. Because of this, there has been a reversal in practice over time, so that a presumption of temporary admission now applies for most asylum seekers, and their detention is less likely overall than for refused visitors. On the other hand, as the responsibility for removing failed applicants remains with immigration officers at ports, this creates a strong incentive to maintain control over the whereabouts of asylum seekers while their claims are being assessed.

Research findings on the decision-making process

The question which remains is why certain asylum applicants continue to be singled out for detention. Official detention guidelines are permissive in character and, in deference to the autonomy of individual ports, are issued on the understanding that they are to be interpreted in the light of 'operational priorities'. The guidelines have no statutory basis and apply both to refused visitors and to asylum seekers, in a wide variety of decision-making contexts at ports and after entry.[6] In common with many other studies on discretion, our research found that organisational actors, particularly IOs, tend to rely more on accepted local practice than on formal guidelines when deciding whether to grant temporary admission or detain.[7] From their accounts of detention practices, it was possible to identify that judgments were made along two primary dimensions – one related to the perceived moral character of the applicant and the other based on practical and procedural considerations, a finding which is also in broad agreement with the socio-legal literature.[8]

Judgments about whether an asylum seeker is likely to abscond if granted temporary admission (i.e. pose an 'immigration risk') are related to perceptions of the applicant's character, and are represented in Figure 1 on the 'personal dimension'. These judgments are highly subjective, and there was considerable variability in what was seen to indicate a 'reasonable risk' of absconding. Poor immigration history, presentation of false documents or arrival without documents, lack of a suitable sponsor, and making a delayed asylum claim after entry as an ordinary visitor has been refused (which are all mentioned in detention guidelines) were considered the most relevant indicators of unreliability. Practical assessments about removability (represented along the

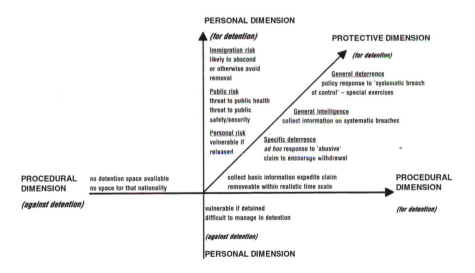

Adapted from (Weber and Gelsthorpe 2000)

Figure 1 *Primary dimensions of the decision-making process*

'procedural dimension' in the model) depend on an immigration officer's detailed knowledge of the complex procedures applying to different categories of applicant, and how they relate to the facts of a particular case. Applicants whose asylum claims are perceived as 'manifestly unfounded' or who are potentially returnable to another European country under the Dublin Convention were particularly likely to be considered 'candidates for detention' on these procedural grounds.

The model also includes factors which may weigh against detention on these primary dimensions. Long-term detention that is considered justified for other reasons may be avoided if the applicant is believed to be vulnerable on the basis of age, gender or physical or mental health. However, alternative secure accommodation (for example in a prison hospital) may be sought where detention is still considered necessary. Prison Service accommodation may also be deliberately sought for individuals who are judged to be too disruptive or dangerous for Immigration Service detention facilities. It may also prove impossible to implement a detention decision for purely practical reasons if detention space is unavailable on the day, or if the detention co-ordinator considers it inadvisable to detain further applicants of a particular nationality, in the interests of the smooth running of detention centres.[9]

A third dimension of decision-making was also apparent, which has emerged from the perception that large numbers of asylum applications are unsubstantiated. The judgment about whether an application is 'abusive' and threatens to 'undermine the integrity of the control' has been represented in the model by the 'protective dimension'.[10] Detention along this dimension is essentially deterrent in character and can follow from policy decisions to detain whole categories of applicant through 'special exercises' directed at particular nationalities, or can be more *ad hoc* and intended to encourage the withdrawal of a particular claim. The use of detention as a general deterrent is intelligence-driven and takes the decision to detain out of the control of individual officers at ports, whereas detention aimed at specific deterrence is highly discretionary.[11]

Detention along this dimension is outside the formal detention guidelines and goes beyond the administrative purpose for detention set out in legislation. The 'public risk' and 'personal risk' elements of the 'personal dimension' in the model are also apparently 'extra-legal', but shortage of space prevents their discussion here. Suffice to say that certain uses of detention in relation to asylum seekers are highly controversial (including long detentions which nevertheless fall within the guidelines), and confirm the perception that the discretion to detain is extremely wide.[12]

Importantly for this discussion, individual immigration officers reported manifestly different approaches to detention decisions. Some tried to avoid long detentions by considering removability from the outset, while others said they leave estimates of the likely length of detention for subsequent reviews. Some thought that risks to the public or the applicant were relevant, while others considered only 'immigration risk'. A minority did not believe that risk of absconding justified detention, which they supported only on substantial public safety grounds, or once an applicant was able to be removed. And some officers were opposed to detaining to 'maintain the integrity of the control', either on principle or because they thought detention was ineffective at deterring asylum applications in the long term. There were also considerable differences in the way individuals interpreted specific factors weighing for and against detention. For example, some immigration officers were prepared to take into account the reasons that may have led asylum seekers to behave deceptively, while others adopted a 'strict liability' approach.

This observed variability suggests the presence of distinct decision-making styles, where both organisational rules and incentives, and individual values seem to play a role. The remainder of this chapter seeks to provide a systematic account of these differences, drawing on a typology developed by social psychologists Herbert Kelman and Lee Hamilton (Kelman and Hamilton 1989). It is proposed that different orientations to the various sources of authority within the Immigration Service are influential in shaping how immigration officers exercise their discretion to detain. Before outlining these orientations, some discussion is needed of Kelman and Hamilton's ideas and of the relative contributions of individual and systemic factors in what might be termed the 'routine production of harm'.

Individuals, bureaucracies and the routine production of harm

Modern societies rely on bureaucracies to carry out a wide range of administrative functions, most of them either positive or benign in their effects. However, since the Holocaust, a body of critical literature has emerged which seeks to explain the role of bureaucracies in the perpetration of large-scale, humanly-created harm.[13] These analyses have raised awareness of the tendency of bureaucracies to elevate efficiency over ethical concerns, and to diffuse individual responsibility:

> ... one can do something and continue doing it without having to take personal responsibility for it. It is as if one were acting while being personally absent. One acts physically, without acting morally or politically. The generalized other – the system – acts within and through oneself.
>
> (Beck 1992: 33)

Socio-legal studies of decision-making within large organisations typically concentrate on the influence of routine practices which develop in response to large, repetitive workloads.[14] However, analyses which concentrate exclusively on organisational processes risk losing sight of the role of individual agency.[15] Organisational actors may indeed be 'personally absent' from the decision-making process where their actions are determined by unreflective, routine practice, and this moral disengagement can have negative consequences where their decisions affect the well-being of others in ways which are not apparent to them. But decision-makers may also behave within a system in a way which actively expresses accepted occupational norms, so that detrimental outcomes for some individuals are rationalised and justified as necessary in order to carry out one's duty.[16]

Kelman and Hamilton set out to explain differences between individuals in their propensity to take part in, or approve of, large-scale 'crimes of obedience'. The destructive events they studied ranged from the My Lai massacre, to the Watergate scandal, to the crash of the *Challenger* space shuttle. While these examples appear very different on the surface, closer analysis reveals many similarities in the role played by systemic factors, and the authors argue that the key issue that differentiates them is merely 'the explicitness with which the goal involves or necessitates harm to a victim' (Kelman and Hamilton 1989: 313).

The authors contend that individuals vary in their susceptibility to the obedience-inducing effects of 'authorisation' (which absolves individuals from making personal moral choices), 'routinisation' (which dissociates acts from their consequences and meanings) and 'neutralisation' and 'dehumanisation' (whereby the humanity of those who are the targets of harm comes to be overlooked or explicitly denied). In the face of illegitimate uses of authority, organisational actors may experience a conflict between the (organisational) duty to obey and the (moral) duty not to obey. The authors argue that a high threshold for disobedience generally applies where perceptions about the overall legitimacy of the system result in authorities being given the benefit of the doubt. But, against this background of obedience, some individuals seem able to resist instructions which they judge to be illegitimate or harmful.[17]

Kelman and Hamilton derived three scales from population survey data that reflected different 'socio-political orientations' towards authority, which they labelled 'rule-orientation', 'role-orientation' and 'value-orientation'. Individuals often displayed combinations of each, but it was possible to identify people who were high on one scale only (particularly on the value scale), from whom 'ideal types' were constructed. Rule and role orientations were found to be quite closely associated in practice, and seemed to characterise individuals who might be described, respectively, as conventional or authoritarian. Value-orientated individuals were distinguishable largely by their disagreement with the attitudes and opinions expressed by the others.

Rule-orientated individuals were found to be only loosely socialised into prevailing norms, and tended to obey rules (whether formal or informal) in order to stay out of trouble. An organisational actor adopting a rule-orientated approach to authority might be expected to comply passively with directions, and to act from a position of indifference or perceived powerlessness. As they are emotionally disengaged, moral principles are less relevant in guiding their actions than pragmatic considerations, and the rule-orientated individual would tend to follow the lead of superiors and colleagues.

Role-orientated individuals were distinguished by a strong identification with organisational or societal norms. They were likely to obey in order to do their duty, and out of a sense of obligation and emotional attachment to their role. In an organisational setting, they might be expected to follow instructions more reliably and enthusiastically than their more detached colleagues, since 'defending the system becomes tantamount to defending their total way of life'. Compared with value-orientated individuals, they might be seen to act, not as personal agents, but as extensions of authority, and to feel at ease as agents of social control.

Value-orientation was characterised by a questioning attitude toward authority and a tendency to focus on the meaning and consequences of actions. Value-orientated individuals operating within large organisations might be expected to retain a sense of individual responsibility and personal agency, and to resist policies which are manifestly at odds with their own values. Kelman and Hamilton posited that these individuals have the 'moral, social and cognitive resources' to position themselves close to authority, while managing to escape 'entrapment in its mystique and its perspective'.

They conclude that both rule and role orientations create a propensity to obey the illegitimate demands of authority: in the first case due to mere compliance and, in the second, because of active identification with the authoritative perspective. In contrast, they argue that the support of value-driven individuals for the policies of the organisations in which they work can only ever be conditional, depending on the degree of congruence between organisational objectives and the individual's deeply internalised beliefs.

Roles, rules and values amongst immigration officers

In order to apply Kelman and Hamilton's concepts, the detention of asylum seekers must be likened to the illegitimate or harmful exercise of power. The earlier discussion identified some specific uses of Immigration Act detention which were of questionable legality, notably detention aimed at deterring applications perceived to be abusive. It can also be argued that the administrative powers created by the Immigration Act were never intended by legislators to authorise the indeterminate detention of individuals who were not in a position to be removed, which raises more general questions about the legitimacy of detaining before applications for refugee status have even been considered.

In addition, those involved in representing or visiting detained asylum seekers are unanimous in their recognition of the harm which results. The debilitating effects of detention on the mental health of asylum seekers have been well documented (Pourgirides, Sashidharan and Bracken 1996), as has the detention of minors (Amnesty International 1999) and of torture victims (Medical Foundation 1994). A former Chief Inspector of Prisons noted the 'settled misery' of detainees who had little idea why they had been singled out for detention, when their detention would end, and whether or not they would be returned to their country of origin (HMIP 1995).

It would therefore seem reasonable to conclude that Kelman and Hamilton's analysis of obedience to authority is an appropriate method for examining differences between immigration officers in their approaches to detention decisions. A re-examination of interview records revealed that role, rule and value orientated individuals were readily apparent amongst immigration officers, but that the three orientations did not appear to operate as mutually exclusive categories.[18] A more complex explanatory model was therefore developed, which treats role and rule orientation as a basic distinction, with layers of value orientation conceptually 'overlaid' on this foundation. Shortage of space precludes a full discussion of the research evidence which supports this modified typology, but the main characteristics of each 'ideal type' have been summarised in Figure 2.[19]

Since a certain amount of voluntary choice is involved in becoming, and remaining, an immigration officer, it is not surprising that the individuals interviewed all showed some degree of role and/or rule orientation. Many officers described their detention practices without any reference to external values, therefore attracting the label of being either a role-orientated 'border guard' (with a focus on controlling entry, and a primary interest in making judgments about the moral character of asylum seekers) or a rule-orientated 'civil servant' (with an emphasis on administering rules and procedures and making efficient use of resources). Broadly speaking, these orientations can be aligned with the two fundamental dimensions of decision-making depicted in Figure 1.

Fundamental orientation to *internal* values i.e. occupational norms and formal rules

Border guards
Authority derives from immigration officer role.
Identify emotionally with duty to control entry to UK and respond to undermining of controls as personal affront.
Outcome orientated - prepared to interpret vaguely defined rules or create alternative, informal rules as means to an end.
Emphasis on Personal (and Protective) Dimensions (Fig 1).
Actively seek detention to maintain control and respond to 'abuse'.

Civil servants
Authority derives from immigration law and policy.
Emotionally detached, have life outside the job.
Focus on efficient use of resources and passive implementation of government policy.
Process orientated - rules and procedures as ends in themselves. Emphasis on Procedural Dimension (Fig 1).
Use detention unreflectively or seek to use it efficiently.

Awareness of *external* values i.e. human consequences and wider context
↓   ↓

Humanitarians
Show personal/emotional empathy towards (most) asylum seekers, particularly if perceived as vulnerable or morally blameless.
Tend to personalise, not analyse, their experience.
Conscientious towards their work, so that tension between sense of duty and moral unease over detention creates confusion.
Unlikely seek detention personally but maintain faith in propriety of colleagues and overall legitimacy and necessity of system.

Professionals
Show situational/cognitive empathy towards asylum seekers and appreciate context and power differentials.
Understand constraints on applicants' actions arising from personal circumstances and policy regimes.
Analytical and able to consider multiple perspectives.
Exhibit balance and care in own decision-making, but not overly critical of system. Seek to use detention fairly.

+   +
Personal values *mobilised* due to perceived illegitimacy of some official practices

↓

Individualists
Some humanitarian characteristics, but more analytical and critical.
Tend to articulate views in terms of personal politics rather than morality.
Highly individualistic and perceive clear incompatibility between some personal values and organisational goals and practices.
Prepared to dissent openly from prevailing detention practices and possibly to seek to influence the decisions of others.
Limit detention to those immediately removable or demonstrably dangerous.

Figure 2   *Orientations towards authority amongst immigration officers*

But some immigration officers expressed values which supplement and modify these basic orientations. As shown in Figure 2, value orientation may manifest as a 'humanitarian' outlook when overlaid onto a role-orientated approach, and as 'professionalism' when associated with a more rule-orientated disposition. Humanitarians seem to share with border guards a tendency for emotional engagement and a focus on human behaviour, while professionals and civil servants both exhibit a more detached, procedurally orientated approach. What unites humanitarians and professionals as value-driven individuals is that both are influenced by wider considerations which help them to avoid total immersion in occupational objectives (of the kind demonstrated by border guards) or unreflective adherence to routine practices (as exhibited by civil servants).

A further distinction is needed between these two ideal types and a third category of value-driven immigration officer labelled here as 'individualists'. These officers were easily identified in interviews by their readiness to express open dissent from occupational practices which were at odds with their personal values. Elements of both humanitarianism and professionalism were usually apparent, but individualists tended to express their views in analytical, rather than moralistic, terms – at times articulating what amounted to a well developed and consistent 'personal politics'.[20] Recalling Kelman and Hamilton's words, humanitarians could be said to have the 'moral resources' and professionals the 'cognitive resources' to avoid entrapment in the organisational perspective, but only individualists displayed the 'social resources' needed to actively transgress accepted norms. In effect, individualists adopt personal policies which seek to avoid the punitive or unreflective uses of detention which are most readily attributable to border guards and civil servants.

Although many immigration officers displayed combinations of characteristics, including combinations which cross the fundamental role/rule distinction, some individuals were so distinctive in their orientation that it is possible to include them here as case studies, in order to illustrate each of the ideal types.

Immigration officer case studies

CIO Number 60: Border guard

This CIO has worked in the Immigration Service for more than 30 years. He greatly values practical experience and considers it important to have a thorough knowledge of the rules, while also being aware of 'what shortcuts you can take'. He describes his discretion to detain as 'limited in theory' but 'open to interpretation'. This CIO is a hands-on operator, appearing to identify with the IOs under his supervision. He claims to be 'one for having a happy office' and, unusually for his grade, says he often helps out in dealing with passengers. He repeats frequently that IOs are 'good at their job' but bemoans the fact that younger officers are spending so much time dealing with asylum seekers that they are not learning the 'real bread and butter work'.

> I must say this dark cloud of asylum seekers is not doing their morale much good … They know when people are lying and they're quite able to show it. But they don't get the chance with asylum seekers who just spin out the old story and, the IO having done his eight hours on an asylum case – it's off to the Home Office and that's the end of it and, as they see it, it's into a pit.

He says he is 'dispirited' by the high level of absconding from temporary admission (TA) and says he 'can't see any way of getting rid of people who should be removed'. He deplores any actions by asylum seekers which are designed to frustrate removal, and jokes that he may go as far as dragging 'likely looking customers' off the plane or confronting them on the way into the 'gent's toilet' in order to stop them disposing of their documents. He feels that his experience has given him the ability and authority to make predictions about the outcome of asylum claims, and is confident that his colleagues feel the same way.

> If this person to my mind is of a category who will not win his appeal – but officially I'm not allowed to say that because I don't make that decision – but I've been around so long that I know what sort of people will get asylum and which won't. If it's a person who we think, or I think, will get refused asylum and lose his appeal and I think that the incentive for that man to do a runner, that he can't be relied upon to be given TA, that would be one of – in fact the main reason for giving detention.

In fact, he asserts that immigration officers feel 'that the people who are making the decisions are perhaps not as experienced as we are' and rejects outright the possibility that the summary judgments of his colleagues may be fallible: 'God forbid that we hold someone up for all those months and they turn out to be genuine refugees – no it doesn't happen'.

IO Number 20: Civil servant

This IO has worked in the Immigration Service since she graduated from university around 10 years ago. She describes her work almost exclusively in terms of the procedures involved, and distances herself from judgments about asylum and its effect on immigration control.

> Basically it's part of our job, whether we like it or not, to deal with asylum seekers, so therefore I try and not lump them all in as one category. The basic thing is logic. You have paperwork you have to complete. You have computer screens you have to complete. You just basically go through it. Someone arrives, they ask for asylum, you pick up the pink file and off you go … if you let the fact that a lot of asylum seekers are coming in get you down, you're not going to be able to do it as well as others.

She observes that her port is 'more likely to detain later on than earlier these days', which she describes as 'cost effective'. In fact, she refers often to the need to consider costs, both in relation to public expenditure and costs transferred to transport companies through the Carriers' Liability Act.

This IO appears content to allow decisions to be made by others, and believes that judgments about likelihood of absconding can only be made by guesswork: 'Obviously in the majority of on-entry cases you don't know one way or the other – most people you give TA to'. She dissociates herself even further from making judgments about asylum claims and, despite believing she has only seen two 'genuine refugees' in her career (the lowest estimate provided in the interviews), she professes to have no 'great feelings one way or the other' about the outcome of applications.

> I'd rather know less, do the job, go through the logical stages, write it all down and let the people who are the experts up at HQ, who have got the country briefs – know exactly what's happening – make the decisions. We're the go-betweens basically. We collect the information and pass it on.

She appears genuinely able to separate her perceptions about the merits of an application from her thinking about detention, if only because 'if we detained everyone who had a weak asylum claim we wouldn't have enough room'. Even in the face of deliberate attempts to deceive, she shows little interest in making judgments about the character or motives of applicants, and views a delayed asylum claim, not as an attempt to undermine immigration control, but merely as a change of procedure.

> Basically they have asked for asylum. Once they have got to that stage they're going to give you the proper details. It's just a question of time. (What if they haven't asked for asylum until very, very late?) They can ask for it at any time. (That wouldn't alter your feeling about the need to detain?) No. Some people will turn around and say they were frightened to ask for asylum. You just have to deal with it.

IO Number 23: Humanitarian

This IO is a mature university graduate who describes herself as an 'IO by default'. She has worked in the Immigration Service for almost 10 years, which she says is longer than she expected. She consistently responds to interview questions by referring to individual examples, rather than providing more general descriptions of practices. Although she claims to try 'not to get emotional about things' she clearly engages at a personal level with the people she deals with. Her apparent failure to draw general conclusions from these experiences leaves her account of her views and practices confused, and at times contradictory.

This IO's tendency to make moral judgments leads her to form unfavourable as well as favourable views about the asylum seekers she has encountered. She finds it 'morally objectionable' when Albanians pretend to be Kosovans, thereby 'taking up spaces that properly belong to someone else', and is critical of the parents of two unaccompanied minors she has dealt with because 'as a mother, there's no circumstance on this earth, that I could imagine ever leaving my children'. Overall, her views about asylum seekers and their motivations are somewhat fickle. On the one hand she describes the 'odd defector' she would hear about as a child as 'absolutely desperate' and the archetype of a 'real refugee'. On the other, she suggests that the Refugee Convention should be revised to take into account the needs of economic refugees, whom she sees as equally in need of help as those fleeing political or ethnic persecution. However, she does not extend this sympathy to Roma (whose motives are widely perceived amongst immigration officers to be purely economic), towards whom she adopts a typical border guard approach.

> Detention of the head of the family can sometimes work as a deterrent because if you actually look at the huge amount of

paperwork involved here just so that someone can go pickpocketing and have benefits for the whole summer. It can be very upsetting ... I personally think it's terrible. But as long as the system will allow them to do it – well.

Even so, this IO declares herself to be 'personally opposed to detention' – particularly to asylum seekers being 'near anything criminal'. This conviction (although not consistently reflected in her account) appears to stem from her direct experience of working within several detention facilities: 'I saw some terrible things there. Some awful things happened there. And I think that's probably had a fairly seminal influence on my own attitude to detention.'

Despite these experiences, she believes that detention powers are not being misapplied, and says that 'on balance I have a lot of respect for my colleagues, and I do think on the whole the decisions are sound, even though I may not personally agree with the principle'. Overall, the combination of her strong, if somewhat contradictory, principles against the use of detention, her emotional engagement with her work, and her deferential attitude towards departmental authority, leaves her unlikely to actively pursue detention, but unwilling to argue against it.

Unless I feel very very strongly about arguing, I will not have an argument with a CIO if they are insisting on detaining. As I said, unless I'm really in there for a reason, I just let it go. Because this job can be so draining and so stressful that you really don't want to make situations for yourself where you're going to go away feeling all this angst.

IO Number 4: Professional

This young IO is a recent graduate who expresses an interest in management and policy. He found his former public sector employment 'inward looking' and 'claustrophobic' and says he has volunteered to be interviewed because he supports 'having outside people looking at the work that other organisations do, from a hopefully completely neutral standpoint'. He responds to the question about 'what being an IO is all about' by posing a more fundamental question about 'what you want as an immigration control'. He believes that some control is necessary, both for the benefit of the receiving countries and the stability of the sending countries, but ultimately sees his role as administering government policy.

As an IO, basically the job is just to apply the rules in the way the government of the day want them used. It doesn't necessarily mean as an individual IO you're going to agree with everything that's in the rules, one way or the another. You might think they're too soft. You might think they're too hard. But your job at the end of day is to do whatever the job tells you to do.

It is clear, however, that his detachment is a deliberately adopted strategy rather than an unreflective following of rules. He often clarifies whether he is stating a personal view or adopting a departmental stance, and his responses characteristically examine issues from a range of perspectives. His analytical abilities enable him, despite his relatively short experience, to provide the most succinct and balanced (although fairly uncritical) overview of the decision-making process obtained in the interviews.

The thing that actually attracts the attention of the IO to begin with is somebody who really is showing blatant disregard for immigration rules, making attempts to lie and cheat and circumvent rules and procedures in whatever way … But that on it's own isn't enough because if you're going to detain somebody there has to be a reasonable expectation that you're going to be able to remove them … That, again, can be affected by other issues such as documentation. So a lot of things have to be in place for detention to be a justifiable, right decision. Mainly because, with a limited number of detention spaces available, you cannot physically detain everybody we perceive as being a particularly bad egg.

He can't recall a CIO declining to detain when he has recommended it. He claims he would 'not take it personally' if this occurred, although he admits to having been more easily 'wound up' when he first started. On the other hand, he recalls having once 'persuaded the CIO' to transfer an asylum seeker from bail to the less restrictive status of temporary admission, because the applicant had complied with all restrictions placed on him.

Although he sees deception as pointing towards detention, he understands that asylum seekers who 'maybe don't have much experience in dealing with people in perceived positions of authority, may well think the best option is to deceive and hide things from us'. He doesn't consider clandestine entry to be a reason on its own for detention 'although I'm sure they'd probably love to', hinting at some recognition of harsher attitudes amongst his colleagues or political masters. At this stage in his career, however, he says he is 'comfortable' about the decisions the department is making: 'From my experience being in the Immigration Service so far, that opportunity to use common sense is used well, and not generally abused … It's far more useful to have a lot more discretion as long as, obviously, discretion is used carefully.'

CIO Number 48: Individualist

This CIO has worked in the Immigration Service for over 20 years, having been recruited almost straight from school. He sees his main challenge as helping to manage the organisational changes which have been dictated by the increased volume of work, and have been met with some resistance by IOs and other colleagues. He contends that the Immigration Service has been 'stopped from doing the job' in some ways over the years, but broadly accepts changes such as increased legal scrutiny and the unprecedented use of temporary admission in relation to asylum seekers.

He considers the operational aspects of the job to be 'not really demanding' and believes that most experienced IOs are just as capable as CIOs of making appropriate decisions. However, he is prepared to challenge them when he thinks their conclusions are wrong. He says he frequently decides not to detain when an IO has recommended it, and claims there is a 'slight culture to penalise people for arriving without passports … or being rude to the IO or whatever it might be'. Several IOs interviewed at the same port said that one CIO is nicknamed 'The Gaoler' and another 'The Liberator'. This CIO comes across in the interview as a likely candidate for 'The Liberator'.

> I'll say here and now, I am by no means the firmest when it comes to detention. I think detention is appropriate when there is a purpose in it. That is not necessarily the view of several of my colleagues who take a harder view of detention – I'm not saying they're right or wrong. But I can only apply my standards.

His individualist stance is apparent throughout the interview. He considers he has been doing the job long enough to be prepared to 'back my own judgment' and 'do the job the way I see it'. In relation to detention this means: 'If it were me, I'd be detaining someone I could remove tomorrow, and therefore it probably wouldn't be an asylum seeker'. This stance is put to the test most noticeably at detention reviews, where CIOs consider whether long-term detention, which has been authorised and repeatedly endorsed by their peers, should be continued in particular cases.

> People seem afraid to let people out sometimes, even when it's going nowhere … Because colleagues will say to you 'What did you let him out for?' 'Because I didn't think it was worth locking him up any more.' … There comes a point when you just can't go on ad infinitum. There is a temptation to do that – to go on ad infinitum … People do get into this mindset.

This CIO is conscious of the 'open-ended power' he exercises and observes that asylum seekers may end up being detained under immigration powers for 'longer than they would have got for a fairly serious crime had they gone to court': 'I can just lock people up for months on end and no-one can really challenge it – not very effectively. I think you've got to be very mindful of that.'

He appears not to take a personal interest in the merits of applications, but is concerned that genuine cases may be 'getting a little bit lost in the overwhelming numbers that perhaps don't have a genuine claim'. He attributes his reluctance to use long-term detention not to 'laudable' principles but to 'realism', which seems to be founded on a series of empirical observations which run counter to prevailing occupational wisdom. He claims that 'research shows that 95 per cent, or even higher, of people we grant TA to do abide by the terms' and that 'experience is showing us that perhaps bail is a viable option'. He asserts that 'the facts don't bear out' the widespread belief that no-one is removed unless they are detained, and is therefore relatively unconcerned when he is unable to detain because of lack of detention space: 'Like I say, I'm not God. I'm not that phased by it. If I can't detain them and they abscond there's not a lot I can do about it … I don't get neurotic about it.'

Implications for detention

In light of the permissive nature of detention instructions and the relative lack of external constraints on discretion, the individual characteristics of decision-makers are likely to have a significant impact on detention practices at ports.

Broadly speaking, this analysis suggests that 'border guards', who see their role in terms of controlling entry, might seek to detain on arrival relatively frequently, in order to protect the integrity of the immigration control and guarantee removal of at least some unsuccessful applicants;

that 'professional' and 'individualist' officers might consciously seek to limit their own use of detention and, in the case of individualists, possibly influence the practice of others; and that 'humanitarians' and 'civil servants' might acquiesce to detention (in the first case reluctantly, in the second indifferently) while being unlikely to argue for detention themselves.[21]

It is therefore possible that a small number of enthusiastic detainers may be responsible for a disproportionate number of detention decisions at ports. While this research provides some qualitative evidence that this is indeed the case, it is a proposition worthy of further empirical testing.

Notes

1 The term 'immigration officer' is used to refer to both Immigration Officer (IO) and Chief Immigration Officer (CIO) grades. In general, IOs have more direct contact with asylum seekers than CIOs, and have some decision-making powers, while CIOs supervise and authorise their decisions.

2 Initial decisions are made with reference to the United Nations Convention Relating to the Status of Refugees (1951). This international instrument has not been incorporated into UK law, although appeals are provided in domestic law. See Refugee Legal Centre (1998a), Refugee Legal Centre (1998b) and Justice/ILPA/ARC (1997) for critical analyses of the UK asylum determination system.

3 Schedule 2, paragraph 16(1) authorises detention on arrival. 'Removal' (as opposed to deportation) is the term used for the expulsion of individuals who have not been legally admitted to the UK.

4 Detention instructions are contained in disparate documents which have only been available in the public domain for a few years. The main instructions are ISC 26/91, ISC 6/94 and IDI Jan/97 Section 1 – Annex A. (see Appendix 2 in Weber and Gelsthorpe 2000) and IND Operational Enforcement Manual Chapter 38 (see Appendix 2 in Weber and Landman 2002).

5 An individual is deemed 'removable' if there are no legal or practical impediments to their removal – normally when all in-country appeals have been exhausted and the necessary travel documents obtained.

6 Many asylum seekers make their applications once they have entered the country either by presenting themselves at Immigration Service head-quarters or after being detected as an 'overstayer' or 'illegal entrant'.

7 For example, Manning has described as a 'useful legal fiction' the idea of decision-makers thoughtfully applying formal rules (Manning 1992).

8 Hawkins has described these aspects of decision-making as the 'moral frame' and 'organisational frame' (Hawkins 1983).

9 Critics such as the UNHCR and Amnesty International have argued that space limitations are more influential in limiting the use of detention than either formal rules or general principles. (See, for example, their submissions to the Special Standing Committee which examined the early stages of the Immigration and Asylum Act 1999.)

10 Note that the term 'protection' refers here to protection of the system of immigration controls, not to the protection of individual refugees.

11 The status of special exercises as government policy is unclear. One CIO described them as 'informal, formal instruction', but successive governments have denied sanctioning the use of detention as a deterrent.

12 It must be acknowledged that discretion has also narrowed the use of detention, for example due to 'normalisation' of arrival without documents at some ports, in the face of large numbers of undocumented applicants.

13 See for example (Hilberg 1985).

14 See for example (Feldman 1992), (Manning 1992), (Sainsbury 1992).

15 For example, Goldhagen criticises most analyses of the Holocaust, including the seminal work of Hilberg, as failing to account for the active support for Nazi policies throughout German society and the excessive and uncoerced actions of many individuals (Goldhagen 1996).

16 Hannah Arendt famously described Adolf Eichmann as a 'colourless bureaucrat'. However, she also noted that he was ambitious, and was particularly dedicated to fulfilling his duties to the satisfaction of his superiors, suggesting that both these characteristics were present (Arendt, 1963).

17 A pertinent historical example is that of Frank Foley, a respected British Intelligence operative posing as a visa officer in pre-war Germany, whose decisions to issue visas to German Jews in contravention of immigration policies are credited with saving thousands of lives (Smith 1999).

18 The examination involved a systematic *post hoc* analysis of 60 interview scripts using NUD*IST, but did not seek to replicate Kelman and Hamilton's rigorous quantitative approach.

19 A more detailed discussion of the research evidence can be found in Weber and Landman (2002).

20 This term is used by Crawley (1999) in her discussion of immigration officers' attitudes towards asylum seekers.

21 It is important to note that only CIOs have the direct authority to put their views on detention into practice, but IOs may still influence decisions through their gatekeeping role.

References

Amnesty International (1995) *Prisoners Without a Voice* (revised edition). London: Amnesty International British Section.

Amnesty International (1996) *Cell Culture: The Detention and Imprisonment of*

Asylum-Seekers in the United Kingdom. London: Amnesty International United Kingdom.

Amnesty International (1999) *Most vulnerable of all: the treatment of unaccompanied refugee children in the UK.* London: Amnesty International.

Arendt, H. (1963) *Eichmann in Jerusalem: A report on the banality of evil.* London: Faber and Faber.

Beck, U. (1992) *Risk Society: Towards a New Modernity.* London: Sage.

Crawley, H. (1999) *Breaking down the barriers: a report on the conduct of asylum interviews at ports.* London: Immigration Law Practitioners' Association.

Feldman, M. (1992) 'Social limits to discretion: an organizational perspective' in K. Hawkins (ed.) *The Uses of Discretion.* Oxford: Clarendon Press.

Goldhagen, D. (1996) *Hitler's Willing Executioners: Ordinary Germans and the Holocaust.* London: Little, Brown and Company.

Hawkins, K. (1983) 'Thinking about legal decision making' in J. Shapland (ed.) *Decision Making in the Legal System.* Leicester: British Psychological Society.

Hilberg, R. (1985) *The Destruction of the European Jews.* London: Homes and Meier.

Her Majesty's Inspectorate of Prisons (1995) *Report of an Unannounced Short Visit by Her Majesty's Inspectorate of Prisons: Immigration Detention Centre Campsfield House.* London: Home Office.

Justice/ILPA/ARC (1997) *Providing protection: towards fair and effective asylum procedures.* London: Justice/ILPA/ARC.

Kelman, H. and Hamilton, V. (1989) *Crimes of Obedience: Toward a Social Psychology of Authority and Obedience.* London: Yale University Press.

Manning, P. (1992) "Big Bang" Decisions: Notes on a Naturalistic Approach' in K. Hawkins (ed.) *The Uses of Discretion.* Oxford: Clarendon Press.

Medical Foundation for the Care of Victims of Torture (1994) *A Betrayal of Hope and Trust: The detention of victims of torture in the United Kingdom.* London: Medical Foundation.

Pourgirides, C., Sashidharan, S. and Bracken, P. (1996) *A Second Exile: The Mental Health Implications of Detention of Asylum Seekers in the United Kingdom.* Birmingham: University of Birmingham/The Barrow Cadbury Trust.

Refugee Legal Centre (1998a) *Reviewing the asylum determination procedures – a casework study. Part One: Initial decision making.* London: Refugee Legal Centre.

Refugee Legal Centre (1998b) *Reviewing the asylum determination procedures – a casework study. Part Two: Procedures for challenge and review.* London: Refugee Legal Centre.

Sainsbury, R. (1992) 'Administrative Justice: Discretion and Procedure in Social Security Decision-making' in K. Hawkins (ed.) *The Uses of Discretion.* Oxford: Clarendon Press.

Smith, M. (1999) *Foley: The spy who saved 10,000 Jews.* London: Hodder & Stoughton.

Weber, L. and Gelsthorpe, L. (2000) *Deciding to Detain: How Decisions to Detain Asylum Seekers are Made at Ports of Entry.* Cambridge: Institute of Criminology.

Weber, L. and Landman, T. (2002) *Deciding to Detain: the organisational context for decisions to detain asylum seekers at UK ports.* Colchester: Human Rights Centre, University of Essex.

Chapter 9

Order, rationality and silence: some reflections on criminal justice decision-making

Keith Hawkins

This book presents a series of valuable essays on decision-making in criminal justice which draw attention to a rich set of features found in some of the less considered areas in which legal officials make profoundly important choices. Criminal justice decision-making is a species of legal decision-making generally, and these essays explore processes observable in other arenas of legal life. In a variety of studies, by a variety of hands, and with a variety of methods, many common themes emerge which deserve further reflection. The emphasis in the present book on decision-making in neglected, mostly post-conviction, sites of criminal justice is very welcome. I intend to focus in particular upon issues arising from two of the questions which Loraine Gelsthorpe and Nicola Padfield pose at the beginning of their Introduction: how discretion is exercised in different parts of the criminal justice system, and what may actually constrain it. In doing so, I shall suggest some lines for further enquiry. I take as self-evident the importance of understanding legal decision-making in its different arenas, for the practical reality of law, and its consequences, reside in the ways in which its words are translated into action.

These essays show in their different ways the importance of exploring empirically a complex socio-legal phenomenon like legal decision-making. In general, the existing literature tends to cluster around two research approaches. Studies in the positivist tradition have been concerned with outcomes and what seems to produce them. This research is correlational in character, and conducted using quantitative methods in which identified 'factors' or 'criteria' are statistically associated with decision outcomes. Studies here have tended to focus on post-conviction decision-making, particularly on sentencing or on parole decision-making (which has a particularly lengthy provenance, since some studies go back to the 1920s and 1930s). One problem with the positivist approach, however, is that it is not enough to suggest what seems empirically to determine outcomes by correlating input data with decision outcome, since this does not address analytically any connection between the two. To focus on a single decision point, or on a single type of decision, risks excluding the social context in which criminal justice decision-making takes place, the field in which the decision is set and viewed, as well as the interpretive and classificatory processes of individual decision-makers. Furthermore, decision-making in the criminal justice system takes place within an organisational context which imposes a set of particular objectives and introduces new constraints upon the decision-maker.

The other approach to decision-making research, that in the interpretive tradition, has emphasised decision-making processes (rather than outcomes), using qualitative techniques of research. The focus here has been largely on the pre-trial criminal process. Indeed, a great deal of what we currently know about discretionary behaviour has emerged in particular from research into policing and prosecution decision-making[1] and law enforcement in regulatory regimes.[2]

To engage with the task of identifying the place and character of criminal justice discretion demands not only a theoretical framework to provide a means of understanding decision behaviour, but also a fine-grained analysis of the character and exercise of discretion on the ground, where decision-making practices in actual cases need close exploration. On the ground, legal rules or bureaucratic policy become merely one force in a field of forces which act upon criminal justice decision-makers and shape outcomes in a decisive way. To focus upon formal arrangements or formal practices will often mislead. Padfield, Liebling, and Arnold (Chapter 5) observe of Parole Board lifer panels, for example, that the actual decision-making about a case is not confined to the hearing, but may begin long before that point, and continue afterwards. Indeed, many of these essays point to the relative independence from legal or bureaucratic policy of the individual decision-maker who is formally accorded discretion.

A perspective

I do not propose to say much about the problems involved in defining discretion, which Gelsthorpe and Padfield address in their introductory chapter at some length, except to note that the definition of discretion has been a preoccupation of a number of lawyers (Davis 1969; Dworkin 1977; Galligan 1986; Handler 1986). However, to take discretion as the focus raises questions about what we recognise as discretion. If our real concern is how outcomes are produced in handling cases in criminal justice (or in other parts of the legal system) a good case can be made for the necessity of studying not discretion, but the decision-making of legal actors (see Hawkins 1992: Chapter 1). The point of this is to allow an approach which gets away from the central place accorded to legal rules (see Dworkin's (1977: 39) 'surrounding belt of restriction'). This should avoid debate on the unhelpful question, which arises when actors seem to decide on the basis of forces other than legal rules, as to whether discretion is authorised or not. If the task is to understand how outcomes are produced, the issue is not so much one of understanding the 'mandated flexibility' of legal actors, as Gelsthorpe and Padfield put it (Chapter 1), so much as their decision-making, mandated or otherwise.

However, Padfield, Liebling and Arnold (Chapter 5) are right to emphasise that one task in any research concerned with process and decision-making is to identify where formal discretion lies. This can be a complex matter. The lawyer's tendency is to present a formal map of institutional arrangements, marking out the boundaries where rules seem to end and discretion seems to begin. Thomas in Chapter 3, for example, analyses formal efforts made over the years to allocate sentencing authority, highlighting the rise of judicial discretion and the subsequent increasingly intrusive legislation intended to remove a measure of discretion in sentencing from the courts. Sentencing is treated as a central decision in the criminal justice process, not least because it is the occasion for the disposal of the convicted person by the judge or magistrate to the post-conviction penal system. Many sentencing decisions, however, involve the exercise of a residual discretion, since the question of sentence is the culmination of several consequential decisions made earlier in the handling of cases. Where pre-trial bargaining takes place, for example, the case presented to the court is the case already worked on by prosecution and defence and shaped in such a way as to avoid – to subvert – the court's full sentencing discretion. The case goes to court already set on a particular course by the decisions made pre-trial with bargains about plea, number or type of charge, or forum struck between prosecution and defence (see, for example, Hawkins 2002). The authority of judges in such circumstances is thus constrained by the decision practices of those located earlier in the system.

Yet identifying the formal locus of discretion is best seen as a preliminary, if the task is to understand actual decision practices, and what shapes them. One way of thinking about legal decision-making seeks to get away from approaches which focus on 'criteria' or 'factors' said to have been taken into account in making a particular choice. The argument, instead, is that decisions can only be understood by reference to their broad environment, particular context, and interpretive practices: their surrounds, fields and frames (Hawkins 2002; Hawkins and Manning, forthcoming).[3]

On this view, criminal justice decisions are made in the broader setting of a surround and within a context, or field, defined by legal and organisational mandates. Such decisions are made in a rich and complex environment, which acts as the setting for the play of shifting currents of broad political and economic values and forces. Decision frames, the interpretative and classificatory devices operating in particular instances, are shaped by both surround and field. To understand the nature of criminal justice decision-making better, a connection needs to be forged between forces in the decision-making environment, and the interpretive processes that individuals engage in when deciding a particular case.

The surround is the broad setting in which decision-making activity takes place, serving as an environment both for individual decision-making, and for the activities of the criminal justice bureaucracies in which such decision-making occurs. The surround is not immutable. Political and economic forces may shift, and in these circumstances the social surround of the criminal justice system may change. The altered condition now replaces the earlier surround, becoming part of a new organisational and decision-making environment for officials. Changes that occur in the surround can prompt changes in the decision field. Equally, a change in the surround may cause a change in the frame, altering the way in which certain events are interpreted and classified. The decision-making surround is not open to control by the criminal justice bureaucracy. All it can do is to react to events and problems as they pop up, or respond to gradual shifts in the surround that become apprehended differently. The media are central to the transmission and interpretation of such events.

The decision field is a defined setting in which decisions are made. Decision fields sit within the social surround. While events in the surround are not open to control, the field, in contrast, is something defined by and acted on by the organisation. The law determines the contours and reach of the field of the criminal justice system by establishing and defining a mandate. The field also contains sets of ideas about how the ends of the law are to be pursued. These may exist at a formal level in the form of policies expressing the organisation's mandate and how it should be attained. But they also exist in an informal way in the values, expectations and aims held by staff at all levels in the criminal justice organisation. For practical purposes, legal and organisational aspects of the mandate come together to be defined by the decision-maker in occupational terms. Fields constitute both the 'background' and 'foreground' for decision-making activity, with foreground matters being seen against a background of assumptions in the field. The contents of the field are, like those of the surround, open to change. The decision field remains relatively stable in the criminal justice system, however, anchored by the fixed occupational roles and tasks sanctioned by the legal bureaucracy, and the routine ways in which people make sense of what they encounter (Manning 1992), though fields vary according to location within the criminal justice system.

If a decision field describes the legally and organisationally defined setting in which decision-makers work, frame speaks to the interpretive behaviour involved in decision-making about a specific matter. The frame describes how features in a particular problem or case are understood, placed and accorded relevance. A frame is a structure of knowledge, experience, values and meanings that decision-makers employ in deciding. It addresses the question, 'What is going on here?' (Goffman 1974). Framing involves a variety of processes. Human beings always seek to impose meaning and order upon events they experience and it is the frame that provides the rules and principles that guide that understanding of what events experienced mean. A frame can be seen as a set of rules for steering the performance of a task, or for organising the ascription of meaning to events or for classifying as relevant other raw material in the field. There can be framing by means of interpretation (making sense of what is presented); classification (what kind of a case is this?); or task, which is organisationally determined in settings of greater decision-making heterogeneity. Framing is the means by which the everyday world is linked with the legal world.

Social surround, decision field and decision frame are in mutual interaction. Surround and field influence which frames move from background to foreground and vice versa. For example, features in the surround, such as the political climate likely to be created by the release of a notorious offender, may intrude into the frame used by decision-makers in an individual case. Field affects frame, as when the introduction of a new policy shapes the way that a particular case, event or problem is regarded.

Frames organise the content and meaning of cases, the conventional units by which the criminal justice system knows its raw material, and which reduce unique human experience to ritualised formal accounts amenable to the application of legal and organisational understanding and handling. The frame is rather like a code that not only shapes the nature of the response, but also informs and even confirms it. The existence of a frame, however, does not in itself isolate the particular facts needed to make a decision. A frame must be applied to an event and its 'facts' selectively retrieved and organised by the application of the frame. Facts and frame are reflexive: facts narrow the potential frame while the frame provisionally applied may cause some facts to be discarded or disabled, others to be introduced, and yet others to be reinterpreted. Put another way, frames are reflexive in the sense that they both constitute 'reality' and they selectively identify the facts that sustain a social reality.

Frames are shaped by a variety of features, such as image and belief. Beliefs about good and bad, right and wrong, for example, help to instruct a decision-maker how to understand a case, problem or person. Frames are influenced in part by occupational and professional ideology, varying according to the view of the world held by decision-makers as a result of their professional training and socialisation: psychiatrists often frame some matters in terms of 'mental health', judges frame some matters in terms of what is 'legal'. Another shaping feature can be the type of decision subject, one of the reasons why criminal justice decision-makers generally regard adults differently from children. Frame can also be influenced by status or office. The way in which a junior official makes sense of a problem might not necessarily coincide with the way a more senior person with other occupational responsibilities might. Conceptions of purpose are also significant. The exercise of gathering, reporting and assessing information is itself a form of framing operation in which the frame determines what material is sought, seen as relevant and significant, and what that information conveys (a good example of this occurs with the police 'construction of the case' for the Crown Prosecution Service: Sanders 1987). The personal disposition of the decision-maker can also lead to the adoption of distinctive frames. Differences in framing of this sort may well result in differences in decision outcome.

Framing involves making sense of signals from the surround and field. The frame prompts action and a decision outcome rendered appropriate by it. Frames are 'keyed', that is, they are indicated by cues or signs such as a word, action or event. How such cues or signs are recognised and what they mean depends on the frame employed. The dominant decision frame to be adopted can be negotiable. For example, in a bargaining relationship in criminal justice there may be negotiations early on about the key and the frame that are to govern the transaction or to mark out the territory on which matters are to be conducted. When keyed, however, the frame is provisional and what is keyed may be re-keyed or transformed so that a new frame is brought into play. Frames are always contingent and there is always room for negotiation and redefinition within a frame. This occurs when a field is penetrated by events occurring in the social surround, leading to a questioning of the established relationship between a key and a frame. A change in the frame may lead to the reinterpretation of existing facts or the selection of different facts.

This process may or may not prompt a different outcome, for when frames change, outcomes do not necessarily change. A change in frame provides, rather, an occasion for the development of a new basis for defining material as relevant (and discarding other, previously relevant, material) as well as a new basis for interpreting the decision to make the outcome rational. Though frames may change, they do vary in the extent to which they are resistant to disruption that threatens the definition of the situation they have in part created. Certain frames can be said to be more resistant to negotiation or change than others. For example, a person, event or matter framed by a decision-maker as 'a bad case' is resistant to reframing.

Framing is not only an interpretative act, a way of making sense for decision-making purposes, it is also a classificatory act, prompting particular decision outcomes or forms of action. What information suppliers choose to present for decision, and how they choose to present it – what they focus on, emphasise or omit, for example – frames reality for the ultimate decision-makers, those who occupy those places where authority to decide is formally allocated. Frames penetrate records, and given their durability, spread their effects across time and different hands (for an example, see Hawkins 1983a). This attribute of framing is especially important in organisations, where there is extensive reliance on the paper record, with its accounts, evaluations and recom-mendations. Within organisations, information suppliers are important actors because they are at the heart of those decision-making processes that frame in certain facts potentially bearing on the composition of a case to be decided about, or frame out those other materials deemed irrelevant or otherwise unnecessary. Such processual framing is a powerful screening or persuasive device.

Frames control and organise the raw material for decision. They include facts, omit or discard them, or change their meaning. Extant facts can be framed in or out over the career of a case in a serial legal decision-making process in which cases are handed on from one decision-maker to another, until the matter is discarded or finally disposed of (see below). This leads to differences in framing which occur as information and evaluation moves through an organisation or between organisations. Changes may occur as a case moves to different parts of the organisation. A matter framed in one way at the point where it crosses the organisational threshold and becomes a 'case', may be framed in a contrasting way by decision-makers who act later in the system (Manning and Hawkins 1989). At different points in the process, different frames will be dominant. Legal frames that define particular facts as legally relevant and have potential for authoritative consequences can overlap with organisational frames. Legal framing involves assembling the legally relevant facts and applying them; the frame constructs and selectively integrates knowledge and justifies its presence (Hawkins 2002). The process creates a context for framing by others, shaping the way in which it is presented to colleagues for decision. In each context, a frame is used, often retrospectively, to define the meaning of the problem or event and to link facts and actions to outcomes and consequences. Once settled upon, the frame provides a clear way of thinking about the offender or event.[4]

This framework can be used to understand the processes analysed in this book. For instance, one illustration of the importance of the decision field appears in Chapter 7, in which it is reported that the type of mental hospital in which a patient was detained was associated with the decision to discharge. An institution which is known to hold a particular type of prisoner or patient sets up expectations in decision-makers about the types of person and problem they are likely to encounter. This may well explain the finding that there were likely to be fewer discharges from the maximum security hospital, which may be the result of a *perception* that the hospital held more dangerous patients (though the researchers found that this may not *actually* have been the case). One important policy implication arising from this is that it is quite possible that a 'good' patient from a maximum security hospital (or prison) may be regarded more stringently or restrictively by decision-makers than a 'bad' patient from an institution of lesser security where there are correspondingly more favourable expectations of the population as a whole. Another is that the key decision affecting outcome is in practice more likely to be the one that allocates the patient to the particular hospital (or prison).

Analysis of the broader contextual forces and their relationship to the exercise of discretion in particular cases is essential, as Gelsthorpe and Padfield recognise (Chapter 1), since they act to alter the decision-making field in which decision-makers operate, and the decision-making frames which they bring to bear in interpreting the meanings deemed relevant in any case. For example, the 'sharp idiosyncratic differences' which Grounds, Howes and Gelsthorpe (Chapter 6) observed among clinicians can be explained by reference to the different decision frames that were in operation. This is significant from a policy point of view, of course, since in such circumstances it is in effect the identity of the person dealing with the case that determines the outcome. Put another way, decision outcomes can be shaped not so much by those making the decision as by those who allocate decision-makers to deal with particular cases.

The organisation of criminal justice decision-making

Analysis of criminal justice decision-making has tended to take the individual case and the individual decision-maker as the primary unit of analysis when attempting to explain decision behaviour (Emerson 1983).[5] One implication of a claim that a case is decided 'on its merits' is that a case exists as a discrete entity, and decisions are made about its fate quite independently of wider forces and constraints. Thus it is often taken for granted that criminal justice decisions are made by individuals, except where institutional arrangements demand that they be made collectively (as in the jury room or by a parole board). In fact, while an individual may readily be seen as responsible for making a particular decision, a very great deal of legal decision-making is a collective enterprise in which several people, either formally or informally, take part in deciding. The concern for the individual case is not surprising, however, since criminal justice officials and bureaucracies (as well as criminological researchers) think about and typically assemble problems for decision into individual 'cases', each relating to a particular and concrete matter and existing in the form of a discrete unit by which each one may be recorded, worked on, referred to, stored or passed on. This individualistic view is partial, however, and fails to describe the real character of criminal justice decision-making which has instead to be seen in an holistic or systemic perspective (Hawkins 1992a; Hawkins 1992b; Reiss 1974). This avoids treating criminal justice decisions as the work of individual legal actors behaving autonomously and independently of others. The idea of the 'case' needs to recognise that a criminal justice decision is often the product of different officials acting at different times making decisions serially in the context of other decisions. These may be decisions already made or about to be made about the particular case, or decisions made about other actual or hypothetical cases (Emerson 1983; Hawkins 1992a), or in anticipation of what subsequent decision-makers might do (Emerson and Paley 1992).

In general, it is decision-making of an anticipatory kind that makes possible the bargaining on which so much of the criminal and civil justice systems rely for their continued viability. In adversarial legal systems legal actors often decide in anticipation of what 'the other side' will do – for example, in opting to settle out of court (Ross 1970), or in anticipation of what others, to whom cases will be handed on for further processing, will do (Emerson and Paley 1992). Similarly, regulatory inspectors contemplating court action have to anticipate questions from their principals, or problems that might arise concerning the nature or sufficiency of available evidence and decide on their enforcement strategy accordingly. Sometimes anticipatory behaviour may be used in an artful way by one decision-maker to attain a particular kind of preferred outcome in a decision to be made by another, as when listing clerks route certain criminal cases for trial by particular judges with known sentencing proclivities in particular kinds of case which are regarded as especially appropriate (Emerson and Paley 1992; Lovegrove 1984; see also Utz 1978).

Organisational decisions are not usually made independently of each other, then, but in ways that take account of the implications of the handling of the present case in a particular way for the handling of other cases, and vice versa (Emerson 1983; Emerson and Paley 1992). A particular case which is decided within the context of a set of cases may produce caseload effects (Emerson 1983). Or there may be sequence effects which act on an individual decision, arising from the order in which cases are decided, in which previous decisions constrain present ones, or where the anticipation of a future decision shapes the outcome in the present case (Emerson 1991). Organisational context serves powerfully to constrain and shape decisions, for each case is not dealt with on its merits, 'independently of the properties and organisational implications of other cases' (Emerson 1983: 425). Indeed, features in the individual case may not be the most important factor in assessing and disposing of cases. A problem may be decided about in a particular way for reasons that have little to do with intrinsic features in the case, but a lot to do with the pressures upon the decision-maker (Lipsky 1980). For example, there is evidence of possible caseload effects in Chapter 6, with a reference to pressure on beds, and the existence of 'bed management' techniques. This is a vivid illustration of the fact that important 'clinical' decisions are not determined solely by features inherent in the individual case. Similarly, in Chapter 8 we read of the recognition by an immigration official that if everyone with a weak asylum claim were detained, there would not be enough room to house them all. Resource constraints can be an important influence in decision-making.

Too close a focus on the individual case and its fate also risks obscuring the fact that different areas of the criminal justice system are organised to require that decisions be made serially, allowing us to think of cases following careers within a decision-making system, of criminal justice officials as part of a network of relationships existing within and between various segments of the system, and of criminal justice itself as a serial referral system in which cases are handed on from one organisational actor or segment to another until the matter is disposed of in some conclusive way. The sequence of decision outcomes contributes to the final outcome, whatever that outcome might be, whenever it arrives.

The implications of a serial conception of criminal justice decision-making are important. First, it recognises that power is dispersed across criminal justice institutions and individuals. It is not the case that people have an equal influence in shaping outcomes. A decision by an individual frequently does not settle matters (though a particular individual may set a case on a particular course which will lead, sometimes inexorably, to a particular destination), but merely decides that the case be handed on to another segment of the system. However, it should be noted that individual actors in a serial referral system like criminal justice often exercise a decisive, indeed final, authority: to drop the case. Power resides in the structural position of the individual at the point at which choice is made, in the capacity of decision-makers to discard cases or not to create them in the first place, or to redefine a matter. In the criminal process, for example, a matter may be redefined as a 'dispute' or 'problem' rather than an 'offence', thereby diverting the case, putting it beyond the reach of the criminal justice system. Indeed, the whole criminal process is shaped from its earliest stages by decisions taken about the creation, handling and discarding of cases. The authors in Chapter 5 note, for example, that decisions about life sentences are the culmination of a long series of prior decisions or recommendations about the fate of a case. Such cases could be tracked back to the point of their creation in the decision of a victim or observer to report to the police the occurrence of an untoward event.

Second, a decision made at one point in the system may close off or profoundly restrict the choices open to a later decision-maker. Plea-bargaining frequently restricts what judges may do in imposing sentence, as it is intended to. Parole boards work near the end of an attenuated process of decision-making in the criminal justice system, and as such operate in a setting where their discretion is severely constrained by the decisions of those who have preceded them in deciding about the handling and sentencing of an individual, whether as suspect, defendant or prisoner. The diffusion of decision-making power again means that serial procedures tend to concentrate greatest effective power in the hands of those, like police officers, who act at the periphery of their organisation, controlling access to it in a setting in which it is generally less visible, thus less controllable.

Third, it is often the case that effective power to decide is frequently assumed by actors other than the official allocated formal legal authority to exercise discretion. For example, real power is afforded by the legal system to those who create or assemble material relevant to a decision for those formally allocated authority to decide. Those supplying information may create a frame for the subsequent exercise of discretion by describing or presenting the case in a particular fashion, thereby setting it off in a particular direction, and in doing so, sometimes producing clear and specific expectations in later decision-makers as to what the 'right' decision should be.

Related to this, a fourth consequence of serial decision-making is that what is described as a 'decision' finally reached is sometimes nothing more than a ratification of an earlier decision or set of decisions made in the handling of a case. This may be so, even though that prior decision may appear – if it appears in the records at all – in the guise of a recommendation or a mere expression of opinion (Hawkins 1986). Indeed, some people who supply information or evaluation may have such an enormous influence on the subsequent handling of a case that it becomes difficult to conceive of the visible, formal point of decision as being the place at which real power to determine an outcome was exercised.

Serial decision-making poses problems which arise from framing effects in loosely-coupled systems. Initial frames informing decisions about case creation or case handling may be overlaid by subsequent frames which reflect different values and sets of priorities (Manning and Hawkins 1989). This process can result in an earlier decision framed in one way being trumped by a subsequent decision reflecting other values. Alternatively, earlier framing can be recruited by subsequent decision-makers as a means of justifying their later decision. However, it is also possible that an opposite effect occurs in a serial decision-making system, and instead of an earlier decision being trumped by a subsequent one, the effect of an earlier decision may be compounded by a subsequent one that may be shaped by the prior outcome reached or modes of reasoning employed. A form of labelling may operate. Thus in decisions about the release of life sentence prisoners, the authors observe in Chapter 5 that being a 'failure' in prison may become a self-fulfilling prophecy. It is as if it becomes more difficult to persuade the decision-maker to break away from a particular rationale adopted by earlier decision-makers the more frequently a further decision has to be made. Labelling is a practice that deserves more research attention since the label or institutional category ('lifer', for example) sets up expectations in decision-makers and interested audiences which may affect subsequent framing behaviour. This may also happen with decisions about how to categorise cases. Padfield, Liebling and Arnold (Chapter 5) observe, for example, that security categorisation is a decision made early on in the career of the newly sentenced life prisoner, and that this decision seemed to be the key to understanding the release decision. The authors reached this conclusion because no prisoner not in open conditions was released, while only one prisoner in open conditions was not released. Similarly, Holloway and Grounds (Chapter 7) report that one of the two most significant features associated with the outcomes of the decisions made by the Mental Health Review Tribunals they studied was the type of hospital in which the patient was detained, indicating the consolidating labelling effect of an earlier decision. The authors also provide another interesting example of the way in which past decisions are used as raw material for present decisions in reporting the observation by Feder (1994) that the matter most closely associated with the decision to parole was the incidence of psychiatric hospitalisation during incarceration. This is interesting, not least because the matter is itself a decision outcome, not an objective condition. Since allocation in the past to a particular category or type is taken as a relevant indicator for present purposes, the crucial decision, then, is often one to allocate a case to a particular category, since membership of a category often presupposes a particular outcome. In the case of life prisoners, the key matter is less the decision about release, and more the decision to allocate prisoners to a particular security category. The practice may be regarded by decision-makers as subject to a norm, a form of presumptive decision-making: 'do not release unless …'. As the authors point out, certain types of decisions carry procedural protections while others do not, and, inevitably, due process procedures tend to be attached to formal, visible points at which disposal decisions are made. Of course, categorisation can also be achieved by less formal means. Grounds, Howes and Gelsthorpe (Chapter 6) observe that some sorts of psychiatric patients were categorised according to general features, such as age, disability or potential vulnerability.

Whereas in decision-making organised serially there may be both competition between frames and consolidation of prior framing intended to serve quite other purposes, differences between decision-makers and their competing frames may be found in systems of parallel decision-making, and may be resolved through the working of social features such as status, expertise and charisma when outcomes are negotiated. The working of status and expertise in interpersonal relations can be seen in Chapter 7 by Holloway and Grounds in which they report the significance of the reputation of the independent psychiatrists making recommendations about the discharge of patients detained in hospital under restriction orders. The particular example they quote is telling: when asked about the patient's propensity for arson, the medical member of the panel said, 'that won't happen. [The IP] is a superb psychiatrist. It just won't happen.' In other words, the identity and assumed expertise of the person making the recom-mendation combines with the status and assumed expertise of the person on the panel to set up an almost irresistible push towards a particular decision outcome. The importance of status is also evident in the authors' finding that the Tribunal president tended to dominate hearings and deliberations, while lay members of the Tribunals were regularly ignored, or were inactive participants in the deliberations. After all, such people cannot make claims to expertise, and as a result will not enjoy any particular status in the interactions.

Interpersonal features like status, expertise and charisma operate in both parallel and serial decision-making systems. Kemp and Gelsthorpe (Chapter 2) reveal the importance of interpersonal relationships within an organisational context in their analysis of the decision-making of custody officers and process-markers in a police force. They seem to suggest that stronger claims to status and expertise from the custody officers were responsible for a shift in the decision-making relationship between the two sets of officials. They found that the decisions of custody officers were 'dominant', and that the majority of their recommendations to process-markers were accepted. This effect would be expected since these officials handed on the cases they had worked on to the process-markers. The high level of congruence between the two sets of decision-makers may well indicate a lack of rigorous and independent review, as the authors suggest, though it is extremely difficult for those who are structurally dependent upon earlier decision-makers to act independently of them. Since those who occupy an earlier decision point in a serial decision-making system are able to frame the practical reality of the case – its content and meaning – for those who have to receive their recommendations (Sanders 1987), this leads to the irony that those who come earlier in the process can severely constrain the discretion of those who come later. Note that earlier decision-makers are frequently regarded as in some sense subordinate or less 'senior', and they often operate in less visible settings.

One other explanation for such an effect (though not one necessarily true in this context) could be that congruence occurs as a result of the earlier decision-makers anticipating what would be an acceptable outcome for those to whom they pass their recommendations. Decisions are often made in criminal justice settings in a way which does not look back to some act or event in the past, but anticipates the fate of the present case were a particular decision reached. This may be more noticeable in decision-making systems where decisions are made relatively frequently and repetitively, allowing those making recommendations to learn the decision-making proclivities of their colleagues, and to anticipate their preferences (Emerson and Paley 1992). An excellent example of this effect is to be found in Chapter 7, where it is clear that certain members of the Mental Health Tribunals researched enjoyed attributed reputations for being more or less willing to discharge patients. Another example is found in Chapter 8, where Leanne Weber reports that experience had given her immigration officials confidence in being able to predict the likely outcomes of asylum claims. I am reminded of the problems that befell a parole board in one American state several years ago when its members decided that greater procedural openness in their decision-making was desirable. This entailed allowing parole candidates not only to be told the result of their parole hearing, but actually to remain in the hearing room listening while the board members deliberated. Members of the parole board soon discovered that institutional managers were telephoning them before parole hearings took place to find out who would be on the panel to visit the prison next. The purpose of this was believed to be to enable prison staff to school the prisoners into the 'right' things to say, and possibly to organise the line-up of candidates so that those they wished to have released would be heard by a board member thought likely to be sympathetic to those types of case. The use of such anticipatory decision-making is likely to be found elsewhere in serial handling systems, and is a practice deserving of further research.

Three sorts of silence

To argue in favour of an holistic approach to the analysis of criminal justice decision-making implies attention to matters neglected in current work. The first area where most criminal justice decision-making research is silent arises with the lack of attention to the wider forces at play when individual cases are being considered. It is essential that analysis is not fixated upon the discrete case, and the role that 'criteria' or 'factors' might play in producing a particular outcome in a particular case. Instead, more emphasis needs to be placed upon those features in the local surround within which decision-makers operate (Hawkins 2002) which in turn shape their decision field and may alter their framing behaviour. This is especially important in criminal justice, where changing elements in the surround, such as the dominance of ideas of 'populist punitiveness' or media campaigns, can have a significant impact on the decision-makers' field, in the form of changes in law or policy. These latter changes can in turn affect decision-making in actual cases, suggesting that the connections between legal rule and policy, on the one hand, and actual case decision-making, on the other, deserves closer analysis. Kemp and Gelsthorpe present some examples of this effect in Chapter 2. They observe that diversion of juveniles from court and custody was repeatedly advocated by government. (Where did this policy come from? Was it the product of a welfare ideology, or was there a hidden economic force at work? Or did economics make welfarism an attractive ideology?) They also mention the change in political mood in the 1990s as the reason for a change in police cautioning policy. Similarly, they suggest that increased pressure exerted upon custody officers to reduce delays in decision-making may have led to an increase in prosecutions (presumably as an effect of the precautionary principle in decision-making to err on the side of caution). Leanne Weber in Chapter 8 provides a second example. She observes that changes in policy in decision-making about immigrants at ports of entry have been prompted by a rapidly growing number of arrivals. Here, a change in the surround has led to a change in the field which has almost certainly led to a corresponding change in officials' framing behaviour in individual cases. A third example of the operation of this principle is in Chapter 5, in which Padfield, Liebling and Arnold discuss the release of life sentence prisoners. They describe the parole board's culture as risk averse. This adoption of the precautionary principle may well be a feature of criminal justice decision-making involving offenders, especially in settings of some public visibility, since the typical decision-maker is likely to feel a degree of vulnerability when dealing with a risky, threatening and discredited population.

Second, analyses of criminal justice decisions frequently overlook other important interested individuals or groups, real or virtual. They often do not attend to the behaviour of the subjects of decisions, and they also tend to ignore the audiences for criminal justice decisions. Their natural focus is upon the exercise of choice and the use of reasoning of those officials who are legally empowered to exercise discretion. But decision subjects are rarely, if ever, totally passive participants in the decision-making process, even if their 'participation' is often unwitting or inadvertent. Padfield, Liebling and Arnold point out (Chapter 5), for example, that prisoners do themselves play a part in decisions about the release of lifers, with those presenting a co-operative and compliant front being more sympathetically viewed. In a decision like parole release, however, the presentation of self can be a very precarious interpretive business. A display of 'remorse' or a dispassionate account of one's crime can be positively or pejoratively interpreted. For example:

> The prisoner had been convicted of homicide, first degree. He had struggled with his victim in a swimming pool before killing him by beating him over the head with a baseball bat. According to the official record, the struggle was the result of an attack by the prisoner on his victim. The prisoner's account, given in what seemed a straightforward manner, was that the victim had persisted in making vigorous homosexual advances towards him which he was trying to repel, when he finally resorted to the baseball bat. The reports on the prisoner's activities in the institution were very positive, as was his psychiatric evaluation. The inmate claimed during his hearing to have had a religious conversion, which he described at length, while imprisoned. When the prisoner left the room, the interviewing board member, who by the convention operated by the parole board in question would nominate the decision for the three-member panel, began by saying: 'Well, he seems to have developed some controls …'. At this point the second panel member grimaced to the third and, without any debate, interrupted before the first speaker could continue to say that he did not accept the prisoner's account of his crime, that it was a fabrication, and that his story about his religious conversion was merely a tactic designed to impress the board. The third panel member then intervened to support this view. Parole was denied.
>
> (Hawkins 1971)

Padfield, Liebling and Arnold draw particular attention to the problems caused when prisoners deny that they were guilty of an offence. Denial can be framed by decision-makers in terms that satisfy concerns both of instrumentalism (such behaviour does not bode well for the person's responsiveness to treatment) and expressivism (such behaviour deserves extra punishment for a failure to acknowledge the wrong done). The subject of the decision slips easily into a double bind, since the paradox is that if the prisoner does not deny, but recognises his or her guilt, that too can be pejoratively framed.

Similarly, criminal justice decision-makers perform in front of an audience, another important element in legal decisions. Audiences may be both real and virtual. The real audiences are comprised of those with a direct interest in the fate of a particular case (in the example of parole, for instance, the inmate, family members, other prisoners, prison and supervisory staff, and so on). The virtual audience, the imagined audience with an interest in criminal justice decisions, in general as well as in particular cases, might consist of the media, potential victims and the like. The criminal justice bureaucracy is an actor on a public stage whose audiences constantly scrutinise its activities and accomplishments, thereby placing demands on it to display various signs of its impact and effectiveness. And like all of those who play to audiences, the institutions of criminal justice are concerned with how well they are received. Displaying and underlining various values to the public in a familiar moral framework helps decision-makers cement public beliefs, values and expectations about what is right and proper.

A third silence in the research literature is of close analysis of parallel decision-making. It is essential to understand better the interaction observable when decision-makers work together to produce a single outcome (Hawkins 1983a). In Chapter 7, by Holloway and Grounds, there is an indication of the way in which a medical officer was characterised by the medical member of the Tribunal. In this example, it seems that a decision outcome – ostensibly one to be produced by a group – rested on the persuasiveness of a particular decision-maker, especially as this person, as the medical member, was able to make a claim of expertise. Similarly, the authors report that hearings when independent psychiatrists were present were significantly more likely to result in a decision to discharge than hearings where no independent psychiatrist was present. Not only is it tempting, when debating the issues, for lay or non-medical decision-makers to take refuge in the presumed expertise of a particular decision-maker, but the availability of a body of knowledge and expertise can confer particular credibility upon the decision outcome because it can be made to seem rational.

It is also the case, however, that differences in individual decision-making, of the sort Weber identified (Chapter 8), need further attention from researchers in both parallel and serial forms of decision-making. Different approaches to decision-making – different framing behaviour – are not necessarily visible in differences in outcome. Different approaches may yield the same outcome, even in decisions where outcomes are binary, and therefore simple. Equally, the same framing behaviour may produce different outcomes. Much depends on the systems of meaning employed by each decision-maker in making sense of features deemed relevant in the case, for decision-makers do not approach each decision task with, as it were, carte blanche, and go on to consider a number of apparently relevant 'factors' in turn. Instead they go about the task with a worldview, a system of meanings, beliefs, assumptions and ideas which makes sense of the world as they experience it.

Policy concerns and the preoccupation with consistency in decision outcomes

The words 'arbitrary', 'inconsistent' and 'unfair' appear in a number of chapters in this book in connection with decision outcomes, just as cases about which decisions have to be made are sometimes described as 'similar' or 'different'. The use of such terms is not surprising when a major concern of researchers is to remedy current perceived deficiencies. Sometimes, however, I wonder whether we are not a little too cavalier in our use of these terms in the absence of a close analysis of a particular decision-making process and the practices and systems of meaning employed by those deciding. Another reason to explore the phenomenon of discretion empirically is to understand better the conditions under which matters that exercise lawyers such as 'consistency' or 'inconsistency', 'discrimination' or 'disparity' are to be discerned.

Let us take the idea of inconsistency. The first point to make is that consistency is an aspect of order in decision-making, but inconsistency is inevitable in the criminal justice system. This is because discretion, like matter, is indestructible. Inconsistency of outcome may be regarded as (among other things) a functional response to scarce resources. There is an irony in the fact that much decision-making (especially in law enforcement) depends on the artful use of inconsistency by selectively suspending the formalities of the criminal law where certain types of people, acts or events are concerned. Second, 'consistency' or 'inconsistency' are not always readily discernible as attributes of decision outcomes, but are recognised in different ways by different legal actors. Furthermore, the situated rationality of the decision-maker may not fit with the conceptions of rationality held by the researcher or critic. Holloway and Grounds (Chapter 7) make the point that the possibility that similar cases are dealt with in different ways is a cause for concern.

One problem here, however, is that critics discern 'similarity' in a case where none may have existed for the decision-maker. This creates major problems for those concerned with the practical control of discretion. Kemp and Gelsthorpe present a number of examples of different outcomes arising in the 'same' case, suggesting that they serve as instances of inconsistency in the application of rules. They may indeed be examples of inconsistency, though to assert this is to assume that there were no differences in the cases as framed by the decision-makers, whereas it is perfectly possible that two decision-makers were responding rationally – and consistently – to what they (but not the researchers) regarded as differences in key features in the cases. There are, of course, methodological implications here.

Kemp and Gelsthorpe give an interesting example in Chapter 2 of an effort to introduce greater consistency into decision-making with the use of the decision-making matrix in the Northamptonshire Police Force. Put another way, this can be seen as an effort to systematise the decision-making frame of police officers in deciding about prosecution. In the matrix intended to guide and control the exercise of discretion, the existence of latitude afforded the decision-maker in rating an offence may well lead, as the authors suggest, to what appears to be inconsistency and unfairness. But these are not necessary conditions, since without such latitude inconsistencies may still arise, as decision-makers are perfectly capable of framing the same phenomenon (in this case criminal behaviour) differently. Indeed, the example the authors give (two girls involved in the same criminal transaction, defined in one case as burglary and as criminal damage in the other) makes the point very well. It also suggests that from a policy point of view, efforts to regulate discretion by apparently narrowing its scope will not necessarily solve the problem. Indeed, Thomas observes (Chapter 3) that guidelines which are too rigid will produce 'a mechanical appearance of consistency' which is capable of creating injustice. It often seems to be overlooked that inconsistency of outcome can equally be achieved by treating two apparently unlike cases in like ways, though this is probably less visible than the two apparently like cases that are dealt with in unlike ways.

One conclusion to be drawn from Kemp and Gelsthorpe's interesting chapter is that human aspects of decision-making are extraordinarily resilient in the face of efforts to systematise the control of discretion. Their essay can be read as the story of a struggle to impose, in the interests of greater consistency, systematic decision-making behaviour onto highly resistant organisational and cultural practices. This leads the authors to conclude that such efforts have so far been ineffective in ensuring fairness, consistency and accountability. Furthermore, efforts to regulate discretion, Kemp and Gelsthorpe warn, could encourage a routinised approach to decision-making if decision-makers are under pressure to reduce delay. Certainly, the more that decision-makers decide cases repetitively (the more they become 'repeat players' in Galanter's (1974) terminology), the more inevitable the onset of decision-making routines becomes.

On rules

Rules are regarded by lawyers as an appropriate remedy for the waywardness of discretion (Davis 1969). Rules are sanctified. The centrality of rules presumably reflects an instrumental orientation to them, an assumption that rules are there for some practical, not expressive, end. It is as if their very presence ensures appropriate action. This is not to deny that rules are valuable for decision-makers. They are something that decision-makers can cling to, an anchor in uncertain waters. It is tempting, given celebrated remarks such as Davis' 'where law ends tyranny will begin' (1969: 3), to assume uncritically, as Orwell might have had it, that rules are good, discretion is bad. But, as Thomas shows (Chapter 3) in connection with his discussion of the Criminal Justice Act 1982, formal rules do not of necessity have an impact on practice. Rules used as a device to control inconsistency of decision-making can create their own perversities, since decision-makers react differently to the same rules, with some following rules more closely than others. One form of inconsistent outcome can arise where a rule-following decision-maker decides one way, and a rule-ignoring decision-maker decides an apparently similar case differently. Others, under certain conditions, cannot or will not follow rules (they cannot remember the rules, they find the rule seems not to fit the case, two rules apparently conflict, and so on: Long 1981). Rules can sometimes be tyrannical. Equally, they may simply be poorly crafted, ambiguous or conducive to abusive decision behaviour. Furthermore, it should not be assumed that rules operate upon decision-makers in a simple causal way. It may not be a case that 'the rule is this, therefore I must do that'. It may instead be a matter of 'I do this and justify what I do in terms of this rule' (so-called 'presentational rules', about which, more below). It is worth recalling Zimmerman's observation that 'outcomes are typically effected in an acceptable fashion by actions that are describable ... as in accordance with rules' (Zimmerman 1971).

Systems of formal rules, for all their appearance of precision and specificity, work in only imprecise ways. Indeed, consistent practice is not necessarily assisted by the drafting of ever more elaborate schemes of rules. The criminal justice system is not neatly organised into smoothly functioning institutional arrangements, but in reality, as a loosely coupled set of subsystems, is much more messy, with internal inefficiencies and conflicts. Those enforcing rules may seek to attain the broad aim of a legal mandate in general terms, but the specific question of whether and how a particular rule applies in a particular circumstance will inevitably be reserved for, or assumed within, the discretion of the legal actor concerned. It is important, therefore, to understand better how rules are interpreted and given meaning. In the absence of better understanding of the conditions under which rules are interpreted and acted on in particular ways, it is simplistic of Davis (1969) to imagine that if discretion is reduced, somehow greater justice will be a natural consequence (see further Baldwin and Hawkins 1984).

One of the pervasive findings to have emerged from studies of law enforcement is that it is often the case that rules are not enforced as those who formulated them might have expected. Instead, bargaining is prevalent. Rules are valuable when their enforcement is suspended for they are an important resource that can be surrendered by rule-users in pursuit of some broader goal of social order or the public interest. Order is often attained more efficiently, control agents believe, by sacrificing or forbearing from the enforcement of rules. This is an aspect of the paradox of control, for enforcement of the broad legal mandate is sought in the suspension of narrow legal enforcement (Hawkins 2002: 299). Many officials operate in a symbiotic relationship, whose essence is a bargain with those with whom they work. Thus the enforcement of rules is frequently suspended as part of a tacit or sometimes explicit bargain to achieve the compliance of the target of law enforcement, whether person or organisation. Kemp and Gelsthorpe (Chapter 2) mention the police practice of 'turning a blind eye' to first-time young offenders. This practice is often, doubtless, sanctioned in the hope or expectation that the offender will respond positively to the gesture. Similarly, Liebling and Price (Chapter 4) cite Sykes' (1958) finding that disobedience by prisoners was sometimes deliberately ignored by prison staff who clearly recognised that a calculated decision not to enforce certain rules may actually achieve compliance more easily than insistence upon the formalities of enforcement. Rule breaking may be a threat to order, but rule enforcement is not necessarily conducive to order. The findings of Liebling and Price in their prison world are reminiscent of those from regulatory enforcement, which show that suspension of rules which could be immediately enforced is a familiar way in which legal officials get things done in the longer-term interests of compliance (Hawkins 1984). Liebling and Price argue, as does some of the regulation literature, that less coercive methods may be more effective (Vogel 1986). The dependence of prison staff on the consent of prisoners, compelled by a need to manage the institution, is analogous to the dependence of regulatory inspectors on the businesses they regulate for information about manufacturing processes and work practices and for their ultimate compliance. Their willing suspension of the prosecution with which they could theoretically proceed sets up an expectation of reciprocity from the other side expressed in a willingness to comply, at least in principle (Hawkins 1984). Indeed, the norm of reciprocity is a good illustration of a social rule that sometimes trumps a legal rule. As well as discretion in the use of rules, there are rules in the use of discretion.

This emphasises the important role played in some forms of decision-making by personal relationships, also illustrated in the Chapter by Liebling and Price (Chapter 4). They observe that in the prison wing where there was a lack of informal contact between staff and prisoners, control was more likely to be exerted by staff by resort to formal procedures. This is consistent with the idea of 'relational distance' (Black 1976) which stresses that formal forms of enforcement are more likely to be used the more control agents deal with a population of strangers. The decisions made in bargaining relationships in enforcement are underpinned by reciprocity and trust. Legal control in such settings is managed as a sort of game, where both sides know the rules and trust the other not to depart from established conventions and settled expectations (the 'tactical agreements' to which Liebling and Price refer). Of course, the selective enforcement of rules, though sanctioned as a practical organisational device in various legal settings, runs counter to the desire for the legal value of consistency. Such heavy reliance upon discretion draws attention to the gap between legal word and legal deed which is not an embarrassment, but a resource for rule-users, for it allows them to enforce their conception of their mandate, rather than the breach of a rule.

Some small methodological notes

How is criminal justice decision-making research to be conducted? One of the problems for researchers is to disentangle instrumental and expressive practices in decision-making. Are release decisions, for example, to be seen in instrumental terms as largely governed by some sort of risk assessment? Or can they be interpreted as expressing a concern to condone or condemn the offender or the crime? Padfield, Liebling and Arnold in Chapter 5 observe that an inmate's behaviour in prison was seen as significant by the parole board. A co-operative attitude and a willingness to accept responsibility for the offence were treated as indicators of maturity. Parole board members may well have reasoned in such an instrumental fashion (although even here there are strong expressive elements – accepting responsibility for one's offence is frequently regarded as a symbolically significant indicator of moral repair). But equally such features may be read another way, as an indicator of the primacy of organisational values, since co-operative prisoners are highly valued in institutions preoccupied with the need to maintain control. Parole boards (where they exist) play a key role in furthering in prisons such organisationally-defined values (Hawkins 1972; 1986). Indeed, making sense of what has been observed is often difficult. For example, Padfield, Liebling and Arnold discuss the problem of predicting dangerousness in the context of their analysis of decisions about lifer panels, a very instrumental view of parole board decision-making. Does this emphasis arise because public policy or the law imply some sort of predictive decision-making, and it is therefore assumed that decision-makers respond by behaving in the same fashion? Or could it be that decision-makers are exercising discretion in symbolic ways? After all, decisions about the release of prisoners on parole are bound up with judgments which inevitably appear to condone or condemn a prisoner's acts and behaviour. In other words, far from looking forward to predict future behaviour, is it conceivable that parole board members are actually looking back to reflect on the offence?

One of the problems of correlational research is that 'factors' associated with decision outcomes are assumed to be causally linked with them. Holloway and Grounds (Chapter 7) found that the variable most closely connected with Mental Health Review Tribunal decisions was the written opinion of the patient's responsible medical officer. This is reminiscent of the finding that the variable that used to be most closely associated with parole decisions in England and Wales was the recommendation of the Assistant Governor. But it is important to ask what produces this correlation. Holloway and Grounds suggest that the reputation or experience of the officer were influential. It is also conceivable that a conception of the greater familiarity of the officer with the case, or the officer's assumed greater expertise, were also regarded as important. However, a further possibility is that following a recommendation from a reputable source is a rational and defensible way of deciding, especially when dealing with a risky population. Again, it is worth repeating that recommendations do not necessarily reflect a linear flow from person recommending to decision-maker to outcome. It is quite possible that this is another example of a recommendation sometimes made in anticipation of what the decision-maker may find acceptable. Congruence between recommendation and outcome poses a difficult problem methodologically since it may mask two independent effects. It may indicate a linear relationship in which a recommendation is sufficiently persuasive that the decision-maker acts upon it; but it may also arise where the recommendation is made in anticipation of what is expected by or thought to be tolerable to the later decision-maker.

Conventional correlational analysis would find it hard to disentangle these effects. To make the point another way, in Chapter 7, the authors report the parole study by Heinz et al. (1976) and its finding that features such as inmates' participation in prison programmes, prison misconduct record, prospects for employment after release, and level of intelligence were 'influential' in the decision to grant parole. But it is necessary to know how and why they were influential. Again, the authors' finding that the nature of the prisoner's offence and criminal history were significantly associated with decisions to grant parole is hardly surprising; but what we do not know is what the meaning of these features were for those making the decision – how, in other words, the raw material for decision was framed. Indeed, correlational analysis may lose sight of systems of meaning in a decision. It is very likely that the 'gravity of the crime' does not mean the same thing for the same decision-maker across all cases. To isolate features which correlate with outcome is not to 'explain' the outcome. For example, in Chapter 7 we read that in the study by Burns et al. (1999) failure to appreciate the wrongfulness of offending behaviour and the absence of remorse were viewed by decision-makers as a sign of 'danger'. This may be so, but an alternative explanation is that such features were framed as indicative of a person who inhabited a different moral world, a person who is deserving of blame for his or her moral frailties. The centrality of the moral frame in legal decision-making must not be underestimated. In this connection, it is noteworthy that in Weber's chapter (Chapter 8), immigration decisions were found to be made along two primary dimensions, one of which was the moral (see generally, Hawkins 2002: Chapter 11).

The decision-maker in criminal justice works in a surround characterised by an environment of risk with possible adverse consequences for the decision-maker, potential victims and sometimes the system itself. This encourages cautious, risk averse decision behaviour. The clinicians analysed in Chapter 6 and the members of the

Mental Health Review Tribunals in Chapter 7 were aware that they were working in an environment of potentially great criticism if anything went wrong. One of the unfortunate features of those segments of the criminal justice system that are concerned with the selective lifting of the criminal sanction (in contrast with those who enforce law or impose punishment) is that they are peculiarly vulnerable to criticism, since much of the media and public regard decisions to lift the criminal sanction as expressions of unwarranted leniency, or a symbolic condoning of offence or offender. A successful decision outcome (the released person who readjusts to life in the community, or who successfully completes his or her period of supervision) is invisible; only failure has the potential to come to public attention. To the extent that this setting makes decision-makers more cautious, its effects are unlikely to show in conventional correlational research. In analysing decision-making about the risk of offenders, one aspect to take into account is that conceptions of risk have to be understood also as about risk to the decision-makers themselves, as evidence presented by Grounds, Howes and Gelsthorpe in Chapter 6 suggests.

Criminal justice decision-making as a search for order and rationality

It is important for decision-makers to operate in and help sustain an orderly, that is, a knowable and predictable environment. Ordering devices are conducive to stability. This puts a heavy emphasis on routine, an important feature in discretionary behaviour, since it makes for decision-making efficiency. It may be a commitment to predictability and efficiency that encouraged Leanne Weber's immigration officers to rely more for guidance on accepted local practice than on formal guidelines. Whether or not guidelines are available, decision-makers often 'explain' their decisions by reference to 'intuition', 'hunch' or 'gut feeling' (see Chapter 6) which are derived from previous experience. Such terms may be employed when decision-makers are conscious of a lack of an orderly or seemingly rational way of reasoning. For example, writing of sentencing judges, Ashworth et al. (1984: 50) reported, 'Only a minority ... regarded sentencing as a matter of principles and reasoned conclusions. Most judges described it as an intuitive process, using such terms as "instinct", "hunch" and "feeling".' This form of decision-making often relies on the use of analogy, in which present problems are fitted into past, apparently similar, cases or types. Such decision-making tends to lead to routinised behaviour in which outcomes are largely unexplored and produced relatively quickly, a decision practice adopted particularly by those who have to deal quickly with a large number of cases or problems arising in succession (for an example, see Gilboy 1991).

Decision-makers have to simplify the complexities involved in criminal justice decision-making, even though the matter may be officially portrayed as one of great complexity. They do not confront for practical purposes a unique world of distinctive events, problems and people. Matters are simplified and made sense of by seeking pattern, by using past experience and aligning the present with the past. Decisions are likely to be made intuitively when existing simple decision rules can be employed to allow the matter to be categorised readily, and only made reflectively when a new problem arises, or when the possible implications of a course of action seem serious. One of the characteristic features of the exercise of discretion by legal actors is that the extent of their experience is such that they are readily able to categorise most events according to some existing framing scheme derived from past events and organisational precedents in order to decide what they ought to do in any particular case. The allocation of a certain event, person or problem to a particular type or category itself tends to determine the action to be taken, since specific consequences frequently flow from the type or category settled upon. This simplifies the nature of the problem to be handled.

Organisational work often requires decisions to be made in repetitive ways (Emerson and Paley 1992; Feldman 1992; Manning 1992). The experience of making the same sorts of decisions about the same sorts of people or problems contributes to the emergence of what Skolnick (1966) termed 'perceptual short-hand': ways of classifying and appraising each matter by focusing on the extent to which it presents features held to be typical of other such cases. This is possible because decision-makers develop understandings of what are 'normal cases' and 'normal ways' of deciding (Sudnow 1965) which lead to the development of typification, one of a number of ordering processes in decision-making. Typification arises partly because familiarity with the broad features of routine cases gives decision-makers confidence in being able to see similarities in other cases, and partly for reasons of efficiency, saving the resources and sometimes the anxiety otherwise involved in addressing each new case afresh. It is not only a way of making decisions quickly and at little cost, but a process that becomes simpler and more routine as decision-makers gain experience, hardening with the passage of time (Rubinstein 1973). Typification is another way of providing a rational defence against criticism, since a decision in a particular matter may be aligned with other typical cases, and therefore presented as routine and un-exceptional practice. Routine decision-making arising from repetitive behaviour is also more likely to be stable, consistent, and therefore predictable than the more individualistic decision-making behaviour reserved for those cases that seem unusual in some way, or those decisions not normally made in repetitive ways. Typification leads to a particular decision outcome in routine cases since a matter categorised in a particular way will be routinely dealt with in the way reserved for cases of that kind. The crucial decision here, therefore, is bound up in the typification itself: the allocation of matters to categories or fitting particular cases into a type of case (see, for illustration, Rosett and Cressey 1976; Sudnow 1965). A matter deemed to be 'normal', 'typical' or 'routine' will be dealt with in normal, typical or routine ways.

Weber (Chapter 8) makes the point that socio-legal analyses of decision-making within large organisations draws attention to the routines that develop in response to large workloads and repetitive decisions, but argues that exclusive concentration on organisational processes risks losing sight of the role of individual agency. But this is to give insufficient recognition to the fact that routine is not only efficient, but more importantly in this context, being a member of an organisation inevitably shapes the framing behaviour of officials.[6] Routine is also a useful justificatory mechanism, however, because decision-making processes or outcomes are more readily justifiable or defensible if they can be presented as following 'normal practice' or a 'routine procedure', just as presentational rules are a valuable means of justifying an outcome. The tendency of decision-makers to employ presentational devices is difficult to uncover in conventional correlational analysis. Decision outcomes are defensible when they can be integrated into a rational system of thought and reasoning.

Decision-making behaviour involves a search for order, and one aspect of that conception of order is a need to secure decisions in some conception of rationality. A good example of this practice is found in Chapter 5, with Padfield, Liebling and Arnold's work on discretionary lifer panels of the parole board. What the board looks for both in its parole dossiers and at the hearing is evidence of 'change'. This was the case in my own doctoral research on decision-making by American parole boards conducted more than 30 years ago (Hawkins 1971), and it is interesting to observe the resilience of 'change' as an ostensible feature in boards' decision-making across jurisdictions and over time (time in which there have been profound shifts in official ideology about the penal system and its guiding principles). Change may be suggested to parole boards by indicators such as efforts at self-improvement during imprisonment, realistic release plans and (especially) that subtle and elusive feature of the growth of an offender's 'insight' into his or her behaviour. If decision-makers can also satisfy themselves that such features are present, they can satisfy themselves that a decision to parole will appear rational, not only to themselves, but to their interested audiences. This may be the explanation for the finding in Chapter 7 that the medical members of Mental Health Review Tribunals were heard persuading patients to try new treatments in an effort to help them make progress. An instrumental interpretation of this would be that such treatments might result in a behavioural difference. Expressively, however, such practices give the decision-makers 'something to go on', allowing them a means of justifying a decision, and making it appear rational. One element in this conception of rationality, and one assuming especial importance in areas of decision-making where there is a degree of public visibility and corresponding vulnerability to criticism, is the idea that a decision is defensible. The use of a vocabulary that is recognisable and comprehensible helps make sense of the decision outcome to those with an interest in it. It suggests the application of rationality in an uncertain world.

There are two final remarks to make. First, criminal justice research might give more emphasis to understanding criminal justice law and practice as implicated in expressive as well as instrumental activity. Analysis of criminal justice decision-making often shows both instrumental and expressive conceptions at work. Kemp and Gelsthorpe (Chapter 2) observe, for example, that the establishment of separate courts for juveniles in 1908 was to further the dual role of the court in providing both welfare and justice. Simultaneously doing good and doing justice are two of the major themes of 20th century criminal justice. Many types of criminal justice decisions are a form of communication which takes analysis of its use into the realm of the expressive,[7] for here conveying messages or manufacturing appearances is more important than the instrumental concern to effect some practical and desirable change in the world. Expressive action is important as it maintains the legitimacy of the criminal justice organisation and quietens criticism (Edelman 1964). The expressive use of decision-making sustains moral cohesion in the social world, helping bind people together in a common vision which dictates an appropriate response to problems which constitute a threat.

Second, one of the themes of these essays is the enormous difficulty that exists in trying to regulate the exercise of discretion. Constraints on discretion can be formal, institutionalised and visible, as where legal categories such as eligibility provisions or bureaucratic provisions are used. Equally, constraints may operate informally, when, for example, screening or case-handling decisions are made in a setting of limited resources. Lawyers inevitably think of discretion as constrained only by legal rules and procedures, while social scientists are also interested in other constraints that operate to shape or curtail the exercise of discretion that arise from other sources (Hawkins 2002). It is tempting always to think about changing structures or procedures to change outcomes. But sometimes this may be a vain hope. Thomas, for example (Chapter 3), concludes that the introduction of statutory criteria for sentencing in the Criminal Justice Act 1982 had little impact on sentencing practice. One conclusion to be drawn from all of this is that one way towards more intelligent and sensitive regulation might be by understanding better the phenomenon to be regulated. These essays are an important contribution to this end.

Notes

1 See, for example: Baldwin and McConville 1977; Banton 1964; Black 1980; Ericson and Baranek 1982; Heumann 1978; Law and Society Review 1979; Manning 1977; Mather 1979; Maynard 1984; McConville, Sanders and Leng 1991; Piliavin and Briar 1964; Rosett and Cressey 1976; Skolnick 1966. There are probably fewer studies of field-level decision-making concerned with the behaviour of social workers, probation officers, and the like. See, for example, Asquith 1982; Cicourel 1968; Dingwall, Eekelaar and Murray 1983; Emerson 1969; and Prottas 1979.
2 There is now a sizeable literature on the enforcement of regulation. See, for instance, Bardach and Kagan 1982; Braithwaite 1985; Braithwaite, Walker and Grabosky 1987; Carson 1970a; 1970b; Grabosky and Braithwaite 1986; Hawkins 1983b; 1984; Hawkins and Thomas 1984; Hutter 1988; 1989; 1997; Kagan 1978; 1984; 1989; 1994, Kagan and Scholz 1984; Kelman 1981; Law Commission 1969; Manning 1987a, Reiss 1983; 1984; Richardson, Ogus and Burrows 1982; Scholz 1984; Schuck 1972; Shover, Clelland and Lynxwiler 1986; Shover, Lynxwiler, Groce and Clelland 1984.
3 These ideas are pursued at greater length in Hawkins 2002. I have drawn in this section on earlier work appearing, inter alia, in Hawkins 1986; 1992a; 1992b; Manning 1986; 1992; Manning and Hawkins 1989; 1990.
4 It is essential to understand framing processes better. How is it, for example, that the same person may be characterised by different decision-makers as 'happy-go-lucky' or 'couldn't-care-less', with profoundly important consequences for the outcome (Hawkins 1983a)?
5 The present essays maintain the focus on case decision-making. Attention now needs to be devoted to policy decision-making, in which decisions are made explicitly to produce change in the decision field and thereby in

framing practices.

6 It is unfortunate that lack of space precludes more than passing discussion of the important role of organisational life and values in criminal justice decision-making. It has to be observed, however, that a great deal of decision-making is heavily imprinted with its organisational provenance. Organisations impose demands of their own upon their actors, who respond in turn by making decisions for their own organisationally motivated reasons.

7 Decision-making by individual criminal justice officials can also be seen as a form of expressive behaviour within an organisational context since, whatever else they do, they are concerned to display their activity and good judgment.

References

Ashworth, et al. (1984) *Sentencing in the Crown Court.* Oxford: Centre for Criminological Research Occasional Paper no. 10.

Asquith, S. (1982) *Children and justice: decision-making in children's hearings and juvenile courts.* Edinburgh: Edinburgh University Press.

Baldwin, J. and McConville, M. (1977) *Negotiated justice.* Oxford: Martin Robertson.

Baldwin, R. and Hawkins, K. (1984) 'Discretionary justice: Davis reconsidered', *Public Law*, Winter, 570–599.

Banton, M. (1964) *The policeman in the community.* London: Tavistock.

Bardach, E. and Kagan, R.A. (1982) *Going by the book: the problem of regulatory unreasonableness.* Philadelphia: Temple University Press.

Black, D. (1976) *The behavior of law.* New York: Academic Press.

Black, D. (1980) *The manners and customs of the police.* New York: Academic Press.

Braithwaite, J. (1985) *To punish or persuade: enforcement of coal mine safety.* Albany, NY: State University of New York Press.

Braithwaite, J., Walker, J. and Grabosky, P. (1987) 'An enforcement taxonomy of regulatory agencies', *Law and Policy*, 9(3), 323–351.

Burns, R. et al. (1999) 'Perspectives on parole: the board members' viewpoint', *Federal Probation*, 63(1), 16–21.

Carson, W.G. (1970a) 'Some sociological aspects of strict liability and the enforcement of factory legislation', *Modern Law Review*, 33(4), 396–412.

Carson, W.G. (1970b) 'White-collar crime and the enforcement of factory legislation', *British Journal of Criminology*, 10(4), 383–398.

Cicourel, A. (1968) *The social organization of juvenile justice.* New York: Wiley.

Davis, K.C. (1969) *Discretionary justice. A preliminary inquiry.* Baton Rouge, LA: Louisiana State University Press.

Dingwall, R., Eekelaar, J. and Murray, T. (1983) *The protection of children: state intervention and family life.* Oxford: Blackwell.

Dworkin, R. (1977) *Taking rights seriously.* Cambridge, MA: Harvard University Press.

Edelman, M. (1964) *The symbolic uses of politics*. Urbana, Ill: University of Illinois Press.

Emerson, R.M. (1969) *Judging delinquents: context and process in the juvenile court*. Chicago: Aldine.

Emerson, R.M. (1983) 'Holistic effects in social control decision-making', *Law and Society Review*, 17(3), 425–455.

Emerson, R.M. (1991) 'Case processing and interorganisational knowledge: detecting the "real reasons" for referrals', *Social Problems*, 38(2), 1101–1115.

Emerson, R.M. and Paley, B. (1992) 'Organisational horizons and complaint-filing' in K. Hawkins (ed.) *The uses of discretion*. Oxford: Clarendon Press.

Ericson, R.V. and Baranek, P.M. (1982) *The ordering of justice*. Toronto: University of Toronto Press.

Feder, L. (1994) 'Psychiatric hospitalization history and parole decisions', *Law and Human Behavior*, 18 (4), 395–410.

Feldman, M. (1992) 'Social limits to discretion: an organisational perspective' in K. Hawkins (ed.) *The uses of discretion*. Oxford: Clarendon Press.

Galanter, M. (1974) 'Why the "haves" come out ahead: speculations on the limits of legal change', *Law and Society Review*, 9, 95–160.

Galligan, D. (1986) *Discretionary powers: a legal study of official discretion*. Oxford: Clarendon Press.

Gilboy, J.A. (1991) 'Deciding who gets in. Decision-making by Immigration Inspectors', *Law and Society Review*, 25(3), 571–599.

Goffman, E. (1974) *Frame analysis: an essay on the organization of experience*. Harmondsworth: Penguin Books.

Grabosky, P. and Braithwaite, J. (1986) *Of manners gentle: enforcement strategies of Australian business regulatory agencies*. Melbourne: Oxford University Press.

Handler, J. (1986) *The conditions of discretion: autonomy, community, bureaucracy*. New York: Russell Sage.

Hawkins, K. (1971) *Parole selection: the American experience* (Ph.D. dissertation, Cambridge University).

Hawkins, K. (1972) 'Some consequences of a parole system for prison management' in D.J. West (ed) *The future of parole*. London: Duckworth.

Hawkins, K. (1983a) 'Assessing evil: decision behaviour and parole board justice', *British Journal of Criminology*, 23(2), 101–127.

Hawkins, K. (1983b) 'Bargain and bluff: compliance strategy and deterrence in the enforcement of regulation', *Law and Policy Quarterly*, 5(1), 35–73.

Hawkins, K. (1984) *Environment and enforcement. Regulation and the social definition of pollution*. Oxford: Clarendon Press.

Hawkins, K. (1986) 'On legal decision-making', *Washington and Lee Law Review*, 43(4), 1161–1242.

Hawkins, K. (1992a) 'The use of legal discretion: perspectives from law and social science' in K. Hawkins (ed.) *The uses of discretion*. Oxford: Clarendon Press.

Hawkins, K. (ed.) (1992b) *The uses of discretion*. Oxford: Clarendon Press.

Hawkins, K. (2002) *Law as last resort: prosecution decision-making in a regulatory agency*. Oxford: Oxford University Press.

Hawkins, K. and Thomas, J.M. (eds.) (1984) *Enforcing regulation.* Boston: Kluwer-Nijhoff.

Heinz, A. et al. (1976) 'Sentencing by parole board: an evaluation', *The Journal of Criminal Law and Criminology,* 67(1), 1–31.

Heumann, M. (1978) *Plea bargaining. The experiences of prosecutors, judges, and defense attorneys.* Chicago: University of Chicago Press.

Hutter, B.M. (1988) *The reasonable arm of the law? The law enforcement procedures of environmental health officers.* Oxford: Clarendon Press.

Hutter, B.M. (1989) 'Variations in regulatory enforcement styles', *Law and Policy,* 11(2), 153–174.

Hutter, B.M. (1997) *Compliance: regulation and environment.* Oxford: Clarendon Press.

Kagan, R.A. (1978) *Regulatory justice. Implementing a wage-price freeze.* New York: Russell Sage Foundation.

Kagan, R.A. (1984) 'On regulatory inspectorates and police' in K. Hawkins and J.M. Thomas (eds.) *Enforcing regulation.* Boston: Kluwer-Nijhoff.

Kagan, R.A. (1989) 'Editor's introduction: understanding regulatory enforcement', *Law and Policy,* 11(2), 89–119.

Kagan, R.A. (1994) 'Regulatory enforcement' in D.H. Rosenbloom and R.D. Schwartz (eds.) *Handbook of regulation and administrative law.* New York: Marcel Dekker.

Kagan, R.A. and Scholz, J.T. (1984) 'The "criminology of the corporation" and regulatory enforcement strategies' in: K. Hawkins and J.M. Thomas (eds.) *Enforcing regulation.* Boston: Kluwer-Nijhoff.

Kelman, S. (1981) *Regulating America, regulating Sweden: a comparative study of occupational safety and health policy.* Cambridge, Mass: MIT Press.

Law and Society Review (1979) Special Issue on plea bargaining, *Law and Society Review,* 13(2).

Law Commission (1969) *Strict liability and the enforcement of the Factories Act 1961* (Working Paper no.30).

Lipsky, M. (1980) *Street-level bureaucracy: dilemmas of the individual in public services.* New York: Russell Sage Foundation.

Long, S. (1981) 'Social control in the cvil law: the case of income tax enforcement' in H.L. Ross (ed.) *Law and deviance.* Beverly Hills: Sage.

Lovegrove, A. (1984) 'The listing of criminal cases in the Crown Court as an administrative discretion', *Criminal Law Review,* 738–749.

Manning, P.K. (1977) *Police work: the social organization of policing.* Cambridge, Mass: MIT Press.

Manning, P.K. (1986) 'The social reality and social organization of natural decision-making', *Washington and Lee Law Review,* 43(4), 1291–1311.

Manning, P.K. (1987a) 'Ironies of compliance' in C. Shearing and P. Stenning (eds.) *Private policing.* Newbury Park, Calif: Sage.

Manning, P.K. (1992) '"Big bang" decisions: notes on a naturalistic approach' in K. Hawkins (ed.) *The uses of discretion.* Oxford: Clarendon Press.

Manning, P.K. and Hawkins, K. (1989) 'Police decision-making' in M. Weatheritt (ed.) *Police research: some future prospects.* Aldershot: Avebury.

Manning, P.K. and Hawkins, K. (1990) 'Legal decisions: a frame analytic perspective' in S. Riggins (ed.) *Beyond Goffman*. Berlin: Aldine DeGruyter.

Mather, L. (1979) *Plea bargaining or trial? The process of criminal case disposition*. Lexington, Mass: DC Heath.

Maynard, D. (1984) *Inside plea bargaining: the language of negotiation*. New York: Plenum.

McConville, M. et al. (1991) *The case for the prosecution*. London: Routledge.

Piliavin, I. and Briar, S. (1964) 'Police encounters with juveniles', *American Journal of Sociology*, 70(2), 206–214.

Prottas, J. (1979) *People-processing: the street-level bureaucrat in public service bureacracies*. Lexington, Mass: Lexington Books.

Reiss, A.J. (1974) 'Discretionary justice' in D. Glaser (ed.) *Handbook of criminology*. Chicago: Scott, Foresman.

Reiss, A.J. (1983) 'The policing of organizational life' in M. Punch (ed.) *Control in the police organization*. Cambridge, Mass: MIT Press.

Reiss, A.J. (1984) 'Selecting strategies of control over organizational life' in K. Hawkins and J.M. Thomas, (eds.) *Enforcing regulation*. Boston: Kluwer-Nijhoff.

Richardson, G., Ogus, A. and Burrows, P. (1982) *Policing pollution: a study of regulation and enforcement*. Oxford: Clarendon Press.

Rosett, A. and Cressey, D.R. (1976) *Justice by consent: plea bargains in the American courthouse*. Philadelphia: JB Lippincott.

Ross, H.L. (1970) *Settled out of court: the social process of insurance claims adjustment*. Chicago: Aldine.

Rubinstein, J. (1973) *City police*. New York: Ballantine Books.

Sanders, A. (1987) 'Constructing the case for the prosecution', *Journal of Law and Society*, 14, 229–243.

Scholz, J.T. (1984) 'Cooperation, deterrence, and the ecology of regulatory enforcement', *Law and Society Review*, 18(2), 179–224.

Schuck, P. (1972) 'The curious case of the indicted meat inspectors', *Harper's*, (September), 81–82.

Shover, N., Clelland, D.A. and Lynxwiler, J. (1986) *Enforcement or negotiation: constructing a regulatory bureaucracy*. Albany, NY: State University of New York Press.

Shover, N. et al. (1984) 'Regional variation in regulatory law enforcement: the Surface Mining Control and Reclamation Act of 1977' in K. Hawkins and J.M. Thomas (eds.) *Enforcing regulation*. Boston: Kluwer-Nijhoff.

Skolnick, J. (1966) *Justice without trial: law enforcement in democratic society*. New York: Wiley.

Sudnow, D. (1965) 'Normal crimes: sociological features of the penal code in a public defender office', *Social Problems*, 12(3), 255–276.

Sykes, G. (1958) *Society of captives*. Princeton, NJ: Princeton University Press.

Utz, P.J. (1978) *Settling the facts: discretion and negotiation in criminal court*. Lexington, Mass: Lexington Books.

Vogel, D. (1986) *National styles of regulation*. Ithaca, NY: Cornell University Press.

Zimmerman, D.H. (1971) 'The practicalities of rule use' in J.D. Douglas (ed.) *Understanding everyday life*. London: Routledge & Kegan Paul.

Index